Healing a Shattered Soul

My Faithful Journey of Courageous
Kindness after the Trauma and
Grief of Domestic Terrorism

Mindy Corporon

To learn more about this book and its author, please visit
MindyCorporon.com

Cover design and illustration by Rick Nease
www.RickNeaseArt.com

Published by Mindy Corporon, LLC

Publishing services by Front Edge Publishing, LLC
42807 Ford Road, Suite 234
Canton, MI

Front Edge Publishing books are available for discount bulk
purchases for events, corporate use and small groups. Special editions,
including books with corporate logos, personalized covers and
customized interiors are available for purchase. For more information,
contact Front Edge Publishing at info@FrontEdgePublishing.com

Dad and Reat
As you were breathing—who you were to one another and others.
In spirit—as a red cardinal, a yellow butterfly and in a song.
Who you are to me, forever—perpetual love.

Teresa LaManno
Daughter, Sister, Wife, Mother, Friend—we will always remember you.

To those hurting, sorrowful and filled with anguish ...
there is a healing path for you.
Keep seeking the peace you deserve.

Contents

Praise for *Healing a Shattered Soul*

As I read this book, I kept thinking: How does Mindy have the strength to relive the worst day of her life and be able to focus on so many painful, detailed moments? I was on the edge of my seat reading each chapter riveted in the suspense of what was going to come next. What really caught me off guard was Mindy's quest to seek out those who were deeply affected by what had happened to digest their experience. Having lost my son to gun violence because of hate, I bow my head to Mindy's courage, tenacity and determination to tell this story and make a difference in the world.

Chris Oneschuk, whose son Andrew, at 18 years old, was killed by an extremist in Florida in 2017

In response to a neo-Nazi's murder of her son and father in 2014, Mindy Corporon has filled her world with love, compassion and kindness. But as *Healing a Shattered Soul* reveals, that doesn't mean she has avoided profound, intense, at-times debilitating pain. Hers is the sort of grievous wound caused by the type of extremism that those of us who are members of 9/11 families know only too well. This book gives you the privilege of sharing both in Mindy's grief and in her remarkable hope, which is rooted in faith. Let this book heal you so you can help heal the world.

Bill Tammeus, journalist and author of *Love, Loss and Endurance: A 9/11 Story of Resilience and Hope in an Age of Anxiety*

Just as Mindy Corporon describes in this memoir, I know the trauma of losing my own children to unjust and unexpected causes. Through the unjust tragedy of personal loss, we have become colleagues with far too many other parents around the world who have suffered similar heartbreak. As grieving, surviving and leading parents, we are Christians, Muslims, Jews and members of other religions as well. All of us share in the faithful call to speak out and advocate for justice, freedom and peace for all. As a Muslim, my faith urges me to save human lives from destructive hostilities. Islam teaches us: Whoever takes an innocent life, it will be as if they killed all of humanity; and whoever saves a life, it will be as if they saved all of humanity. We must inspire others, including our community and political leaders, to take positive actions to build, not destroy. I urge everyone to read Mindy's memoir and let her family's story inspire fresh discussion and action for equality, harmony, and peace across the many lines that divide us in this world.

Izzeldin Abuelaish, MD, author of *I Shall Not Hate: A Gaza Doctor's Journey on the Road to Peace and Human Dignity*

This is a book about how we struggle with faith and how faith, if we are able to believe and hold onto that belief, can be the foundation for healing and finding the way forward when we experience life struggles. Each of us will struggle at some time in life. Some of our struggles are monumental as in Mindy's story. Others are shattering in other ways: a failed relationship, economic downturn, the death of a loved one. Regardless of what causes us to struggle, *Healing a Shattered Soul* can help us discover what we can do to find a way to crawl through what Psalm 23 calls the "valley of darkness." As Mindy shares her personal journey, she does not preach at us. Rather, she opens the door so that we can walk alongside her, revealing that loss and love, hurt and healing, faith and freedom all go hand in hand. As she was advised by her pastor to "keep listening," *Healing a Shattered Soul* is a must-read for all of us who need to keep listening to find healing and hope in a broken world.

Rabbi Arthur Nemitoff, Senior Rabbi of The Temple, Congregation B'nai Jehudah in Overland Park, Kansas

The very day that her son and father were murdered by an evil man who set out to kill Jews, Mindy Corporon showed the world her outer strength. In the days, weeks and years that follow, people continue to marvel at her courage, unaware of how she grapples with intense pain and sadness. Her memoir *Healing a Shattered Soul* gives readers an inside look at how Corporon finds ways to repair her heart while helping others and proving that, for her, faith always wins.

Barbara Bayer, former editor, *Kansas City Jewish Chronicle*

When I heard about the lives lost on April 13, 2014, my heart was broken. As a Muslim who had been working with the Jewish community since 9/11, I had been to these locations several times. Plus, I recently had lost my husband from a sudden death. Losing a loved one is difficult but losing them to violence is even more so. And when it's your child, a mother's heart can never be completely healed from this loss.

A few months later, when Abdisamad "Adam" Sheikh-Hussein was killed after he led the prayers in front of his mosque, I was asked by the Somali community if I could invite Mindy to a community vigil. Mindy came and the most impactful part of the vigil was when the two mothers, Mindy and Adam's mother, hugged. Adam's mother didn't speak English, but the hug of two mothers who lost their sons, whose sons were victims of two separate hate crimes within a year, still resonates in my mind.

Even though Mindy and I come from different faiths, the concept of love and friendship is universal. What I have learned in my personal journey is that the only way to fight hate is to educate and that is what Mindy does in her life's work and through her book.

Mahnaz Shabbir, founder of Shabbir Advisors and community leader

Open to God's whisper, Mindy Corporon's resilient steadfastness to overcome evil with goodness inspires confidence in the reader to trust in their personal ability—along with the grace of God, support and prayer from a strong, loving community—to grow through adversity and effect positive change around us. The central value Mindy placed on tight-knit, loving family relationships and authentic, close friendships propelled her onward to overtake deep, drowning grief with buoyant, inner healing. She kept walking deliberately, one foot in front of the other, out of the fog to bask in the warmth and brilliance of the sun once again. Mindy Corporon's defining story is not one of loss, but of love.

Julie Overlease, author of *Hope Upon Impact: A Miraculous True Story of Faith, Love & God's Goodness*

Throughout this catastrophe, Mindy Corporon anchored herself to a network of caring family, friends and strangers, who soon became friends. She sought answers to questions that should have never been necessary to ask, while simultaneously helping others through their personal losses and resulting grief. It would be understandable if a person who suffered such loss were angry and filled with hate and vengeance. This was not the case with Mindy. By helping and accepting help, Mindy was able to shine some light into darkness. Not only did she find support in her own Christianity but also in Judaism and Islam. *Healing a Shattered Soul* is about a journey none of us would willingly take. It is also about finding a way home from a harrowing journey. Mindy Corporon acts as our personal guide on this trip, demonstrating love and commitment as the best compasses to avoid losing ourselves on the way.

Sylvester "Sly" James Jr., former mayor of Kansas City and co-author of *The Opportunity Agenda*

Mindy Corporon's profound honesty and amazing strength conveying her innermost thoughts and feelings during the most painful time of her life are relevant for each and every one of us. Anyone who has experienced the loss of a loved one knows how desperately God is needed to get through the hurt and suffering that loss brings. Mindy is absolutely inspirational in sharing not only how her Christian faith has helped her heal, but also how becoming educated and respectful of other faiths has enriched her life. Her program SevenDays® Make a Ripple, Change the World has continued to spread and now evolved with the additional layer of racial justice. I truly applaud how brilliantly

Mindy has given birth to a movement that is focusing on kindness and love, making our world a far better place for one and all.

Peggy J. Dunn, mayor of Leawood, Kansas

Even though most of us haven't experienced situations as critical as Mindy, her stories about her faith, family and life are something everyone can learn from. Mindy openly discusses how her lack of exposure to other people and cultures caught her off guard. But, by remaining open to change, she helped to make our community a better place, or as God called her to: "Bring my people together."

Carl Gerlach, mayor of Overland Park, Kansas

While suffering is draining, forgiveness is filling. I believe this. As a Black woman in the U.S., freedom and liberation is a constant struggle. It is an ever-present suffering that appears in big ways at times and in seemingly small ways at some of the most unexpected times. In order to have the energy, passion and commitment to go to battle every day, I need the "filling" that forgiveness brings. I use it to remember the limitations of hate and the expansiveness of love. Hate cannot restore. Only love is restorative. I believe that the solutions to our problems are three-fold: in the heart, in the action and in the legislation. I am inspired that Mindy is relentlessly focused on the heart. We can make a ripple and change the world and *Healing a Shattered Soul* gives us much insight into how we can act on that belief.

Dr. Nicole D. Price, speaker, trainer and author

Mindy Corporon provides an insider's view of a mother's grief, a daughter's sorrow, an activist's intention, a leader's calling and a woman's grit by sharing her story of the murder of her son and father in a religiously motivated hate crime by a white supremacist. Then, readers will be uplifted as Mindy urges all of us to act with kindness, to seek to understand and to come together as a diverse, pluralistic community. By taking us along on her journey, Mindy fulfills her goal to bring people together, and helps us all to make a ripple to change the world.

Alana Muller, business relationship coach and CEO of Coffee Lunch Coffee

When I learned of the murders of Reat Underwood and Dr. William Corporon on a dark day in 2014, I was overcome. As a Jewish man, the son of two Holocaust survivors, and an individual who lost a grandfather and an aunt in the war, this act of misguided modern-day antisemitism went straight to my heart. Through this book, Mindy shares a story about a mother's love for her son and daughter's love for her father. She shares the tragic loss of two beautiful people and her tremendous heartbreak navigated with an unwavering faith. As someone who did not grow up with a strong understanding of what faith in God means, Mindy's words leave me inspired.

Alan Locher, public relations executive and host of *The Locher Room*

Out of horrific pain, Mindy encourages readers to work toward the greater good. Through her story, Mindy calls all of us to examine our theology and our capacity to understand those different than us. Her example to rise up out of the ashes provides an example of light shining in the extreme darkness.

The Rev. Karen Lampe, founding pastor of The Caring Congregation, LLC.

This story will undoubtedly be a source of healing, inspiration and encouragement for many, for years to come. "Live life to the fullest and never give up." I have used Reat's phrase numerous times when trying to encourage and motivate our students. His influence at Blue Valley High School will continue to be ever-present. I can only imagine how pleased Reat must be to see those same attributes being vividly demonstrated by his mom.

Scott Bacon, Principal of Blue Valley High School in Overland Park, Kansas

"Hope and healing after unthinkable tragedy." That may seem impossible, but Mindy Corporon's striking memoir shows how that can happen through God, and those God places in our path during our time on earth. To have had a small part in this transformational journey is truly a blessing. This book will now be a part of the healing path for others.

Diana Chaloux LaCerte, author and co-founder of Hitch Fit in Kansas City

As a white Christian male, I never thought I would experience antisemitism, let alone have my eyes open in such impactful way to racism. Now, my experiences have allowed me to truly live out "love thy neighbor" seeing those who come from different backgrounds whether it be culturally, religiously or even sexual orientation. It has allowed me to understand that, even though I might not agree with others' beliefs and practices, I am still called to love them, listen to them to possibly learn and treat them with dignity. Though I wish this could have been learned through different circumstances, it is important to move forward and recognize how God has invited me to take the good and the bad experiences as opportunities to be a light to others. It is so nice to see how God is using Mindy Corporon. I am excited to see this project go further.

Gian LaManno, son of Terri LaManno who was killed in the same series of shootings in 2014

This is a huge, huge story. It's a textbook for healing. Mindy Corporon has become a healed healer.

Cuky Harvey, owner and director of education at Pacific Rim Lomilomi and Translucent YOU

THREE KILLED IN SHOOTINGS AT KANSAS CITY-AREA JEWISH CENTERS

OVERLAND PARK, Kansas, April 13, 2014—Three people were killed by a shooter outside the Jewish Community Center of Greater Kansas City and the Village Shalom Jewish retirement community on Sunday afternoon. The attacks shocked this peaceful community that is a suburb just over the state line from Kansas City, Missouri. The horrific news quickly reverberated nationwide one day before the Jewish festival of Passover begins.

The shooter began firing a handgun and shotgun in a parking lot of the community center at about 1 p.m., CST. Two men who were targeted initially by the shooter escaped unhurt. Then, the gunman fired into a truck that was approaching a parking place, killing 69-year-old William Lewis Corporon, MD and his 14-year-old grandson, Reat Griffin Underwood. The two were arriving so Reat could take part in auditions for *KC SuperStar*, a singing competition for teenagers that was going on inside the building.

Dr. Corporon practiced medicine in Marlow and Duncan, Okla., from 1976 through 2003, when he and his wife moved to the Overland Park area to be closer to their grandchildren, according to a family statement. He continued to work 40 hours a week and loved spending his free time with his grandchildren. Reat was a Life Scout and a freshman at Blue Valley High School who participated in debate and theater and loved to sing.

The center was filled that day with several programs, including a fitness program for children with autism. In another part of the building, a performance of *To Kill a Mockingbird* was about to begin, and auditions were under way for *KC SuperStar*, an *American Idol*-style contest to find the best local teenage singer. The gunman fired randomly into the building from the parking lot but did not injure anyone inside before he fled the scene. Center staff members were the first to call police and to provide medical assistance to the victims but were unable to save their lives.

The shooter next targeted the retirement center, a mile away, and killed Teresa R. LaManno (Terri) in that parking lot. He also shot at other people, but missed, then fled the scene. He was arrested later in the afternoon by police, making antisemitic remarks as he was led away. FBI agents working with local authorities confirmed his antisemitic motives.

Terri LaManno, 53, was an occupational therapist at the Children's Center for the Visually Impaired in Kansas City and was visiting her mother at Village Shalom as she did each Sunday afternoon.

Overland Park is a community of nearly 200,000 and averages two homicides a year. Police Chief John Douglass said the attacks shocked and galvanized the entire community. While this was a hate crime, he said, "We have no indication that the shooter knew the victims."

Expressions of horror and outrage came from leaders across the nation.

Calling the killings "horrific," President Barack Obama said, "The initial reports are heartbreaking."

"These senseless acts of violence are all the more heartbreaking as they were perpetrated on the eve of the solemn occasion of Passover," said U.S. Attorney General Eric Holder.

Civil rights icon and U.S. Representative John Lewis said, "It is deeply tragic that such senseless brutality should occur on the eve of Passover, the time when Jews all over the world remember their liberation from slavery in Egypt thousands of years ago. Hate itself is a kind of bondage that poisons the well of the soul. Somehow we must finally learn that it can never be a meaningful answer to human problems."

Foreword

The book you are about to read is a story of terrible tragedy, human evil and utter pain. *And* it is the story of survival, healing and redemption. Mindy Corporon has been described as a heroine, superwoman and a force of nature. Her story helps us understand how one survives tragedy, and says to the reader, "If Mindy can survive this, and can do what she has done, then surely I can survive the adversity I face and bring something good to come from it."

It was about 3 p.m. on Palm Sunday afternoon in 2014 when I received a call telling me to turn on the news that there had been a shooting three miles from our church. Shortly after, I learned that two of the victims were members of our congregation, and the third was the aunt of one of our staff. Two of our pastors were on their way to the hospital. I had one last Palm Sunday service left to lead and preach and then I would head to Mindy's parents' home to be with the family.

Palm Sunday usually begins on a joyful note. The children enter the sanctuary waving palm branches as the congregation sings the Hosannas. But as the 5 p.m. service began, I asked the children to wait. Through tears I shared with the congregation that two of their fellow members, a grandfather and his grandson, both of whom were to have been in that very service, had been killed just a few miles away. People began to weep. We paused in silence to pray for the families who had lost loved ones. As I thought of Mindy's family, I was reminded of the words of Jesus from the cross, "My God, my God, why have you forsaken me."

There is no class in seminary on what to say when a terrible act of violence takes the life of your parishioners. There is no scripture that will take away such darkness. Having been with dozens of people at the loss of children, or with a handful of families whose loved ones were murdered, there was one thing I'd learned, "Seek to embody God's love, and listen more than you speak."

That night as I met with the family I sought to listen, and to express love for them. There were two things I wanted to share with Mindy, things I share with most people following a tragic death: This was not God's will—it didn't happen to punish or teach you or as part of God's plan. It was an act of evil that was not the will of God. But while God did not cause this, he will help you survive it, and he will force good to come from it. *Evil will not have the final word.*

In the aftermath of this tragedy, and in preparation for the funeral, I wanted to understand what led to this act of hate. Mindy notes that some have said that the answer to her question, Why? was "an idiot with a gun." But digging deeper, this "idiot with a gun" was a man who spent most of his life reciting a narrative of victimhood for whites and repeating a message of hate directed toward minorities, with a particular disdain for the Jewish people. He'd devoted most of his life to the cause of white supremacy and to fueling racism in others.

As I prepared the funeral message, the scripture that kept coming to mind was Romans 12:21, "Do not be overcome by evil, but overcome evil with good." In the years since the service, Mindy has devoted her life to living this scripture. She has been determined to address the kind of ignorance and hate that led to the death of her son and father. She's sought to defeat evil with good. She has been a living, breathing illustration of God forcing good from evil.

In the process, she's inspired countless people to live lives of kindness. She's brought people together across different faiths to listen and learn from one another. She's hosted dialogues, led marches, conducted interviews, taught both in lectures and in her life, to do all that she could to overcome evil with good. She inspires me by her faith and work. I've considered it a privilege to be one of her pastors.

Reading the opening chapters of this book, I was once more moved to tears as I felt Mindy's pain. But as I continued to read, my heart was once again inspired by the redemptive story of God's grace working through the life of Mindy and her family members as they refused to let evil have the final word. This book is an invitation for the reader to join them in this work.

Adam Hamilton *is the senior pastor of the 22,000-member United Methodist Church of the Resurrection in Leawood, Kansas, the nation's largest United Methodist congregation.*

Preface

In *Healing a Shattered Soul,* Mindy Corporon allows us to see into the trauma, pain and the path forward for herself and many of her loved ones. There is hope for all of us in reading this book.

Mindy explores her personal journey through the unimaginable loss of her father and child to a hate crime. It is an honest depiction of life post-trauma. You have a choice to be crushed by your loss or to move ahead despite and through the grief journey. It is not simple and clean, and there is no real resolution in loss. You gather the shattered pieces of yourself and move forward. You are never the same, but you can find meaning in life.

Mindy has been fortunate in the friends and support networks around her that have bolstered her and encouraged her and her family members through this difficult process. Through her faith and beliefs, she has been able to make use of her life experience to turn her loss into a number of wonderful outreaches to stop hate and help others heal from grief and pain. With her willingness to learn from others, Mindy proactively seeks to bring about understanding and compassion for so many others. Through her loss, she indeed makes a difference. The aftermath of two deaths have helped spread compassion to so many others. Mindy's work exemplifies that journey. She has worked to make the world a better place. When we do that, the loss of our loved one is not in vain.

I especially appreciate that Mindy mentions how attendance at the vigil for her loved ones compared to the vigil attendance for the young Somali refugee who was also murdered in what was likely a hate crime. We understand that not everyone receives the same public outpouring of support that was afforded to both Mindy and me when my own daughter was murdered in a very public hate crime.

Mothers lose their children to violence every day, and yet many have no time to grieve and receive little to no public support or attention. We must hold space in our hearts and minds for them as we continue to overcome hate with love. People say, "Love always wins." I say that is true when we practice that love in meaningful ways that make a difference. I see Mindy Corporon as one of those mothers doing exactly that. We never want other mothers to experience the pain and loss of losing a loved one, especially a child, to hate.

I am honored to call Mindy Corporon my friend. Her book offers hope in a time of pain, pointing the way forward with faith and love. Read it and be encouraged to find your own way forward through pain and loss.

Susan Bro is the mother of Heather Heyer and a Co-Founder of the Heather Heyer Foundation. Susan launched the foundation to carry on the legacy of her daughter, Heather, a young paralegal with a strong sense of justice who was murdered by a domestic terrorist on August 12, 2017, in Charlottesville, Virginia.

About the Cover:

The Swirling Blue Ocean

Many might wonder why I would venture back to the scene of the crime, the location in which hate-filled evil and subsequent death encompassed our lives. A part of my soul considered the same. We were living our lives on April 12 and damned if I would allow ignorance and fear to stop us from continuing the same (I am my father's daughter), albeit with a freshly painted cynicism and more than a thin layer of apprehension. One such aspect of living life was the creation of the Faith Always Wins Foundation and annual production, SevenDays® Make a Ripple, Change the World. Herb Buchbinder, a friend and former colleague and well known in the Jewish community, was hosting a conversation about how to commemorate the tragedy. While our first meetings were held in homes of those who cared deeply, there came a time when our committee outgrew a living room and found the proximity of the Jewish Community Center easy access for all. I agreed.

I had walked the hallway numerous times prior to the murders that took place on April 13, 2014, and was doing so again in 2015, when I found myself in the middle of an art exhibition. What seemed like hundreds of paintings and a variety of sculptures hung on the walls and dotted the hallways of the Jewish Community Center. To be close to my father and son, it was typical of me to park near the same space in which their lives were taken and mine shattered. As I took my normal path from our planning meeting, past the White Theatre and out the same doors that had once been shattered by bullets, I found reason to pause and breathe. On this day, the art stopped me in a moment of awe. The variety of mediums and genres held my interest long enough for me to step in front of 'the swirling blue ocean'. This is my interpretation of the painting purchased by me and now on the cover of *Healing a Shattered Soul*.

After inquiring about purchasing this painting, I had the pleasure of meeting Mrs. Lowenstein. Humbly she told me it was not her intent to sell any paintings. As our conversation continued, she learned my name. I wasn't simply a woman passing through the exhibit. I was the daughter and mother who had lost so much. Her eyes widened as a sadness fell upon her face and shoulders. "I know who you are and you are somebody I wish to have my painting. I am so sorry for your loss." Babs' spirit and energy lifted when I thanked her, letting her know that 'the swirling blue ocean' reminded me of snorkeling during warm beachy vacations with my two boys and husband. My father, too, was a certified scuba diver. The ocean is a healing place for me.

In a brief phone conversation in early 2021, Babs and I laughed and talked with excitement about her painting being on the cover of *Healing a Shattered Soul*.

"Mindy, it makes me happy and thrilled all over that you purchased my painting and now have moved yourself and my painting to the ocean. What a nice story about my painting. I am proud of you and all the good things you do," she said.

About the Artist

Babs Lowenstein (b. 1931, Kansas City, Missouri) lives and works in Leawood, Kansas. Her paintings have been seen in exhibitions at Kansas City's Union Station Gallery, Hook Gallery, Jewish Community Center Art Studio Exhibit, and the Epsten Gallery at the Kansas City Jewish Museum of Contemporary Art.

Employing a variety of palette knives, occasionally her hands, and rarely a brush, Lowenstein's art utilizes thick layers of textured color. While drawing on the rigor of modernism—from Jackson Pollock's hand-thrown paint, to Clyfford Still's sweeping colorscapes—and while nonrepresentational in technique, the paintings often strongly evoke figures, faces, flora, and captured moments of action.

As she has traveled to many places in the world she has always looked for beautiful color. It might be in the translucence of a tulip petal in Holland or the explosion of color in an English garden, in the fiery oranges and reds of Chinese dragons or the color exploding from fireworks on the Fourth of July. She also is in awe of the way light comes bursting through the sky and how it sets gingerly in the mountains.

She has always loved an array of art, from the very contemporary to the Old Dutch masterpieces. Lowenstein has her work in collections in Kansas City, Los Angeles, New York City, Houston, Boston and Florida.

Introduction

In the past seven years since my father, William L. Corporon, M.D., my oldest son, Reat Underwood, and Teresa LaManno were murdered, the trepidation, anxiousness and anger build mostly in the weeks and then days ahead of a significant event. The hollowness I felt on April 13, 2014, while holding hands with my dearest friend, Tarra Freberg, in front of a crowd mourning the unthinkable, finds its way back into my soul as commonly celebrated days announce themselves on my calendar.

The month of May 2020, found me and all of you, literally, in the throes of COVID-19. The familiar feelings of anger and pain, like a couple of distant cousins whom I recall meeting but don't enjoy visiting, get my attention. The first sign of these feelings is slight and irritating. While the news of the pandemic was vast and unrelenting, causing immediate fear of the unknown in all of us, my personal physical changes did not stem from the uncertainty of the newly announced virus.

These intimate feelings were once again working their way through my body. Periodically, as a reminder that healing is a lifelong journey, tears found their way into my eyes and then down my cheeks. During my morning walks, tears started to fall more frequently. When

I say, 'fall,' I mean flow. As grief and sadness take over my heart, I lose control of the tears. I had found a safe place to sit with the pain, or rather, walk through it. Allow me to describe the physical sensations. A heaviness in my chest arrives. My breathing becomes uncomfortable. I am short of breath, enough to feel as if I am out of shape. I will notice the heaviness in my chest and initially contemplate if I am this out of shape. My brain isn't far behind my body. My brain will then take the feeling of heaviness, shortness of breath and a low level of fear, which would be described as anxiety or trepidation, and place a visual memory in view. I am in the parking lot of the Jewish Community Center.

It's at this moment when I succumb to the realization of what I know will be. My typically amiable and thoughtful self will attempt to fight off the pain, push it away, push it down so that I don't go into the darkness. I do not go down the slippery slope of pain and darkness alone. I grab everyone around me, or at least I want to. My irritable mood, erratic behavior, strange decision-making and stream of tears are a clear sign. Conversations with everyone in my life are more difficult as I am mentally grasping for any of them to stop the known and unwanted wrenching pain of loss.

With effort, practice and yes, even time, I have learned to use my breath as a conduit to channel the pain, allowing the pain to progress but not to debilitate me. With concentrated effort, I sit quietly with a pen in hand and a journal on my lap and write. Most times I start with a prayer—the Lord's Prayer. "Our Father … who art in heaven, hallowed be thy name, thy kingdom come, thy will be done on earth as it is in heaven. Give us this day our daily bread, forgive us our trespasses as we forgive those who trespass against us. Lead us, not into temptation but deliver us from evil, for thine is the kingdom, the power, the glory forever and ever. Amen." Calming my soul long enough to begin the process, I allow thoughts to flow onto the page in front of me. Many of my journal pages are dotted with tears, sharing their own thoughts of anguish as they drip onto the paper.

"Bring my people together." *There it is again.* A mantra. A command. I think to myself, *I have.* I have brought people together. *I have turned myself into a damned event planner. What else am I to do?*

On February 23, 2020, Ahmaud Arbery was gunned down by two white men. A third white man was videoing the altercation between Ahmaud, a Black man, and his attackers. This heinous hate crime came to my attention in early May. *Again?! ... Why, again?!* are the words drumming in my ears. Yes, this was a white on Black crime—not a faith crime. To me, they are the same. A hate crime: a hatred so deep inside someone aimed at another person because of their beliefs, skin color or sexual orientation ... now exploded on another unsuspecting family.

I know how far the ripple of hate can reach. Every day, I feel them.

There was a stirring in my soul. Why was my interest so piqued from this crime?

There had been other hate crimes since the tragedy that took the lives of Dad and Reat. Very public crimes, such as Heather Heyer's murder in Charlottesville, Virginia, on August 12, 2017. Sharon Davis, a dear friend of mine, lives in Charlottesville and reached out to me at the time of this horrific hate crime. The KKK was back. They were back and publicly walking in the streets chanting, "Jews will not replace us." Who is us? What do Jews have to do with the removal of the Robert E. Lee monument in the park with the same name? I had these questions and more surrounding the rally that took a life, the life of Heather; but I didn't feel a personal call to a new action.

Only 14 months after our tragedy, a gunman opened fire in the Mother Emanuel African Methodist Episcopal Church in Charleston, South Carolina, murdering nine praying Black Christians. The shooter, a white male, had been sitting with the church group during their Bible study. He had the audacity to place himself in a location considered not only safe but also holy, pray with the nine members and then murder them in cold blood.

I know why I couldn't tackle this. Exhaustion from grieving my own loss.

At the suggestion of my friend, Alana Muller, I did, however, welcome former North Carolina senator Malcolm Graham, brother to Cynthia Graham Hurd, one of the victims, to present his story at our 2016 SevenDays® Make a Ripple, Change the World experience. This was all I could muster.

In Olathe, Kansas, only miles from my own home, Srinivas Kuchibhotla was gunned down at Austins Bar & Grill by a white man yelling, "Get out of my country!" This murderous hate crime was about to become very personal. Three people were shot and Srinu's life was taken unnecessarily—tragically. His widow, Sunayana Dumala (pronounced 'Sue Nyna Due Malla'), whom I now call *chelli*, which means "little sister" in the Telugu language,[1] continues to feel and live through the repercussions of her husband's murder. We have held hands, wept and walked together since our meeting, only months after the murder that forever changed the trajectory of her life. Yet, on the evening of February 22, 2017, when the text appeared on my phone alerting me of the shooting, my body didn't react with the power I had hoped it would. The phone slipped from my hand as I dropped to the floor. In my own backyard? Why is this hatred continuing? What else can I do to stop the hatred? The efforts already being put forth through our Faith Always Wins Foundation had not yet made the impact needed to stop this hate crime.

On October 27, 2018, I was flying to Dallas for a reunion with five of my sorority pledge sisters. We had reunited in August of the same year and were eager to see one another face to face. Waiting in the Orlando airport, I received a phone call from our foundation's public relations director, Ruth Bigus. Had I heard about the shooting in Pittsburgh, Pennsylvania? In Mister Rogers' neighborhood, no less, 11 people had been murdered during Shabbat services at the Tree of Life Synagogue. Familiar tears found their way to my cheeks. In my Uber ride from the airport to Mary Ann Kellam's home, I answered questions from the first of many interviews that I would conduct, reminding humanity that we live amongst evil in our world. Reminding humanity that God can be found in a park or on a bus. God isn't waiting to be found only inside a holy place of worship. Reminding humanity that each new violent hate crime isn't a reminder to me that my father and son were violently murdered by a shooter wanting to kill Jews. I remember every second of every day.

---

1 Telugu is spoken by people from the states of Telangana and Andhra Pradesh in India.

Now, in 2020, I am viewing the video of Ahmaud Arbery losing his life and a stirring is in me. I ache for his mother. I know the pain she is feeling and will continue to feel.

My body is feeling the ache of my own grief and the anxiety is building as my mind drifts to Reat. He should be excited about his 21st birthday. We might have planned a trip to Belize, one of our favorite destinations, or to Las Vegas or New York City! I suppose our plans would be muted due to COVID-19, but they would have been in the works. I would rather be sorely disappointed by having to cancel my son's 21st birthday plans than face reality. He would turn 21 in Heaven. From Reat's age of 15, this is how I call it, how I see it:

There is a choir ... music of many genres can be heard. My father, his parents, my mother's parents, a close friend of mine from high school, Kyle, a friend from my working life, Greer, ... they are all present. They are laughing. They are joyful. I can feel it now, in my chest ... the ache of the joy we were meant to have on Earth, in our own home. My mind races after this vision appears. It always does. The vision tells me to move onward and plan my own party. I can celebrate Reat however I choose.

He loved fudge. Reat loved sweet and salty mixes. He favored strawberry rhubarb pie and s'mores! If given the opportunity, fudge always won the coin toss. I planned to make pink fudge for Reat's birthday. He left this world loving the color pink. We had recently purchased him a suit with three shirts and two ties. One of the shirts was pink and he loved how he looked in it. He felt confident in his style, with the pink shirt and his new fedora. This is why I would not only make fudge, I would make pink fudge. As a gesture of kindness, I would divide it into baggies, write a kindness note and hand it out to small businesses in our town. This seemed to satisfy my urge to "be kind" and take an action to make someone else's day better than mine.

As I awoke from sleep six days prior to May 21, Reat's birthday, I had a new vision. A picture of Black women and white women, together. I heard the mantra "Bring my people together." Ahmaud Arbery's death came to mind. Did the men who murdered him NEVER see Black and white people together? Did the shooter who took the lives of my father and Reat, NEVER see Black, white, Jewish and other people of faith, together? Is this what is needed … for us to be SEEN together? Actions speak louder than words. Actions! What action am I to take to bring Black women and white women together? Since the murders of Dad and Reat, this is common for me, to wake up with thoughts streaming in my brain as if someone is dictating to me. It is common for me to be in my waking state and have a clear vision of something only to realize that vision coming into reality days, months or years afterward. As common as they have become, I am still wary. Why me? and what now? are my typical responses.

Nicole Price, Ed.D. and I met in March via a Zoom meeting as COVID-19 was derailing all our lives. This pandemic was also causing our Faith Always Wins Foundation to take a huge pivot from an in-person annual event to an all-virtual event expected to begin in mid-April. During our first call on March 23, I shared with Dr. Price another idea/vision I had for our upcoming SevenDays® Make a Ripple, Change the World experience. Not only did we move to a virtual platform for six events, we also started them early and added eight more. In the first two months of COVID-19, as many were talking about how their worlds had halted on a dime, mine took off on a jet plane at warp speed. From the safety of our homes, each volunteer committed hours to prepare, rehearse and record numerous interviews and valuable pieces of educational material. We also produced a live LOVE Day interfaith panel on our opening day, April 21, and another live interfaith panel on April 26, which was our final experience of SevenDays® 2020. I am so proud of our committees, volunteers and my friend Jill Andersen, who is also our one employee, for willing this to be so. You can find our production pieces at https://www.youtube.com/c/GiveSevenDays.

Dr. Price, who I now call Nicole, became a friend during those haggard days and nights in March and April. As I contemplated my vision of Black women and white women together, on Friday, May 15, 2020, I texted Nicole, "Would you have time to speak with me today or tomorrow?" Her response, "Yes, I'll be free in about 15 minutes. Does that work for you?" It worked for me and helped me transform my vision into reality within six days. During my morning walk on the phone with Nicole, we vetted my vision and idea of SEEING Black women and white women, together.

I recall the sun shining brightly and birds flitting here and there as I stopped in my tracks to contemplate how many Black women I might know. Hmmm. I had never stopped to think about how many Black women I knew or let alone how many I knew well enough to ask them to join me for this gathering. Nicole chuckled as I proudly announced I could name eight Black women off the top of my head whom I could call or email, asking them to join us for a conversation. I felt stupid. Why had I never reached out prior to now?

Between May 15 and May 21, I created "Respect. Engage. Appreciate. Trust. Black and White Women Friends." I Invited eight Black women and seven other white women to join in conversation about who we are as women, mothers, wives, sisters, daughters and humans. Do you see it? The acronym for REAT? This is what my heart needed. This was the vision placed on my soul only days before my baby would turn 21 in Heaven. "Bring my people together" has been my mantra, my calling and my challenge since the day my soul was shattered.

Allow me to take you on the rest of my journey to date; the healing of my shattered soul.

Top: A joyous occasion to dress up. Reat and his younger brother, Lukas, were ushers for the wedding of Francie Boyer (oldest daughter of Richard Boyer and sister to Laura Boyer Carley). Milburn Country Club in Overland Park, Kansas. 2013

Bottom: Enjoying their final campout together, Mindy and Reat are at one of their most favorite places. H. Roe Bartle Scout Reservation in Osceola, Missouri. 2009

"I Love You Too, Mom"

April 13, 2014, Palm Sunday.

The rays of the morning sun were peeking through the blinds on the windows as I opened the door to Reat's room. On his left side, facing the back wall of the room, he lay still except for the rise and fall of his ribs. Quietly and slowly, I stepped fully into his room, making my way to the edge of his bed. Even sitting myself next to his sleeping body didn't jostle him. Lightly, I began stroking Reat's back, up and down the full length of his torso. The rhythm of his breathing changed as he began to wake.

Reat is old enough to set an alarm. He uses his alarm for school days, the type that shakes his bed wildly and makes rapid beeping sounds. His alarm would send me into cardiac arrest from a deep sleep. Today, there was a request. He wanted me to wake him, not a shaking, quaking alarm. Thankfully, as a 14-year-old boy, he welcomed my attention, he requested my assistance and he was happy to have me in his room. I obliged.

Gently waking, he rolls over with a sly smile on his lips. His first words to me are, "I love you." Ahh, what a great kid. I love him deeply, of course. What a great son I have. I am lucky to be his mom. As he is fully rolled onto his back, I lean in for a hug. "Watch out for drool," are his next words to me. My head stops parallel to his and hovers over the pillow, where the drool must be lying in wait. We chuckle and I remind him of how proud I am of him. He has worked tirelessly for countless hours in preparation for today's audition.

He admits to being nervous. "You should be," I respond, "Today is a big day. Some jitters will keep you focused when you walk on stage. There is nothing wrong with being nervous, even afraid." Quickly, Reat states, "I am not afraid, Mom—gosh, I just said I'm nervous." This is when I realized I was pouring too much parenting philosophy on him. We had chosen his outfit weeks prior—his dapper new black suit; crisply pressed, light-blue shirt and brand new purple and blue tie. During our outing at Men's Warehouse, weeks before, Reat had also selected a fedora, cool grey with stripes, to wear for this audition. Mixed in with the grey and white stripes was a hint of sky blue—my favorite color. As he made his way to the shower, he tasked me with making his favorite sandwich—turkey, provolone and pears.

Typically not a bounding-out-of-bed, or bounding-down-the-stairs type of child, Reat bounded down the stairs with excitement. He looks amazing. I wish I had taken a photo to capture the moment. He has been working with a vocal teacher for the past several months. Her instructions were for him to warm up his vocal chords early and then again just before his audition. He begins with the "me-me-me-me's," as I call them. After using his voice to move up and down the scales, Reat begins to sing his audition song while I listen proudly.

Today's audition marks Reat's third of the spring season. He's feeling encouraged because he received an acceptance notice from audition No. 2 last week. That acceptance ensures 12 months of performances all over the city with the talented group "Starlight Stars." My son is becoming a bona fide performer. I am thrilled for him! Recently enrolling him in dance lessons provides the opportunity for the tri-fecta: Singing—acting—dancing! In the music business, they call that the "triple threat." He has talent and is seeking more, which our family appreciates and encourages.

Last year, Reat landed a role in *Damn Yankees* at The Theater in the Park. That show was a game changer in terms of his (and our) devotion level. We have now transitioned from musicals being Reat's personal ventures to them becoming family affairs. His numerous commitments require wheels and I am the first option driver. I drive him to voice and dance lessons, theater practice and performances. I attend almost every single one, cherishing each moment I get to watch him on stage. My mom is the second option driver. His roles in musicals are beginning to advance from the smaller parts to the more prestigious ones. He is so excited to begin moving up the ranks.

Today Reat is auditioning for *KC SuperStar*, which is our smaller Kansas City version of *American Idol*. It is a benefit for the Jewish Community Center in Overland Park, Kansas. Coincidentally, my wealth management firm has been a sponsor of this event since its inception. We are so proud to have our own rising superstar auditioning in 2014.

Reat and my mom (lovingly referred to as "Yea Yea" by the grandkids) chose his main audition song, "On the Street Where You Live" from *My Fair Lady*. Hence the reason he asked to add the fedora to his audition outfit. In the kitchen, with me as his audience, Reat sang the 32 bars for me. He messed up once, so he started over and finished well. As I was washing the morning dishes, our conversation was light. He said, "Mom, did you know I may get to sing a second audition selection, today?" I didn't know this to be true. I responded, "Really, I wasn't aware. What have you selected?" He then goes on to tell me that, if given the opportunity to sing a second song during his audition, he has chosen, "You're Gonna Miss Me When I'm Gone" (also known as the "Cups" song). With no hesitation, he breaks into the ballad while walking around the kitchen. His gait is easy, his voice is smooth and I am tearful. The beauty of this scene has never been lost on me. A teenage boy in his comfort zone with his loving mom, watchful and hopeful for his talent to be noticed later in the day.

My dad (warmly regarded as "Popeye" to his grandkids) offers one loud knock on the back door before opening it and walking through our eating area and out the sliding door to our porch. Reat had settled himself in front of the computer for some games and offers, "Hey, Popeye." Somehow, I am still at the sink and have managed to begin drying the dishes. After placing the final plate in its allocated home inside our cabinet, I drop the towel on the counter and turn to see my father standing on our porch. With his feet in a wide stance and his hands on his hips, he could be signaling "offside" during a football game. This posture is all Dad. Standing firm with confidence in seemingly any situation, his presence is comfortable. Dad is checking out our newly created pool, which stands mostly empty. We had inserted a hose early that morning, but the small puddle of water in the deep end tells us we have a long time to wait for a full pool.

My father stands at 5'8" and has a belly resembling a small Santa Claus. His haircut is "styled" in his usual buzz cut. My younger son, Lukas, teases Popeye that this short hair is considered "bald." At age 69, Dad's short, typically dark hair has been overtaken by white. His eyes resemble those of Asian descent. When he smiles, they close into tiny slits. Rarely smiling in photos, one of my favorites is when he is laughing so hard, his eyes are wet with tears. I have always gathered his reason to be that he would rather his eyes be open for photos than show any teeth. His skin is olive. As usual, he is wearing his khaki pants, a Hawaiian print shirt and his signature suspenders. Replacing belts with suspenders years prior, they quickly became our favorite Father's Day gift. He does not lack variety in the suspender category because he has them in an assortment of colors and themes.

Dad and I stand on the back porch for a few minutes, discussing his desire to come back over and check on the water level after Reat's audition. We smile as we ponder swimming laps in our new pool. My dad loves to swim laps and taught all three of his children to swim—me, and my older and younger brothers. I'm grateful he passed along his love for swimming. It's a sport I find both strenuous and relaxing. I remember Dad trying other sports—one was an attempt at recreational tennis with my mom. However, it didn't seem to stick like swimming did. Dad and I have belonged to the same gym for years, and I often show up while he is mid-mile in the pool. As he has aged, Dad has grown weary of needing to turn his head to the side to breathe. So, he has invented a new way, which guarantees I can always spot him quickly in the pool. He is, without fail, always the only lap swimmer donning a mask and snorkel.

Back in the kitchen, we continue to talk about our future backyard pool as Dad takes a seat at one of our kitchen stools. We have always talked easily. He has a friendly, bedside manner for his medical patients and an easygoing personality. He is smart—actually, very intellectual—and a voracious reader, a passion he passed along to Reat. Dad is knowledgeable about history, psychology, the human body and parenting. That knowledge base works perfectly for his job as a physician. He graduated medical school from the University of Oklahoma when I was 4 (my older brother Will was 7) and started practicing when I was 5. He passed his board certifications in 1976 when I was 8. Back then you needed a year called internship to practice. He could have taken residency, these were relatively new in family practice ... but we were broke.

I always enjoy my conversations with Dad, even if they are challenging. (Well, if I'm honest, I don't enjoy the tough ones "in the moment," but they tend to have a tremendous impact on my life.) Our conversation that morning is purely chitchat and logistics. We discuss family and schedules.

It is a "divide and conquer" morning for my immediate and extended families. Mom has gone with my sister-in-law Dana and her two kids to take pictures with the Easter bunny. My husband, Len, and I are heading to our son, Lukas', lacrosse game, and Dad is assigned the task of taking Reat to his audition. The evening prior, around our dinner table, I discovered that Lukas wore a sad face when I announced I would be driving Reat to his audition. Their activities were to begin only 30 minutes apart. His big brother, seeing this sad face, offered me permission to go to Lukas' lacrosse game and asked his Yea Yea to drive him to his audition. Announcing her schedule with the Easter bunny photos now placed all eyes on Popeye. He happily obliged to be selected as Reat's driver for the day. They adore one another.

Dad and I talk through expectations of the afternoon. He understands that after Reat's audition, he is to return Reat to our home. Particularly happy about his assignment for the day, Dad mentions that he will check on the water level of the pool later this afternoon. We are all excited about the pool. Perhaps Dad more than I had realized. My parents left a full-sized lap pool on their 40 acres when they made the move from Oklahoma to Kansas to be near us.

We all plan to meet at 5 p.m. for the evening church service. We will celebrate Palm Sunday together and then have an extended family dinner at a Chinese restaurant. For a moment, I consider if Jesus cares what we eat on Palm Sunday. It is my younger brother, Tony's, birthday the following day and my mom still insists on family birthday celebrations ... even for the adults.

Our conversation has moved from logistics to my workload when Reat gets my attention, "You are going to be late to Lukas' game." Ugh. The lacrosse game. Glancing at the clock on the microwave and back again at Dad, I say, "You got this?"

"I got this," he responds.

Now, with a quickness in my step and a small amount of anxiety about leaving my dad to oversee the final and likely most important audition for Reat, I gather my purse and keys. Before walking out the back door to our garage, I stop and take in Reat. The right side of his body is closest to me as he faces the computer monitor, clicking away at the keyboard. With part haste and part trepidation, I lean over enough to plant a kiss on his right cheek.

"Good luck today. I love you," the words leave my mouth without my mind truly considering the depth to which I mean them. I do mean them. I mean them, every day. A few steps back and again headed for the garage door; I hear ...

Reat's loving reply to me in his confident "I know you are anxious, but I have this," kind of way—

"I love you too, Mom."

Left: Thanksgiving Day. Popeye (Bill) and Reat arrived from a successful deer hunt in Oklahoma to Melinda and Bill's home in Overland Park, Kansas in time to join family for what would be our final Thanksgiving with them. 2013

Right: Attending the wedding of her younger brother, Tony Corporon to Dana (Beebe) Corporon in Colorado, Mindy was a single parent but never parented alone. Bill (Popeye) was often present for assistance. 2000

One More Rescue

My earliest memory of my dad is of his forefinger. I am unsure of why we were walking, and I couldn't tell you where we were going or where we had been. My memory is of holding on to my father's right forefinger with my whole left hand. The visual of my small, child-sized hand wrapped around his large, adult finger with my arm swinging slightly as his hand moved in motion with our walking is indelibly etched in my brain. Holding on to his finger was all I needed to make me feel content.

Comfort. Safety. Peace. Knowing I was loved by him. Knowing he was my protector.

Picking up a stranger

When I was about 8, we took a trip to Estes Park, Colorado. The car ride made me sick. My mom's second youngest sister, Barbara, was with us. She often came on family trips as a sitter for my older brother, Will, and me. I fed chipmunks and birds the nuts my parents handed me. The sun shone so brightly and beautifully through the tallest trees I had ever seen. I learned about beer from a brewery tour in Golden, Colorado, the home of Coors. The smell of the hops on the tour and the taste of beer on my young tongue must be the reason I am not a beer drinker. We went on horseback rides in the mountains, stopping for campfire food made by the trail guides. The smell of the horses and the feel of their strong bodies holding me high above the ground was exciting. Later, I would learn to barrel race and compete in a few rodeos.

We were in Colorado for a medical education seminar that Dad needed to attend for continuing education credits. The conference was in a large, beautiful lodge. Something happened to our reservations, so we didn't stay at the lodge. We stayed in a small camping area with cabins. On one of Dad's drives into the conference, I must have asked if I could go with him. He obliged. I don't recall anything about the meeting he attended or didn't attend. I do remember being in the front seat of the car as an adult man walked to the window and noticed me sitting there. He towered over the car, making me feel very small, and I was thankful I was inside and he was not. I heard Dad tell this person to sit in the back; and he said, "My daughter is sitting in the front." The back door opened and the stranger got in the car.

My dad didn't move me to the back seat. Maybe he allowed me to sit in front because I got car sick. Perhaps he felt I was safer in the front, closer to him, with a stranger in the back. What I felt from him was support. As small as this gesture was, he placed me ahead of another adult. He didn't call me his princess or any type of endearing name. He offered me unconditional love and support.

The tar episode

Have you ever been around a road when it is being tarred? The instructions I received from my dad were clear. "Stay away from the tar." Again, he was specific. Our home had white carpet in the front room. Perhaps I was on my way to my friend Lynn's home, or maybe, I was interviewing neighbors for the newsletter I had created. Summer days seemed longer than school days and I was bored. Have you ever tried to get tar off your skin with soap and water? About 9 inches of warm water, the door opening fast and my father's body moving quickly is what I recall. My right wrist was in his right hand as he yanked me from the tub, splashing the water onto the floor. SMACK! His left hand found my wet, naked right butt cheek. The sting took hold as he released my arm, dropping my weight into the waves of water. This was the only time I had or would ever feel his hand on my behind. Quick and to the point. No words … only action.

My father believed in quick resolutions.

I'm a big sister

Close to age 10 on April 14, 1978, I woke up to find a family friend and neighbor in our kitchen. Janet Loveless, mother of Kyle and Lynn and wife of Leroy, was there to inform me that I would become a big sister later that day. She told me Dad had called her in the middle of the night, soliciting her assistance. He was taking Mom to the hospital and didn't want me and Will to wake up alone in the house. My dad had the calm fortitude to call a trusted neighbor to provide comfort for his other two children while knowing my mom's health and the health of his unborn son were potentially unstable. My mom had an emergency C-section; and she lost a significant amount of blood, which placed her and my brother Tony at risk.

Within a week I was caring for my baby brother nightly. He was placed in my bedroom until age 4. My parents trusted this was a good place for Tony.

Pine-Sol and a sharp knife

My mom was quick to scream, "BILL!" on occasion. Several weeks prior my dad had removed a mole from my back that presented as suspicious. Of course, I couldn't see the mole, but trusted Dad knew what he was talking about when he said it needed to be removed. In his office, lying on the patients' table stomach down, I felt the prick of a needle as he numbed the area. His voice was soft and careful as he asked me to stay still. The tug of the stitches being pulled in and out of my skin felt unusual, but there was no pain.

As a competitive gymnast at age 12, I was anxious to return to practice.

Within a few days I had an uncomfortable feeling where the mole had been removed. I could reach the area on the left side of my spine by contorting my right arm around my back. Using my right middle finger, I could press in the space where a scar was supposed to be forming. Hmmm. I went to Dad one evening as he returned from work. Mom was with Will in his bedroom. Our home was not large but Dad was keeping his voice low as he asked me to remove my shirt and wrap a towel around my waist. I didn't yet need to wear a bra but still felt I should cover my chest. Using the shirt I had removed to cover my chest, I leaned on the kitchen counter as I saw a bottle of Pine-Sol being placed in front of me.

Mom's shrill scream came as I was feeling a warm liquid, which I presumed to be blood, streaming down my back. "Bill!" Her scream startled both of us. He shot back, "Jesus, Melinda!" I froze, fearful that any move I made might cause more screaming.

I could feel Dad's breath on my back as he lowered his head close to the area requiring his attention. The sting of tweezers with applied Pine-Sol touching my now raw skin brought tears to my eyes. Unsure of how long this might take, I wanted to ask the question but felt I shouldn't speak. My older brother, Will, must have appeared to see what was happening. I learned explicitly what was going on as Mom explained to Will that Dad had cut me open for some unknown reason. Dad spoke with authority to all of us at once, explaining that my body had rejected the stitches. Therefore, the inside sutures ripped apart rather than heal the wound. The area where the mole had been removed was barely being held together by an outer, thin layer of skin. Infection was possible.

Using the sharp knife with quick precision over the thin layer of skin, he opened the once sutured area. Prick. Prick. Each time he touched the open wound, I felt a prick and sting that lingered. Dad pulled out about six stitches from my raw skin.

Someone asked about him stitching the wound. Nope. There was nothing to stitch together. My skin was too thin and frail to be pulled back together. He placed a bandage on the wound and called it good.

If he was anything, he was pragmatic.

Cheer practice

My senior year in high school our cheer squad had an opportunity to compete in Nashville, Tennessee, at the International Open Cheerleading Competition. Emotions ran high during our final weeks of preparation. Despite the fact it was Christmas break, we worked numerous hours daily. Eventually, stress and tension hit an all-time high and the dam broke. Our coach abruptly stopped the music and hollered instructions for us to sit down on the mat. I don't recall his exact words, but I distinctly remember he directly identified me as a problem. He wasn't saying I was a problem in the routine, but he was singling me out as a problem in a personal way. When I think back to that moment, I easily recall the queasiness in my stomach.

All eyes were on me as I endured his public tirade, which openly attacked my character.

I'm not sure if my coach asked me to leave or if I dismissed myself. Regardless, my heart was broken and my mind was paralyzed by shame as I walked toward the phone in the hallway. My face was marred with sweat and tears. Because my truck was in the shop, I needed a ride home. (Yes, you read correctly. There were no handheld cell phones and I drove a Nissan pickup truck.) I called my dad's office and spoke to his scheduler, who was like an aunt to me. I spoke through tears as I tried to explain the situation. As my words spilled out about needing a ride home, I was coughing back tears boiling up from the embarrassment of being pointedly admonished, without any warning and in front of my peers.

As I was mid-sentence, my dad's voice broke my train of thought. He was on the other end of the phone asking me to repeat what had happened. Taking in a deep breath, I recounted how I had been singled out as a problem for the squad based on a decision made at a meeting attended by parents and cheerleaders a few nights prior. The meeting held at our home was one of many for fundraising plans, travel arrangements, uniform discussions, etc. We were a small-town cheer squad with no special funding from our school. This was 1986. The logistics for this event were monumental. Significant planning was needed on top of hours of practice for a precision routine. A decision had been made to allow only cheerleaders and immediate family members on our bus to and from Nashville, which was about an 11-hour drive one way. He hung up the phone before I understood how I would get home from this auspicious occasion.

The look on my father's face told me he had passed anger and was well on his way to DEFCON 5. My father is not someone you would say is agile. Yet, in the moment it took him to remove his body from his now stopped vehicle and run past me, someone could have described him as such. He was in the room I had just left, which was filled with teens he had known for 10 years and my cheer coach. I couldn't make out his exact words because I chose to stay in the lobby. I can't recall if he asked me to "stay put," which sounds like something he would say, or if I was equally embarrassed that my father was now storming my cheer squad practice. What I could not hear in words, I could hear in volume. As he exited the practice, he motioned for me to climb into his truck. Apparently, he had patients—in his waiting room, exam room and the lab—waiting for his medical services. He needed to get back to work, quickly. I was in awe that he had come to my rescue with the force of a tornado.

Later, I would find out that my dad had unloaded on my coach, but not just about his poor treatment of me. My father was furious that our coach would flaunt his position as a leader in an unacceptable manner. It wasn't only me that my father was representing. He was representing every student in the room when he told our coach that the selected choice of communication to air a personal grievance was highly unprofessional. My dad's heart beat for us kids, every single one in the room. I was so grateful to have him as my father.

The rescue

"Dad, I need an attorney. I'm leaving Gary," I explained.

"Let me make some phone calls. I'll call you right back," Dad answered.

Within minutes, Dad returned my call. "I'll pick you up tomorrow morning at 8:30 a.m. You have an appointment at 9 a.m." This conversation took place four weeks after giving birth to Reat by cesarean.

Several hours later I found myself crying tears of exhaustion, relief and fear of my future as I drove Reat from his birthplace of Norman, Oklahoma to my hometown of Marlow. During the appointment at the attorney's office, I felt numb as I stoically answered questions and explained behavior that had become commonplace to me. Masterfully manipulating me from the time we had married and turning up the heat when I announced I was pregnant, Reat's biological father was emotionally abusive.

I was the frog in the pot of water. Not realizing that I was boiling to death until an infant needed my care, I had succumbed to outlandish lies and behavior. My eyes were dry while my father was wiping his. Reat was working to reach five pounds and struggling because of my malnourishment. As each action taken against me was spoken out loud, my brain struggled to understand why I had stayed so long. And now, a newborn was my responsibility.

Behind my dad, I drove the short hour and 10 minutes to my childhood home. Divorce papers were being drawn up, and I was instructed to find a safe place to live, to sleep and to begin eating well enough to sustain myself and Reat.

As I exited my car and Dad did the same, my mom was on him about why on earth he had me drive by myself in my current state of mind and condition. "It's her car, Melinda. It's her car. She never said she couldn't drive. They are here, aren't they?"

In the end, he saved my life with his

The following quotes came from caring individuals who wrote to Pastor Adam Hamilton, senior pastor of our church, the Church of the Resurrection, prior to the memorial service he would oversee on April 18, 2014.

"Dr. Corporon was the nicest physician I have ever worked with. His compassion for patients and respect for nurses enhanced the respect I had for him." –Daria

"I always envied your family, you had a dad that was constant and true." –Kim (sent to my older brother, Will)

"Dr. Corporon saved my dad after his first heart attack and undoubtedly saved him other times. He also discovered my mom's cancer and saved her life. His love of his patients is unwavering." –Unknown

"Regardless of time, day or night, he offered care to those in need." –Unknown

My father was my hero. He always told me I could be anything and do anything I set my mind to. He didn't waver when I enrolled in aeronautical engineering at the University of Oklahoma. When I switched my major to communications, he believed and trusted in me as I stated, "I will make it work, Dad, I am loving these classes." In none of the above memories did I mention the amazing hugs my dad offered. When asked what I miss about my father the most ... his hugs come to mind just before his belly laughs and how he used to rub his hands together when he was in the throes of a good conversation.

My dad was Comfort, Safety and Peace to me.

The same as "I got this."

Bill and Melinda Corporon attended every home game and several away games during Mindy's tenure as a cheerleader for the University of Oklahoma. Mindy and her father, Bill, are shown here on the field, enjoying a hug after a home game. Norman, Oklahoma. 1989

Remnants of the violence that took the lives of Bill and Reat can be seen in this photo of the truck Bill was driving. Shattered glass and a displaced fedora without its human. Clearly, this was foreshadowing the next years of their lives. April 13, 2014.

3

Your Father's in Heaven ...

April 13, 2014, Palm Sunday.

Earlier that morning, Len and I researched potential pool furniture online. We moved into our home in 2005 after first purchasing a piece of land three months before our wedding in 2001. Finding the design for our home in a magazine, we toiled for months on every aspect of the structure with an architectural engineer before hiring a builder and breaking ground. We are a good team and proved this to one another during the process with each decision made. Len had the flexibility to be on-site almost every day, monitoring the construction. I would pop in about twice each week for a summary, and to listen, ask questions and make suggestions or recommend outright changes. We each brought our uniqueness to the home from beginning to end. Once complete, I truly thought that the decorating would be left to me and whomever we agreed to hire. Not so. Len wanted to be and was part of every decision, from decorative pillows to our bedroom furniture; from the carpet in the boys' playroom (I wanted a laminate tile) to the beautiful wet bar in the basement. In 2013, when we broke ground for our pool, I knew we would design and decorate it, together.

We know we want our backyard (and new pool) to be a hub for family and friends, so we are looking forward to new furnishings.

We can't wait for our backyard to overflow with our loved ones. We envision our boys spending many hours out there—in and out of the pool—with their buddies, so we know comfortable couches are a must.

Reat's 15th birthday will present our first opportunity to break in the pool with a party, including guests and all! As we scrolled through furniture options this morning, we asked Reat's opinion on couch shapes and colors. Our boys are growing up; we want them to be involved and have ownership of family decisions. After all, we love having our boys' friends in our home, and we don't want that to end simply because they are getting older. Feeling a bit dismayed that Reat hastily chose a couch in a neutral color, I asked him for his reasoning behind the "sand" choice. Thoughtfully, he explained, "We should go with a neutral couch color, which then provides us the opportunity to less expensively decorate it each summer with colorful pillows." Yes, this was Reat. His head could sometimes seem far away, maybe even in the clouds, but his reasoning was intact.

"Good call," Len said with a grin and his typical thumbs-up salute. Len was pleased with Reat's comment about "less expensively decorating" and I had to laugh. Reat was no dummy. He knew this comment would be beneficial to him later in the day or week.

Around noon Len and Lukas head out for Lukas' lacrosse game in time for the warm-up. Dad had not yet arrived to pick up Reat. I had the pleasure of being an audience of one when Reat sang his two options for the audition. His second option brought tears of joy and filled my proud-mama heart.

His voice easily, softly and calmly sang these words to me ...

> I got my ticket for the long way 'round
> Two bottle 'a whiskey for the way
> And I sure would like some sweet company
> And I'm leaving tomorrow, wha-do-ya say?
> When I'm gone
> When I'm gone
> You're gonna miss me when I'm gone
> You're gonna miss me by my hair

You're gonna miss me everywhere, oh

You're gonna miss me when I'm gone

I've got my ticket for the long way 'round

The one with the prettiest of views

It's got mountains, it's got rivers, it's got sights to give you shivers

But it sure would be prettier with you

When I'm gone

When I'm gone

You're gonna miss me when I'm gone

You're gonna miss me by my walk

You're gonna miss me by my talk, oh

You're gonna miss me when I'm gone

Source: LyricFind

Songwriters: A.P. Carter / Luisa Gerstein / Heloise Tunstall-Behrens

Cups (Pitch Perfect's "When I'm Gone") lyrics © Universal Music Publishing Group, Peermusic Publishing, BMG Rights Management

As he finished singing, all was right with our world.

It is 12:30 p.m. when I kiss Reat goodbye, jump in my car and head out. I drive faster than I should to the field, but that tends to be my usual routine. Working to get more done in way too little time. Feeling the pressure to be available to everyone and anyone who needed me, I am an overscheduler.

As I walk from my car to the field, I spot another mom I recognize. She is walking towards me. "The game is canceled," she informs me, "There's lightning in the area." Looking up in the sky as children would, we search for the reason the game has been canceled. Seriously, not seeing a dark cloud in the sky, we look at one another and shrug our shoulders. As I continue walking towards the field, I spot Len and a disappointed Lukas heading my way. "Hey sweetie, I am sorry the game was canceled," is all I can muster to my sad-faced 12-year-old. He mutters what we call non-words and shrugs his whole body in disappointment. Not feeling as if there is anything I can do to remedy his feelings or the situation, I announce I will now be driving to Reat's audition. I said, "Len, Reat has my phone with him. Would you call him and let him know I am on my way?"

Not waiting for Len's response, I am already in my car. Stealing a glance at the clock in the car, I am keenly aware I could arrive at the Jewish Community Center (JCC) before Dad and Reat and well before his audition, which is scheduled for 1:30 p.m.

While Reat was an amazingly talented, intellectual, fun, humorous and excelling Boy Scout, he was also normal. A couple weeks prior we realized Reat had used Len's credit card to make a purchase on his Xbox. Since it wasn't parent approved, Reat is without a phone for two weeks. This morning I allowed him to download a pitch pipe on my phone for practice and gave him permission to take it with him to his audition.

"That's OK, I'll just surprise them," I think as I make my way to the JCC. Traffic was light. No need to drive over the speed limit. No reason to hurry. During my 15-minute drive, my only concern is hoping Reat remembers to take deep breaths before he begins to perform.

As I turn the corner from 115th Street into the campus, I spot the celebratory flags lining both sides of the street, leading me to the JCC. I reminisce about the numerous times we have frequented these beautiful facilities. Swimming lessons, the junior triathlon, art classes, baseball lessons and previous theatrical performances have had us visiting this location as a family for about nine years; Reat would have been 5 and Lukas, 3. In 2014, as I am driving into the campus, the JCC is happily celebrating 100 years.

Now, turning right as I enter the parking lot of the JCC, my car is facing west and I am driving through a mostly empty lot. Another quick glance at my clock tells me it is 1:08 p.m. "Great. Plenty of time to make it in to see Reat perform," I mumble to myself. Dad's crimson-colored Sooner truck is noticeable because it is one of the only vehicles I can see parked near the building's White Theatre entrance. His truck is facing south and I notice both doors on the driver's side are open, but I don't see Dad. I can't see anyone walking around. I am curious as to where he is and why he left both doors open.

My speed would have been conducive to typical parking-lot speed. Perhaps a bit faster due to a lack of other vehicles in the parking lot. Within seconds, my eyes find my dad. My heart begins to race. My mind is confused. I can see clearly but not understand why my father is lying on the ground perpendicular to the driver's side door. His body seems motionless. Fear about Reat's whereabouts comes to mind. Where is Reat? Is he calling an ambulance? Has Dad had a heart attack or a stroke? I hear myself speaking in guttural language. "Reat?" "Ambulance." "What happened?" "What happened?"

My body begins to shake violently. A rush of nausea rises up in my stomach, as if it had been there the whole time. Cold. I feel cold. My mind is trying to wrap my head around this horrifying scene. Am I still driving? Yes, I am driving. Be careful but hurry. Hurry … Reat! What happened?

"Reat must be inside, calling an ambulance," I am saying to myself. I start giving myself instructions … Hurry. Stop the car. Grab your keys. Grab your keys. Run. Run fast! Somehow I manage to stop my car, although paying no attention as to how. From sheer muscle memory, I place the car in park as I simultaneously yank my keys from the ignition and run at high speed, albeit in sandals, toward my father.

I hear myself screaming … the words come out without any thought about who might hear me or who might answer me, "WHAT HAPPENED?! WHAT HAPPENED?!"

These are the only words I can find. They rise out of me and dissipate like rain water on a hot, dry sidewalk. No one is near me.

My car wasn't far from Dad's, only two rows behind where he had parked. I didn't have far to run and in seconds I am closing in on his still, unmoving, completely motionless body. Move. Please try to move, I think.

Fear.

A fear in my belly, in my bones, unlike I have ever felt before but I have felt since, overtakes my body. I am close enough now to see the unimaginable. My dad has fallen on his left shoulder. His head and body are facing the building.

Fear. How could this be? What am I seeing?

A pool of blood is forming around his head. My body feels as if I am being suspended in the air. I want to move closer. I want to help him. My dad, he isn't moving. There is blood. How can this be happening? The blood is making a wider circle around his head. I catch my breath. Am I breathing? There are no people, anywhere. I feel afraid and alone, very alone. As I make a step to move closer, in need of touching him and knowing it would be the last time, I am stopped.

Knowing how this felt at the time, I am trying to find the words to describe to you exactly as I felt. It felt as though a person standing in front of me, placed both of their hands on both of my shoulders and stopped me from moving forward. I felt as though a strong person was holding me in place. Stopping me with their own hands and arms.

No one was near me. I was alone in this space, seeing my father for the final time. How could this be? Only half an hour ago I talked with him in my kitchen. We were in my kitchen. This is not real. He was talking to me in my kitchen. He hugged me. We were filling the pool and talking about the water. We were supposed to go to church and have dinner tonight. The memory and visualization of seeing him smiling at me only less than one hour ago was distorted by the image of his motionless body lying in a still forming pool of blood.

I feel paralyzed.

I hear the words, "Your father's in Heaven. Go find Reat."

On Reat's birthday, Bill held Reat and never
let go, with Yea Yea nearby. Norman Regional
Hospital, Norman, Oklahoma. May 21, 1999.

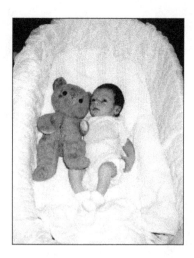

A 1-week-old Reat Griffin Lloyd Underwood
in the Gordy/Corporon family bassinet with
the comfort of Mindy's teddy bear, Tommy,
at his home in Norman, Oklahoma. 1999

Four Weeks

My firstborn child, a boy, Reat was born May 21, 1999. It was a beautiful, sunny day in Norman, Oklahoma. I was married to Gary Underwood. We had decided not to find out our baby's gender and there were no gender reveal parties in 1999. We could do without the uncertainty of his gender due to all the uncertainty in our marriage. Baby boy remained nameless for the first four days of his little life. The entire time I was in the hospital, we argued over his name. I had previously gathered a list of family names before the birth, but we could not come to an agreement on two names. After many disastrous conversations, I realized the name "Lloyd" was being thrust upon me to include somewhere in the name. Gary took a hard stand and it was a deal breaker for him.

After four days of negotiations, we finally agreed on Reat Griffin Lloyd Underwood. "Reat" came from Gary's side of the family. Gary's great-grandfather on his mother's side of the family was named Reat Ira Medcalf. "Griffin" was my maternal grandmother's maiden name. "Lloyd" was Gary's middle name and had been in the Underwood family for several generations, hence the deal breaker.

Once we finally agreed, we signed the document for submission to the state of Oklahoma for his birth certificate; and we were ultimately released to go home. I absolutely loved Reat's name and often referred to him as Reat Griffin, just because I loved the sound of it.

Nameless for four days, contentious conversations, arguing in the hospital … our marriage was ending at the time I became pregnant with Reat. His birth catapulted me into the reality of my failing marriage, which was as significant as the new responsibilities I now had as a mother.

Reinforcements were called in when intervention was needed most.

My mom was an amazing caregiver. She pampered me and took care of Reat while I slept. Thankfully, Reat latched on as soon as my milk came in and nursing was going well. Having this ONE thing go well kept me moving forward. After cooking, cleaning and caring for me and Reat for over a day and a half, she departed only because I insisted she had given me what I needed.

Shortly, after my mom left our home, Reat and I were awoken by a loud commotion in the kitchen. Our house was filled with deafening crashes of breaking glass and Gary's voice screaming obscenities. As I grabbed Reat from his bassinet, I heard more glass breaking. With my heart racing and my newborn infant in my arms, I slowly and silently approached the kitchen. My discerning the fragrant smells of chicken and spinach did not coincide with what I was witnessing.

God bless my mom. She had made me two of my favorite dishes— buttermilk chicken and spinach casserole. Not one bite had been eaten from either of them, as I had gone to sleep just as she pulled them from the oven and left for her home.

One by one, he was dropping glass baking dishes full of food into a trash bag. I asked him to stop. He continued without looking at me.

I was witnessing the explosion.

Retreating into my bedroom, we took shelter and began considering our options for a safer place. Reat and I now had each other.

During my pregnancy I had only gained 19 pounds. After four weeks of having less than adequate food, sleep and quality of care for myself, I lost 23 pounds. Giving life to another human is a huge feat. Feeding another human in any capacity, an infant, a toddler, a teenager, a homeless person … food is the substance of life. I was giving life. Giving life to Reat helped me see how I had given my life away. I was nourishing him while I was being deprived of nourishment in the form of love, emotional and physical support and yes, nutrients.

My embarrassment of allowing myself to be treated as less than by my spouse had kept me from divorcing him prior to our pregnancy. My stubborn and hardheaded nature had placed me in a predicament already unsafe for me and now noticeably unsafe for Reat.

Why is it that I allowed myself to drop deeper into a darkness, an abyss, having no association with whom I had once been? How many bad decisions, not poor decisions but BAD decisions, had I made in the previous seven (yes, seven) years of my marriage, which felt wrong at the time YET ... YET, I made them ... for myself, for someone else? I had to come clean with myself. I had to come clean and reach for help. Drowning myself in pity and sorrow, I felt anger raising its head in the pit of my stomach. My gut was telling me, "Push it down. Push it down."

I was not to show anger. Why? Why was I not supposed to be angry about how badly I was being treated? Why was I allowing myself to be fed bullshit day in and day out from a man who was supposed to love me unconditionally? And now ... look at what I have done. I have brought a child into this world—a child. I can't defend myself. How am I going to defend him?

A voice inside me said, "I am here." This voice was small and unfamiliar to me. I heard this voice again. It said, "You are not alone." Sitting in the middle of my living room, alone, I phoned a friend.

Tandi Ball and I had met when we tried out for the Kansas City Chiefs Cheer squad in 1991. We cheered on the squad together for two seasons, but it felt like we had known one another for years. She had since married and had a baby of her own now. Brennan was the first baby of my immediate friends whom I knew in utero and on day 1. Tandi knew me. We could confide in and cherish one another in the same conversation. She had relied on my advice in the past. It was my turn to ask for help.

With tears in my eyes, shame in my throat and shaking hands, I dialed Tandi's number. She listened. I didn't know how many stories I planned to tell her but I told her EVERYTHING. My heart ached and my tears dried as I found an inner strength with each new story of misogynistic, manipulative incursion. Finally, I paused and took a breath. The other side of the phone line was quiet. "Tandi?" I said. She responded with one sentence so meaningful, full of love, care and strength … the lifeline I needed. For some reason I couldn't do this on my own. I had to ask permission. She said, "Mindy, you should leave him."

When my dad answered the phone, I only made the following statement, "Dad, I need an attorney. I'm leaving Gary."

"Let me make some phone calls. I'll call you right back," Dad answered.

Within minutes, Dad returned my call. "I'll pick you up tomorrow morning at 8:30 a.m. You have an appointment at 9 a.m." Reat and I were asleep when Gary returned from wherever he had been. The next morning he had a strange, disheveled look about him. I looked at him with a new sense of ownership of myself and said calmly, "I'm leaving you. I have a meeting with an attorney today."

He didn't get angry. He simply replied, "You can't leave me now. We have a child."

"This is precisely why I'm leaving you," I explained. "We will not raise him together." He left the room and then left the house.

Reat was just four weeks old when I left his biological dad.

It was agonizing to explain the reality of what I had lived through during my nine months of pregnancy. Both the attorney and my dad listened intently as I recounted story after story. Dad wiped tears from his cheeks as he rocked his newborn grandbaby in his arms.

My attorney shared one pleasant observation about Gary that day. She explained, "He is doing everything he can not to hit you. You need to vacate the premises—and quickly." I knew Gary didn't hate me or Reat. He had just become incredibly miserable, to a point of such intolerance for himself, that he was pushing everyone and everything away. Sometimes when words don't work, we show our love (and disgust) with actions.

Thus began my life as a single parent. Single parenting was certainly not on my wish list of accomplishments. Talk about a failure … not only was I getting divorced, but I was also getting divorced with a newborn. Thankfully, my parents welcomed us with open arms. I would describe my time with them over the next 10 months as "living in the cradle of love." Reat and I received generous amounts of love, wonderful food (Have I mentioned how important food is?) and some much-needed attention during our respite.

My attorney advised me to move back to the Kansas City area as soon as possible in order to reestablish my residency in Kansas. Although, I was working from Oklahoma City, my wealth management career and business partner were located in Overland Park, Kansas. In August of 1999, I leased a long-term stay location with three bedrooms, a kitchen and a garage for me, my mom (who had become our nanny) and Reat.

My divorce was finalized in February 2000.

Top: Dawson Gardner and Reat Underwood ready to attend their first H. Roe Bartle Boy Scout summer camp in Osceola, Missouri. 2010

Left: Camellot Academy cast Reat in his first production as the Baby Elephant Bird in *Seussical the Musical*. At age 4, his love of performing was born. Kansas City, Missouri. 2003

Bottom: Reat auditioned in January 2014, and was overjoyed to receive his acceptance letter into the Starlight Stars program in early April. Courtesy Starlight Theatre, Kansas City, Missouri. 2014

"LIVE LIFE TO THE FULLEST AND NEVER GIVE UP."
— REAT UNDERWOOD

5

Passionate About Life

Baby Reat

When Reat came out of my womb, he resembled Yoda. Yes, Yoda from *Star Wars*. Dad even emailed all our family and friends to share the news.

My father became Reat's surrogate father. They would go on walks together on the acreage seeking the blackberry bushes. Dad would take Reat to the pond to watch the ducks and the turtles swim. He would walk miles with Reat either strapped onto his chest, which placed Reat on the top of Dad's belly, or Reat would be riding on Dad's back in a hiker's pack made for carrying little ones. No matter what, when Dad arrived home from work, Reat was ready for their time together.

We spent 10 months in my parents' home in Marlow, Oklahoma—the cradle of love. His first words were not Mom or Momma, although he did end up calling me Mom-Mom. Reat's first word was Popeye. He named my father "Popeye." We never truly understood from where Reat heard this name because we didn't watch the cartoon, *Popeye the Sailor Man*. It was clear that it was what Reat called him, so we all followed suit. I hardly called my dad, "Dad" any longer. We all referred to him as Popeye.

We trekked the I-35 corridor often from Marlow to Overland Park, Kansas during the same months that babies learn to sleep through the night. Country music singers Garth Brooks and Shania Twain became our nightly ritual to lull Reat to sleep. "From This Moment On" and "Whose Bed Have Your Boots Been Under?" from Ms. Twain played over and over as I walked, rocked, patted and soothed in any way I could to assist Reat in sleeping through the night. If you are a Garth fan, you know that any song we played was a winner for Reat and our nightly rituals.

Len Losen came into our lives in March of 2000, when Reat was 10 months old. Len and I met serendipitously in Dallas, Texas due to a wedding and a work conference. A close high school friend, Carol Skaggs, invited me and another friend, Sandy Strong Beall to her wedding. The "after-the-wedding" party found me, a newly single woman, dancing into the wee hours of the morning with a man I dubbed, "Eye Candy." With Reat under the watchful care of my parents, I felt comfortable for the first time in over 19 months to have some fun. Initially, Eye Candy had his eye on Sandy. Finding out she was married, he was relocating himself when she insisted he stay to meet her, 'cute, single friend'. Eye Candy, also known as Len Losen, was enjoying himself prior to a weeklong conference with his company. Finding ourselves at a coffee shop the next morning led to phone calls during the following week upon my return to my parents' home in Marlow. We managed to meet the following weekend in Norman, Oklahoma, a neutral location. During our first real meal together, I fed and entertained Reat as he sat in his high chair while Len and I learned about one another. As Len was about to pay the bill, I excused myself to the restroom, but not without asking Len to hold Reat and feed him his bottle. There was no intention on my part to "test" Len with Reat or vice versa. I needed to potty and Reat needed his bottle. Much like my father, I'm pragmatic. Upon returning to the table, Len informed me that Reat was the first baby he had ever held. Lukas became the second, when he made us a family of four on March 5, 2002.

Toddler Reat

As a handsome little boy, way past his Yoda days, Reat wore dimples and a quick smile. All I had to say to him before a photo was snapped was, "Put on your angel smile, sweet boy." Reat brought an enormous amount of laughter and joy into our lives.

It wasn't long before we realized Reat's talent of being able to memorize the books that were being read to him. He was precocious, learning everything quickly. My parents were totally into musical theatre. Their talent skipped me and landed smack on Reat Griffin. At age 4, he had his first role in *Seussical the Musical*. Reat played the baby elephant bird hatched by Horton the elephant. His love of acting, performing, singing and dancing was born earlier. At age 2, he would recite the Eric Carle books read to him and then act them out for anyone, anywhere.

Fascinated with dinosaurs and museums, Reat was a sponge and a prolific learner ... one dinosaur at a time. In an elevator with Len, Reat was explaining the difference between a Triceratops and a Tyrannosaurus Rex. Another passenger in the elevator was stunned to find out that Reat was only 3 years old. I can't say the word museum without phonetically saying mew-zay-em—Reat's pronunciation.

Loving M&M's—we were tickled that Reat called them em-oh-em's. We still call them this today.

One of Reat's nannies sent a message to us shortly after his death telling us how much she adored the opportunity to spend time with him as a youngster. "Reat had a heart of gold, and was a very happy child," Audra shared with us.

At age 2 years and 10 months, Reat became a big brother to Lukas.

Elementary and Middle School Reat

Little League started as early as age 5, in kindergarten. Reat played in the Stilwell League. We found friends fast while benching it two evenings a week and each weekend from March to July. Our boys played catch in the front and back yards with one another before each practice and we played "games" as a family on many evenings that were free from a scheduled practice or game.

My dad wrote this message in 2008, at the time Reat was 9, and Lukas, 6.

> Father's Day, Sunday, June 15, 2008, email sent by William L Corporon—excerpt taken from a longer email.
>
> Reat has pitching aspirations and pitched for the second time yesterday. This is the first year for KID PITCH; he's 9 y/o. He has been working on form and delivery and really looks good in the stretch, windup and delivery. And his delivery is pretty good. In his one inning to pitch, he struck out two, walked three, hit one and allowed no hits. That is about par. The kid who pitched after he did, hit three and walked another and was so upset he had to leave the game. The second batter Reat faced, hit a one-bounce shot back to him. He backhanded the ball and, taking his time, turned and threw to first. Two away. I'll have to say that I've seen that play a thousand times over the years, but I've never seen it done better. And maybe he'll never do it again, but it was a thing of beauty! We are beginning to mutter about the coaching on his team because he's always stuck in the outfield and he plays well at 2nd and short. They move the boys around a lot. But mostly he's outfield.

Competitive baseball crept into our home the summer Reat turned 13. He was a good enough player to be on a competitive team. However, his desire to play at this level of the sport lasted only as long as that very drawn-out, hot season. After finishing 120 games, he made the decision to drop baseball and focus on singing, acting and dancing for his plan to perform year-round.

Therefore, we were surprised when he asked to join the eighth grade, middle school football team. What? Reat knew he would never play football in high school. His stature dictated this, as well as his disinterest in being hit by another boy with intention and aspiration. However, Reat joined the team and immersed himself into the camaraderie of the players. He was on the B team and I believe in one game he managed to make one tackle. There was just no disappointing this young man. He was thankful to have had the opportunity to try football, and we were thankful he finished with no injuries.

Reat looked forward to the end-of-year talent show every year. One highlight from his elementary days was his performance with his friend Dawson in the Abbott & Costello "Who's on First?" comedy routine. My parents, especially my father, worked with the boys for days in preparation for their time on stage. They knocked it out of the park! Reat enjoyed collaborating so much that he engaged another friend, Danny. They played their respective instruments one year—Reat on the violin and Danny on cello. They performed well enough to garner the attention of their fourth grade teacher, Kala. She asked them to play pre-wedding music as guests arrived for her wedding!

Cinderella, *Wizard of Oz*, *Annie* and *Peter Pan* … he loved every one of these musicals, from the lines he learned to the friends he made. He cherished his people and most people were his people.

Cub Scouts was a HUGE part of life for us during elementary years. Len and I had an arrangement whereby any overnight camping was my responsibility. Y'all, I love to camp! Our theatre kid, who could memorize his lines quickly and spent many hours playing computer games and learning to dance, also LOVED to camp.

Bobcat, Tiger, Wolf, Bear and Webelos—we did it all! Reat relished every moment. The achievement, responsibility and interaction with his peers was a passion. I loved every moment as much as he did. In fifth grade, he crossed over to Boy Scouts and began camping without me. Some minor emotional upset swirled inside of me during this transition. When Reat recognized I was sad to have less of a role with him, he offered my name to the troop as a potential leader. Reat selected Troop 37 with his close friends Dawson and Dirk and our new chapter in scouting was born. As an active parent in his scouting career, I encouraged him to reach Eagle by age 14 or 15, before he might be a licensed driver. In the state of Kansas, you can legally obtain a permit to drive by age 14; farming is still prevalent in a majority of the state.

In 2005 our family had adopted a charity. Operation Breakthrough provides a safe, loving and enriching environment for children in need and empowers families though advocacy, emergency aid and education.

They provide a safe, loving and educational environment for children in need and empower families through advocacy, emergency aid and education. Touring their location, we fell in love with the children and their families, as well as with their mission to help others. Reat and Lukas were keenly aware that their gently used toys and clothes all found their way to the children there. We also adopted a family of four every Christmas. My parents had taught me the importance of helping others, giving back to our community, paying it forward and generally sharing LOVE with everyone. Len and I taught our boys the same values with the help of Operation Breakthrough and scouting.

As Reat achieved Life Scout, his next level would be Eagle. Thus, he had to create an Eagle project, planned and implemented by him, with guidance from an adult mentor. I was thrilled when Reat told me he wanted to fill the food pantry at Operation Breakthrough for his Eagle project. This is an email from Reat to Lee Duckett, a dear friend who continues to serve as Development Director at their location in Kansas City, Missouri.

> February 17, 2014 From Reat to Lee Duckett
>
> Hi Mrs. Duckett this is Reat. I just wanted to email you about the eagle project that we have briefly talked about in the past. I would like to collect household items and food from different neighborhoods and businesses. If this is alright with you i will need to fax over a document to get your signature. Also, I was wondering if along with being the cause for my project you could donate some barrels to help with collection at the businesses. I was thinking some barrels along the lines of the barrels from Harvesters. If maybe your kids could make two of them and maybe put pictures or designs they have made on them i think that would really help the donations. If any of this is possible just shoot me an email back and we can talk about it through email or over the phone. Thanks Mrs. Duckett!
>
> —Reat Underwood

High School Reat

As a freshman at Blue Valley High School, Reat excelled at debate! His first semester of high school he attended seven debate competitions. This meant he was out the door before 7 a.m. on Saturdays and sometimes Sundays over seven weekends that fall semester. Friends, there were about 17 weekends total that fall semester of high school. He loved debate, the camaraderie, the competition and the winning … it was a wonderful experience. He was so engaged and immersed, and he excelled—his efforts earned him the National Forensic League's Degree of Excellence.

As our 2014 began, we had an articulate and intellectual young man in our midst.

> January 22, 2014—9:08 a.m.
>
> Sent from Reat to Mindy.
>
> "Hey mom, I was just looking at my watch list for stocks and I wanted to know if I would be able to open a TD Ameritrade or stock trading account. I have started to become really interested in it. I would like to talk to you tonight about it. Thank-you!"

"His smile lit up the room in the pre-K class at Church of the Resurrection. He touched so many of the little kids' lives, he loved God and loved others," we heard from Amy, one of the adult volunteers who supervised Reat at KiDSCOR.

Guys & Dolls was one of the high school performances in March 2014. Playing a minor role as a freshman didn't deter Reat from involving himself with each and every student associated with the production. I recall one evening—only one evening—when the show had ended and they were striking the set. I met Reat just off stage. His eyes were red and puffy. Immediately I knew he had been crying. Having no idea what would have caused his tears, I wrapped him in my arms hoping to offer solace for his sadness. "Mom, I'm OK," he said over my shoulder. Reat was now about 6 inches taller than me. He held me and squeezed a bit more. "Mom, I love performing. I love singing and acting. I can't wait to be here the next three years and on this stage!"

We had active lives. Reat was involved in activities that engaged him with his peers, adults and family. He adored his theatre, scouting and baseball; but his love and his passion was most certainly performing with a song.

Athena Sullivan, Reat's gifted education teacher at Blue Valley High School, sent this message to Pastor Adam Hamilton, senior pastor of the Church of the Resurrection, for him to understand who she knew Reat to be. "Reat was smart, talented and easygoing. Above all else, he was compassionate, he cared about people, all people. You could see it in the little things he did every day. He felt intense empathy for people, especially victims of social injustice. He wanted everyone around him to be treated with kindness and respect."

Personally, I was active on the Blue Valley Educational Foundation board and had taken part on a planning committee for our annual breakfast. This breakfast was popular and well attended. Each year, about 1,000 people, representing corporations, small businesses, a vast variety of teachers, administrators and students from the school district attended. Our superintendent was given a platform for a "state of the school district" message, awards were presented, achievements were celebrated and eggs were served with coffee. It was a fun, enjoyable experience to plan and be part of as a member of the board and as a supporting sponsor through my wealth management firm.

Anne Blessing, the executive director of the foundation, had heard me talk about Reat's singing talents. She was aware he seemingly had no fear of performing in front of a crowd. In 2012, when I brought up the fact that Reat would be entering his freshman year of high school in 2013, would be a Life Scout and would have the maturity to sing in front of this crowd, she offered him the opportunity to perform. His voice coach attended, along with our family, including my parents, younger brother and sister-in-law. So, in late August as a freshman representing Blue Valley High School, Reat sang our National Anthem in front of 1,000 people! Not only did we record this, but it is also on YouTube!

On the cusp of greatness ... the Kansas City Starlight Theatre Program accepted Reat into their 2014 program for high school youth—Starlight Stars. He was one of 24 who would learn musical routines composed of song, dance and some acting for the sole purpose of PERFORMING around the metropolitan area. What an honor and an exciting opportunity for this young man. We were all thrilled at the possibilities that lay in front of him.

Reat had also tried out and been selected for a role in The Theatre in the Park's summer 2014 production of Tom Sawyer.

Reat's best friend at the time of his death, Jake Svilarich, shared this message with Pastor Adam Hamilton, days before our memorial service. "He was always there for me when I needed him ... He was an extraordinary person ... A super talented singer and actor and an amazing friend ... We all love him and he will have an impact on all of our lives".

On April 13, 2014, Reat was auditioning for *KC SuperStar* at the Jewish Community Center.

Each audition requires a headshot of the talent. Reat sat for his headshots in March with aspirations of many more auditions. TheRYEstudio, Stilwell, Kansas, March 2014.

This photo taken one year prior to his being murdered captures Reat's essence of joy. Photo courtesy Francie Boyer at Milburn Country Club in Overland Park, Kansas. April 13, 2013.

6

Finding Reat

April 13, 2014, Palm Sunday.

"Your father's in Heaven, go find Reat." Strong. Decisive. Pragmatic. I felt none of these as I was staring down at the pool of blood still forming around my father's head. He was lying on his left shoulder—motionless, lifeless. I know now that he had just stepped out of his beloved truck as a gunman opened fire. Boom! One pull of the trigger from only 3 to 4 feet in front of him. He was murdered. His life was taken out of fear and the hatred of Jews.

Looking around to see who spoke these words to me, I see no one. The air was cooling off. The storm that had canceled Lukas' lacrosse game was lurking. Immediately to my left there were no vehicles. I could have taken a few steps in that direction to go around my father's still warm, yet deceased, body.

Not understanding anything at all … what happened to my father or where to find Reat … I take a few steps backward and to the right. As I am walking behind and around the back of my father's truck, the world is spinning and fog is creeping into my brain.

As I step around his truck, I find two men holding Reat in their arms. The man on my right is holding Reat's head and shoulders. The man on my left is also close to Reat and seems to be leaning over his body. There he is. My baby boy. Reat is on his back … lying down in a small grassy area in the arms of these two men. I don't recognize either of them. He looks asleep.

Fear. Disbelief. I feel sick. Oh my God! What has happened?

Physically, I am already close to them. They are only a few feet away from the right side of my father's truck. These two strangers seem to be caring for him. I scream, "What happened?" which startles me and both of them. One of the men looks directly at me and asks, "Who are you?"

As I point in the direction of my father's lifeless body, I tell them, "That is my father and he is in Heaven. This is my son. Is he still alive?" Reat looks asleep. Thirty minutes ago he was smiling at me. He was singing to me. Singing. The word "singing" is in my brain and fearful of being noticed.

There was no smile on his angelic face. No movements that I could see. Moving close enough to lean over the two men, I could see red spots covering his face. His face looked as if he had a case of measles or chickenpox. At the moment, I fail to realize these spots are blood.

My brain is working to reconcile what my eyes are seeing. My body seems to be present, but not present, at the same time. Suddenly, I am physically grabbed by a man who came from behind me. He came out of nowhere and almost toppled me. With my full attention directed at two men holding my seemingly injured son, I am shaken by the full brunt of another large man. His arms go around me; he is holding me and at the same time pushing me lower. There is some sort of nonverbal exchange between the man holding me in a crouching position and the men caring for Reat. I see their mouths moving but hear nothing. My head turns to look at the truck, which is now to my immediate left. Not so close that I could touch it … but close.

While my gaze is on the truck, working to assimilate my view, I feel my body standing up and out of the crouched position. The man stands me up and I hear him say, "I have to take you to a safer place. There is a live shooter in the area."

When I hear the word "shooter," my eyes and brain work to focus on what I see around and near Dad's truck. The passenger side door is open. Reat would have been sitting in the passenger seat. The window is shattered. Glass from the window has exploded into thousands of small fragments on the ground below the open door.

I look toward the Jewish Community Center and don't see a shooter coming our way.

My gaze manages to fixate on Reat for a long enough moment to see his beautiful face. He only looks asleep. Asleep with red dots on his face. What happened? Why?

The man who grabbed me from behind now has me in an upright position. Although I am standing, he continues to hold my arms firmly and his stomach is against my back and body. He is strong and much taller than me. His voice is telling me to walk. What?

He is mostly holding me up. I feel hands and arms tightly gripping my arms, working to move me. My body does begin to move, as he is directing our pace. He is practically carrying me as we walk around Reat and the two men.

I hear a voice ask me why I am here. We have reached the entrance to the White Theatre. Reat was to be auditioning in the White Theatre.

"Why are you here?" "How do you know them?" The stranger has come from behind me and is now holding me from the side. We are in a side hug, except my arms are limp at my side. I am looking at the scene we just left and see the two men moving their hands, lifting Reat's head and shoulders from the ground. My legs are weak.

My view allows for me to see Reat, the truck and my father all at the same time. I am leaning against the stranger. I am bewildered. My body is shaking. I feel nauseous.

The question is repeated by the stranger, "Why are you here?"

I attempt to lift my head to look at him. A whoosh of nausea inside me is about to make an appearance. Without realizing how quickly I want to stop this feeling inside of me, I bend over, desperately seeking relief from the dizzying nausea.

From a bent-over position with the stranger's hand on my back, I explain that they are my dad and my son. I hear the man ask me if there is someone I can call. Then he asks, "Another family member?"

Still bent over with my hands on my knees and the stranger still extremely attentive to me, I look over at the full scene. Reat is unresponsive to the two men. I think to myself, "What is wrong with him?"

My father's truck is sitting idle and somehow holding the secret to what happened in this parking lot. His body is still. Disbelief.

The world seems to be spinning around my head. I need it to stop so that I can think.

"Was he shot?" I ask the man as I begin to take steps, walking back toward Reat. The man on the right of Reat's body, now to my left, waves his hand in a motion that says nonverbally, "Don't come over here." I ask the stranger standing with me, "Can I hold my son's hand?" My request is relayed from one stranger helping me to another stranger helping Reat. His arm and hand are firmly in a "stop" motion. Holding Reat with one arm and holding his other arm up in a "stop" motion, I am told to stay away.

My stranger escorts me the few steps back to the entrance of the White Theatre. He says that an ambulance has been called and they should be here shortly. I'm having trouble standing up. I've become so wobbly and disoriented that he continues to keep me in his grasp as he locates a metal chair from somewhere.

He sets me in the chair and asks again if I have someone I can call. "Yes, I do," I tell him. "What I don't have is my phone to make a call. My phone is in the truck," I hear myself say as I work to raise my arm and point at the vehicle that holds the secrets in the parking lot. Thoughts of walking to the truck and retrieving the phone are fleeting. Even in my desperate state of shock, I realize this parking lot has become a crime scene. The truck, the keeper of the secrets to what happened, is part of a crime scene. I know I shouldn't try to retrieve my phone.

My stranger hands me his phone. Immediately, the phone is popping up and down in my unsteady hands and I struggle to hold on to it. My body, shaking uncontrollably, won't allow me to hold on to his phone. I make a futile attempt to hold it steady while I type in the numbers. I can't hold the phone steady enough, so I hand it back to him. He watches this take place and reaches for the phone. I offer it to him with both of my hands, as if in a prayer position asking for communion. Without him asking me, I begin to recite the number I was attempting to dial.

Len answers the phone. I hear his voice on the other end of the phone, sounding a bit suspicious about answering a call from a number he did not recognize. My stranger explains that he is with me and that I need to talk to Len. Handing me the phone again, I take it with both hands and hold it to my ear, still holding it with both hands. I ask Len if he is driving. He says he is. I then ask him to drive carefully while I speak to him. The words I need to speak begin to come out of my mouth. As I speak the words, I am hurting. My stomach is aching. My body is shaking as if I have been placed in a freezer. I say as clearly as I can, "Len, there has been a shooting at the Jewish Community Center. My dad was shot and killed. Len, my dad is dead. I think Reat was shot too, but I can't tell. There are men working on him. He is sitting up, but I think they are holding him up."

My eyes are on Reat and the two men caring for him. While I am deeply concerned for Reat, I don't have the urge to rush over for fear of interrupting their care. I watch the two men with Reat as I talk to Len. They are wrapping a white towel or some sort of fabric around Reat's head. He doesn't seem to be conscious. I tell Len, "A man is wrapping something around Reat's head. Dear God, he may have been shot in the head. There is a lot of broken glass everywhere."

Len responds to me, but I have no recollection of what he said, nor does he recall what he said to me. He remembers being confused by what I was saying to him. He remembers me screaming into the phone. It wasn't a calm phone call. He could tell I was extremely upset. My words were coming so quickly and, of course, none of what I was saying was expected and didn't make sense to him. He heard me say, "My dad is dead and Reat is shot. I don't know if he is alive." Unfortunately, 12-year-old Lukas also heard me say these words.

Reminding Len that Reat had my phone in my dad's truck, I ask him to call my mother. Again, there is no recollection of any words he said to me. I give the phone back to my stranger helping me and ask him to tell Len where we are. Saying out loud that my dad was dead was too much to process. Evidently, Len was in the car still heading home from the canceled lacrosse game. He and Lukas were listening to me screaming on the other end of the phone, trying to assimilate the meaning of my words. They were heading in the opposite direction from where I needed them to be.

After my stranger offers Len directions to where we are, I say to my stranger, "My dad is dead. We need to pray for Reat." Rain begins to fall lightly on me, the ground and my dad. The storm. The storm that canceled the lacrosse game has found me. The wind picks up. My eyes move from my dad's body to Reat while my brain is filled with a flurry of thoughts about how this could happen. Is this real?

I don't remember praying.

A woman walks outside and stares at us with an expression of utter disbelief. I don't recall what she said to me, but I remember asking her to cover my father. Specifically, I asked for a tarp or some sort of covering that would keep my family members from seeing what I saw. "My family will be arriving soon. I don't want them to see him this way," was how I phrased my first sentences about my father's death.

My stranger asks if he can depart and check on something. With my permission, he leaves me alone on the chair. The air turns cooler. I am shaking. A few people gather around me. Their faces look as shocked as I feel. Someone takes me by the hand and walks me inside. They tell me there is a shooter in the area and I need to be inside. They led me to the theater. I find a seat in the back row. The theatre is dark and quiet … eerie. There are people present, but they are voiceless. Do they know what happened? I feel as though I walked into the middle of a production just before the stage curtain is to be raised. Darkness, silence and anticipation hang in the air. The fogginess in my brain continues to be present.

After only a few moments of sitting by myself in the back of the theatre, my nausea makes a comeback. Feeling as though the nausea will win this time, I want to ask where I might find the restroom. There was a man standing near me. I ask him for assistance. This man places his arm around me and I spot his nametag. His name is Jacob. "Jacob, I know you. Don't I know you?" "Yes," he responds, "We know one another." I tell Jacob my dad is in Heaven and my son, Reat, is being cared for in the grassy area outside. I ask Jacob if he knows when the ambulance will arrive. He assures me he doesn't know but that one is on the way. I think I ask him to make sure he comes and gets me when they arrive so that I can be in the ambulance with Reat.

While he nods to me, he also looks deeply troubled. He walks me to an area where there is light—a bright light which makes me squint. I hear Jacob ask someone to assist me in finding the women's restroom. A woman takes me by my right elbow and walks me some steps into a bathroom. As she leads me, I notice there are people all around me. These are young people. My brain remembers something important. Reat was supposed to be one of these young people. They are talking, but I can't make out their words. There are whispers and soft crying. I feel uneasy walking through them, as if I have interrupted their production. I shouldn't be here. This is not where I am supposed to be right now. I am supposed to be sitting in the theatre waiting to watch my son audition.

Only looking up to see the door, I catch a glimpse of a few faces. Tears have streaked their cheeks, makeup is streaming down their faces and their expressions are of disbelief. The nausea is about to win as I make my way into a bathroom stall. Sitting rather than standing, or leaning over … my body has decided to potty rather than vomit; and I relieve myself as the crying grows louder in the room just outside the bathroom.

The reality of being too far away from Reat when the ambulance arrives comes to mind. My nausea disappears.

Somehow, I make it back into the darkness of the theater. As I walk toward the back of the room, my mom rushes through the doors. She screams when she sees me, "Mindy! Oh my god!" She is screaming, "Was that your dad? Was that your father? I saw his shoe under the tarp! What happened? Where is Reat?"

Breaking into sobs, I reach for her and pull myself into her embrace. Hugging her tightly, I began to say what I had felt but could not put into words. "I am so sorry, Mom. I am so sorry. I should have been the one driving Reat. I should have driven him. I am so sorry."

The guilt had been stewing in me. Now it was flowing out of me. I needed a release. While I want to keep repeating these words in a way to somehow reverse the death of my father, my mom interrupts me.

"Where is Reat?" she asks over and over into my shoulder. We are embraced, shaking and crying. The darkness of the theatre envelops me more as I push away, look her in to her eyes and yell …

"What do you mean, 'Where is Reat?'"

Top Left: Reverend Lewis and Helen Corporon, Mindy's paternal grandparents, also known as Pepaw and Memaw. Photo taken for the Central Christian Church directory in Enid, Oklahoma. 1998

Bottom Left: Bill, Melinda, Will, Mindy and Tony Corporon pose for a family photo. 1978

Right: Travis and Rita Gordy, Mindy's maternal grandparents, also known as GrandDaddy and Muthie. This photo was taken for the United Methodist Church directory in Ponca City, Oklahoma. Early 1990s.

7

A Good Enough Christian

The Bible Belt is defined as those areas of the Southern and Midwestern United States and Western Canada where Protestant fundamentalism is widely practiced.

As a young girl, I lived and felt the definition of the Bible Belt, but didn't come to understand it fully until I reached my 40s.

Every Sunday in our small town, people scattered to worship in the churches they had attended for generations. In Marlow, Oklahoma, you would find Baptist, Catholic, Church of Christ, Methodist, Pentecostal and Presbyterian services. Everyone was one form or another of Christian, at least everyone I knew.

It felt as if each place of worship competed to fill their pews, choirs and youth groups.

In conversations with friends either on my elementary school playground or in the cafeteria in middle school, I was made aware of the goings-on in everyone's own place of worship. There was a focus on volunteering and giving to those in need among all the congregations. Funnel cake sales for this need and garage sales for that need occurred often. There were also parking lot car washes and bake sales to fund a missionary passing through on their way to a far-off country spreading the word of Jesus. Invitations to the First Baptist Church came often and sometimes I would be able to attend.

Vacation Bible school was a rite of passage in my church and every other church in town. The stories were taught with puppets, songs and craft materials—oh those craft materials. God must love crafts, I surmised. When I became a mom, my childhood craft days in Sunday school and vacation Bible school came roaring back to me. I filled an entire cabinet of items from Hobby Lobby and Michaels with craft materials like popsicle sticks, markers, glue (there always had to be glue), construction paper and pipe cleaners. Jingle bells, puffy balls in a variety of colors and wooden cutouts were always part of my collection because you never know when you might need a wooden cutout to decorate.

Everyone I knew was enrolled in some fashion of Bible school or weeklong Bible camp in the summers during our elementary years, while Sunday school was expected year-round.

How many ways could a room full of sweaty 8-year-old kids create the Last Supper? Answer: as many ways as there were children tasked with the project. Dioramas, poster boards and puppet shows were my favorite ways to learn the stories of the Bible.

Virgin Mary presented with the task to bring baby Jesus into the world, John the Baptist and his dunking of those willing to be baptized, Jesus healing seemingly anyone and everyone who said they "believed" in Him and "do unto others as you would have done unto you," the Golden Rule … these were ingrained in my young mind as I sat in the First United Methodist Church and then the First Cumberland Presbyterian Church from age 7 to 17.

As a youngster and to this day, reciting the verse of the day was torture for me.

Memorizing and reciting Scriptures has never been in my DNA. Unfortunately, memorizing and reciting Scriptures was part of the criteria for gold stars and attagirls at vacation Bible school. I never felt the permission to ad lib my thoughts or ideas associated with the verse of the day. This would have been a game changer for me. My inability to recite the verse of the day or the Scripture of the week, specifically associated with its definitive chapter in the Bible, led me to believe I was not a good enough Christian. Whether I felt this from the teachers, the students or from my own competitive nature, it doesn't matter.

In fact, I am certain that none of the teachers explicitly intended on laying any Christian shame on me for not knowing the verse of the day.

I am certain how I felt about not being able to remember the verses well enough to recite them back to my class or small group in the specific format requested: chapter, verse and then the language. For instance, I can recite the Lord's Prayer and could from the age of about 6. However, I couldn't tell you where to find it in the Bible. I could tell you it is found somewhere in Matthew, Mark, Luke or John—the Gospels. I felt I was not a good enough Christian.

My first memory of the Golden Rule wasn't at all golden, nor was it initially associated with the Bible or church. I am sure I was misbehaving in some fashion, being the independent, sassy girl that I was. My Muthie, (Mom's mother, my grandmother) quickly spoke these words to me as I entered her kitchen, most likely running from my older brother, who was after me for something I did to him. Also known as "poking the bear."

Muthie would say, "MindyDoll, what have you done? Do unto others as you would have them do unto you." I saw this as a Muthie-ism and not as a Bible verse. As a result, I didn't associate this message with a location in the Bible. This message was a family message and, therefore, a family value. Learning this verse came from the Bible during a Sunday school lesson only lifted my Muthie to saint status in my mind. My Muthie not only knew verses from the Bible, she used them in her daily conversations.

As a high schooler, I often entered the Methodist church on a Friday night after home football games. Coined the "Friday night dances," these social outings were held in the basement of the Methodist church.

Since the Baptists weren't allowed to dance at their own churches, these students also found their way to the basement of the Methodist church on Friday nights. Having never attended the Catholic church in Marlow, my only recollection of any Catholic students I knew was one of stoicism. They talked about attending "mass," but my interest was not piqued enough to explore further.

Another "baptism into Christianity," as it was known in my church and my town, was to attend summer youth church camp. I heard all about it prior to being old enough to attend myself. The cabins, woods and camp food intrigued me immensely. The idea that we would gather around a campfire and sing our favorite hymns was appealing. Older youth would return from camp and be invited on stage to share their experiences with our own youth group and others they met during their weeklong adventure. I wanted to be them. I craved to have experiences in nature with God, like I had heard explained to me from the stage in our small church. Attending summer youth church camp was sure to make me a good enough Christian.

There was always a reason I couldn't attend summer youth church camp.

They ranged from gymnastics to cheerleading to "that's not our church" camp.

From age 7 to 12, competitive gymnastics was significant in my life. I loved gymnastics and, like many girls my age, dreamed of being Nadia Comaneci. In 1976, when she was claiming her individual gold medals at the Olympics, I was 8. This dream lasted another four years for me as I traveled to various summer camps in the United States and competed during the school year on our local team.

Cheerleading entered my life when I was 10 and in fifth grade.

Cheering became my religion.

It kept me in a group during high school, prepared me for and helped me win a national championship, launched me into friendships, leadership positions and fun in college and allowed me employment over several high school summers and after college.

"That's not our church," was my parents' response regarding my desire to attend ANY church camp available at the same time I had an open week. My assumption was that whatever was going on in the "other church" summer camp was not intended for me.

I had two specific thoughts about "that's not our church," spoken by my parents. First, I took this to mean that I didn't measure up to the "other church's" standards of Christianity. Second, I considered that what I was being taught in the short amount of time I had available with my own youth group was enough for me. Waffling back and forth between these two ways of thinking kept me in a position of feeling I didn't measure up to being a good enough Christian. My thoughts about myself as a Christian morphed into me thinking because I was not a good enough Christian, I didn't qualify for what other churches provided Christians, and I had been taught enough in the time I spent and wasn't worth having more education provided in the realm of Christianity.

A small lifeline came in the form of an angel, literally. During my high school years, my mom oversaw the music programs in our church. This included the adult choir, children's choir and any youth programs throughout the year, namely Christmas. My mom placed me in the position of the lead angel in our live Nativity scene for Christmas. Music was playing in the background and someone was narrating the story. My lines were, "Do not be afraid. I bring you good news of great joy that will be for all the people. Today in the town of David a Savior has been born to you; he is Christ the Lord." Without having to remember from which Bible verse these words came, I learned these lines quickly. Standing on at least two bales of hay, I stood above the other humans in the program, as well as the donkey who had brought in our Mary.

Playing this angel and repeating these words for others to hear meant something to me. Somehow I could feel that I could talk to God on my own. Standing on the hay bale several nights in a row, being what many called "a witness" to my faith, helped me witness myself.

My mom's parents, Travis and Rita Gordy, lived two hours and 45 minutes away in Ponca City. We visited "Muthie and GrandDaddy" (my older brother, Will, named them) often. We loved to watch them sing in the choir at their United Methodist Church. They had beautiful voices. GrandDaddy sang so well that he displayed his talent as part of a barbershop quartet when my mom was a young girl.

My mom always wears a smile when we talk about GrandDaddy's barbershop quartet practices and performances. These are fond memories for her and her three sisters. My Muthie stayed home to raise her four girls, my mom being the oldest. Muthie and GrandDaddy volunteered often at their church and in their community. My mom must have learned her generous ways from them.

Communion was important in all the churches I attended. Communion in any church symbolizes the scene that took place at the

Last Supper. Bread, or small wafers representing bread, were present. These represented the body of Jesus. There was wine involved, or in our case, grape juice. Grape juice was poured into small individual cups, which were placed in a large, round brass tray with holes made for these cups. The wine or grape juice represented the blood of Christ.

Communion represents giving your life to Christ. Each time I take communion I am committing myself to follow the teachings of Jesus, Son of God. As a grown woman, each time I take communion I am transported to the United Methodist Church basement in Ponca City, Oklahoma, where my Muthie taught me how to prepare communion and its importance in our lives.

In my younger years, whenever we visited them, I went to church on Saturdays with Muthie. At this time in her life, it was her responsibility to prepare Sunday's communion trays. I'll never forget all she taught me about the beauty of communion in that church basement.

Her voice eloquently explained the importance of communion. She explained that it meant I was a Christian, a believer in Jesus Christ. And not only do we believe in His teachings, but also more importantly, in His sacrificial death and resurrection.

While I was worried about not remembering Scriptures and verses, my Muthie was comforting me about how I was accepted by God through having faith.

"Now MindyDoll," Muthie would say, "This is the blood of Christ. We don't want to make a mess of it. We want to live up to the expectations of what Christ asks us to do."

"This is the blood of Christ," I would repeat to myself, "Don't make a mess with it."

Pour, pour, pour—we were pouring the grape juice into the small, very tiny cups, which were nestled in the round, brass (I have since found these come in a silver finish, too) communion tray. Once each of the cups were filled in one tray, we would fill another and stack one on top of the other. We had to be meticulous so as to NOT make a mess of the grape juice.

As a 7- or 8-year-old, the room seemed large, the countertop was high and those small cups were numerous. The allure of this moment came from the outside windows. Rays of light filled the room, glistening on the brass communion trays as they lay in wait to be filled to the brim and then stacked.

I felt like those trays then, and sometimes, now. I want to be filled to the brim with goodness and love. I want to be poured into by someone who cares so deeply they don't want to make a mess of me. I need to feel sturdy in how I stand and where I stand, just like the stacked communion trays.

The desire to have attention from anyone, let alone my grandmother, was important and filled me. Our task was great. She enveloped me in her world, allowing me to be her helper and to learn the mystery of communion.

Muthie and GrandDaddy talked openly about their faith in God, the expectations of being a good Christian and their expectations of me as one of theirs.

The Rev. Lewis and Helen Corporon, my father's parents, were just as active in their church and community. I remember traveling to Concord, California, picking oranges and frolicking in very green grass. Memories also take me into more church services in California and in Enid, Oklahoma. My Pepaw was an educator and then a minister. Dad used to joke with me that he had attended more church in his teenage years than I would in my whole lifetime.

Being parents to six children, my father being the second and only boy, they had their hands and home full for many years.

Church, family and living all wrapped into one for me. With Pepaw as a senior minister at the First Christian Church in Concord, California, from 1969 to 1976, I didn't see them often. When we did visit, church was part of our visit. Memaw and Pepaw returned to Enid, Oklahoma in 1976, so he could take the position as associate minister with the Central Christian Church.

Again, every time I saw them over a period of one day or three or more days, at some point church, church friends or a church luncheon were included. I never knew them without God and Christianity being involved.

I know Dad tired of being the preacher's son. Yet when Dad and Mom had us kids, Sunday church became a weekly staple for our family. My dad even stood at the pulpit and delivered sermons occasionally when our pastor was away.

During my college years in Norman, Oklahoma, I enjoyed the freedom of driving to Enid for long lunches and peach ice cream with Memaw and Pepaw. I was never there very long before a knock at the door would present a loving neighbor from their retirement community. They didn't know a stranger and welcomed all people with open arms. It was a blessing to watch them interact with their friends.

Filled with nostalgia as I drove from Enid to Norman, I knew those conversations with Memaw and Pepaw were shaping me. As I pondered our talks and their advice on my way back to the University of Oklahoma, I was deeply grateful for my time with them. The message I heard from them was patience, fortitude, resilience and above all— faith in God. At the time I was engaging with them, they were past their child-rearing years and enjoying retirement at the Golden Oaks Retirement Village. They had time for patience and had learned over the years that square pegs don't go in round holes. It takes fortitude to lift your family from one location, a location you have known much of your life, and move far away because God asked you to ... FAITH. Using my own father as an example of resilience, they reminded me of the hard work he had endured to become a physician while raising a family along the route.

Everything I was taught by my maternal and paternal grandparents seemingly came from their being Christian.

The town in which I grew up hosted only Christian locations for worship.

My worship experiences were swaddled in Christianity.

Therefore, when I made the move from college to adult life, finding myself in the Kansas City metropolitan area and employed with a wealth management firm at the age of 24, I knowingly had my first encounter with Jewish people.

As an employee at Kidder, Peabody & Company, I worked for two male brokers. One of which later became my business partner for a period of 24 years, Richard W. Boyer. Richard was friends with people of the Jewish faith. Some of these friends had become clients of his; therefore, I began engaging with Jewish people on a weekly basis.

Having no experience with Judaism, I stumbled mightily as I learned about their holidays, rituals and vernacular, such as calling their place of worship a temple, rather than a church. One horribly embarrassing mistake I made was in conversation with (lucky for me) only Richard. I don't recall the context but we were discussing something about money and haggling. The words, "Why don't you jew him down?" came out of my mouth, with no sensitivity whatsoever for the clients we worked with daily. Richard's face turned red as a beet as he began to admonish me for what I had said.

Here's the deal: I had no idea that what I had said was of negative connotation to Jews. This term had been used as frequently in my life as "I feel rode hard and put up wet," was used when anyone had a long, exhausting day. Richard was right to correct me. It pained me to realize I was lacking in understanding about this entire faith and culture of people with whom I now relied on for some of my own income.

In the same few months that I was being indoctrinated into working at a wealth management firm and engaging with Jewish people who were clients, I was invited to attend a college friend's wedding.

Jennifer Douglas and I were Tri Delta pledge sisters. Jennifer was Christian and Jennifer's fiance, Mark Ephraim, was Jewish. When I interviewed Jennifer for this book, I asked her if we had talked about Mark being Jewish when they met. We had not. They married at the Oak Tree Golf and Country Club in Edmond, Oklahoma, with a rabbi performing the ceremony. This was my first introduction to any type of Jewish ceremony. When Mark stomped on a wine glass wrapped in a cloth as they stood under a canopy called a chuppah (sounds like huppāh), I almost jumped out of my seat. This was as much Jewishness as I saw because as soon as we were released from the ceremony, I was deeply engaged with all my Tri Delta sisters in hugs, laughter and sharing our current lives.

Jennifer and Mark have been married 29 years and are raising two children, who are flying from their nest, despite COVID-19. Jennifer shared with me that no one had meaningful or caring questions for her before her marriage to Mark. In fact, she vividly remembers a coworker saying, "You know if you marry him and have kids, your kids will go to hell." She was living in Oklahoma City, Oklahoma, the same state in which both of us had been raised—smack dab in the middle of the Bible Belt. The Bible Belt is not the Torah Belt.

In recent years, the caring, meaningful questions started to appear, such as how they raised their children: Christian or Jewish? She said *Jewish*. Do they celebrate Christmas or Hanukkah? Her response was *Hanukkah*. They had a girl and a boy. They attended Jewish preschool and a Hebrew school and hosted bat and bar mitzvahs at the age of 13. Jennifer and Mark continued their children's Jewish education with confirmation ceremonies at the end of their sophomore year of high school. Jennifer shared with me that while she visited her family during Christmas and Easter, these times together were "family" time, not religious time for her family of four. She and Mark raised their children with the Jewish faith. Judaism has been her religion.

The importance of my sharing this chapter with you is this: I don't remember a time when I was not Christian. While I never heard my grandparents or my parents say "Jesus is the only way," or "you will go to Hell if Jesus is not your Savior," this was said from the pulpits and then relayed to me on the playground, in vacation Bible school and youth group. These statements defined Christianity for me.

When my mother heard me speak publicly about how I remember my childhood teachings of Christianity, she reminded me that on Sundays after church we sat at the kitchen table discussing the sermon.

She also reminded me that during any family conversations, I could be present, but yet not present. I have been told that discussions on any topic could ensue, perhaps plans would be made based on these discussions and yet even while I was physically present, I wouldn't know the result of the discussion. This happened often enough that I became known for "not paying attention."

The message I received from my mom as an adult, after the murders of Dad and Reat, has been that our family has always been friendly and open to those of other religions. After all, my parents had Jewish Orthodox friends when we lived in Oklahoma City. Of course, this meant they were open to other religions. I was 3 years old when we lived in Oklahoma City. One of my memories is of stepping on a tack with bare feet. There is no recollection of our neighbors having a different religion than the one in my heritage.

While this is a lovely and meaningful message to receive now, it didn't soak in with me as a child, teenager or young adult. Whether this was because I wasn't fully present during our family conversations or whether the messages from the pulpit and life in the Bible Belt were louder, it is moot at this point.

My religion taught me that our religion was the ONLY way to not end up in Hell.

I had believed this, or at least had not questioned it enough to create any other avenue of belief. Dutifully, I was following the Christian life and teachings I heard from the pulpit and learned from other churchgoers. Charity, community involvement and "loving my neighbor as myself" were more than an appearance, they were who I was in my adult years. As the wife and mother in my own home, the chief executive officer of a business, the values I learned in the pew, on the lap of my grandparents and parents was that as a Christian my faith in Jesus, God and the Holy Spirit had saved me. And because of this belief there was no way I would go to Hell. Hell was for sinners and those who didn't believe in Jesus as the Son of God. Yet, here I was living in Hell.

Had I not been a good enough Christian to keep my father and son alive?

Top: Melinda and Bill Corporon, along with Len, Mindy, Reat and Lukas attending Reat's Cub Scout Blue & Gold Banquet. A family unit of six. 2009

Left: Doing what they loved most, being with their grandchildren, Melinda and Bill are surrounded by Travis Corporon, Reat Underwood, Lukas Losen, Katy and Andrew Corporon and baby Olivia Corporon. Location not remembered because that wasn't what was important about this photo. 2012

8

Devastation

"Reat is on the grass! Reat is on the grass next to Dad's truck! Two men are caring for him." My response is fast and fearful to my mom, who is questioning where Reat is.

She shrieks back at me, "No! He is not there." Mom explains that when she was pulling into the parking lot, an ambulance was pulling out. She says they were driving slowly. She screams it over and over, "The ambulance was driving slowly."

My brain is on fire now—the nausea from my stomach is now anger in my heart and brain. What does she mean? What ambulance? "I asked them to come get me. I asked to be with Reat. Are you sure you didn't see him on the grass next to the truck?" I ask her.

We have fully released one another and I am now directing her to the door from where she came only 10 minutes or so after me. Into the hallway we walk freely, aiming for the shattered glass doors near the entrance to the White Theatre.

Our conversation is fast, disjointed and filled with anger and disbelief from each of us. I am deeply concerned that my mom could have seen my father in the way I did. I am mystified as to why NO ONE came to get me to ride in the ambulance with my child.

They knew I was there. Where are the two men who were caring for him? Where is my stranger? How long had I been in the darkness of the theater?

As we approach the glass doors and attempt to go outside, the police stop us. The police are here. While we physically stop when asked, we continue our disjointed conversation about the "slowly moving ambulance," "my dad's body under the tarp," and "where are they taking Reat?"

Disbelief. Anger. Sickness.

Many police officers have arrived on the scene. A blonde female officer is outside walking quickly around and marking the area. There are officers scattered throughout the hallway. I walk up to one and ask, "Where is the boy? Where did you take him?"

The officer says he cannot tell me where they took the young man because he didn't have an ID on him. I scream back at him, "He is not a young man! What? What are you talking about? I saw him. I am his mother. I wanted to be with him. I was with him until someone led me away. Why didn't they come get me? Where is my son? Tell me where you took him!" I am yelling at the officer, shaking, my whole body is filled with anger, fear and frustration.

Jacob, the man with the name tag from the theater, comes around the corner and pulls the officer away from me to speak with him.

Physically retreating a few feet away from the police officer and Jacob, I am now standing next to my mom. We are looking frantically for anyone else who will help us. We need to know where they took Reat.

My mom is tenacious and outspoken as she continues to ask out loud why they won't tell us where the ambulance has taken Reat. Her voice is loud as she states again, "He is not a man; he is a boy. He is only 14 years old. She is his mother!"

Her tenacity allows me a moment to steal a look outside. I am looking for a secret way to bolt out the back door, hoping to find the men who were caring for Reat. They will speak to me. They will remember I was there.

My heart sinks. Reat is no longer on the grassy space. The red truck with the secrets from the parking lot rests untouched, with shattered glass around it like a nest. Someone did place a blue tarp over my father's body. "I am sorry, Dad," I say aloud and to myself. "I am sorry, Dad," are words I hear myself saying today.

Soaking wet and breathless, my younger brother Tony runs toward us from another entrance to the building. Quickly, I give Tony an update on what I know. He and I embrace. Apparently, the perimeter is already blocked off and the state trooper wouldn't let Tony drive into the area because, as the officer explained, "It's a crime scene."

My mom says she is going to be sick, so all three of us walk into the women's restroom. My mom goes inside a stall as Tony succumbs to anger. A bathroom stall receives the blow.

"What is happening?" I ask myself again. I feel responsible for this, but I can't help. "I should have been driving Reat," I say aloud.

As the daughter of a physician, I know in my heart that the medical team working with Reat will do all they can to help him. My heart will not allow my brain to think negatively.

Chaos. Fear. And now torrential rain. I feel as though my spirit is fading.

We walk out of the bathroom and back into the hallway. Len and Lukas appear. Their faces are filled with fear. I am so very frightened to tell Lukas that Reat, his big brother, was shot with a gun.

Time passes slowly as we continue to try and ascertain where our Reat was taken. Law enforcement stands firm in their unwillingness to share any information. In their minds, we could all be potential suspects. And, since Reat had no identification, they remain silent.

After what seems like hours, somebody finally shares the invaluable information that, typically, victims of head trauma are transported to Overland Park Regional Medical Center.

My mind shifts to the familiarity of that hospital.

Lukas was born there in 2002, and Len helped them place pneumatic tubing in their new building several years prior. I am also familiar with the previous CEO. We know that hospital well. Surely, they will save Reat.

Our hearts pound as we long to know Reat's condition, but the torrential downpour is forcing us to stay put. As I stand still for a moment to ponder my new reality, a man with a familiar face runs up to me. I recognize that he is the man who practically tackled me to the ground in the parking lot. This time he is running toward us with keys to our car. He has pulled it up under the overhang to shield us from the pelting rain and placed several other men on either side of our vehicle, blocking us from the already arriving media. Even in my numbing shock and desperate grief, I recognize him as a hero.

As my stranger approaches, he introduces himself to our small, frightened family. Mickey. Mickey Blount is my hero and no longer my stranger.

Len and Lukas come in close for a hug. I am shaking uncontrollably. Len holds me tightly. He explains to me that another person has also been shot. They saw the body in the parking lot at Village Shalom, which is just a couple blocks away. They had accidentally turned into Village Shalom, thinking that it was the Jewish Community Center. They heard sirens and saw flashing lights, so they followed the police into the incorrect location. He is explaining why they took so long to arrive at the Jewish Community Center.

Another person dead. Another body in a parking lot. As I try to take this in, I am being ushered into our vehicle and into the back seat. My mom and I always get car sick ... she worse than me. So, on this drive, her placement in the front seat takes precedence over my car sickness.

Len gets behind the wheel as mom takes the passenger's seat. I lower myself into the seat behind Len and Tony takes the other back seat behind Mom. Lukas retreats silently to the third row. My mom and Len have a conversation about the route to the hospital, but my mind is so deeply distraught that I can't hear or understand them. Lukas is silent during the entire car ride. I use Len's phone to call Richard Boyer, my business partner of 22 years.

Richard doesn't answer his phone, so I leave a message. "Rich, this is Mindy. You may have heard there was a shooting at the Jewish Community Center this afternoon. My dad was with Reat at the 'J' for the KC SuperStar auditions. My dad was shot and killed and Reat has been taken to Overland Park Regional Medical Center. Rich, my dad is dead and we don't know how badly Reat is injured. I don't have my phone, so please call me back on Len's phone."

I hang up the phone. I can't believe the words I have just spoken. Shock must be overcoming me because I feel myself shutting down.

The ride to the hospital is heavy with fear and disbelief. Internally, I keep reliving the scene I came upon in the parking lot—the sight of my dad, blood still pooling around him as he lay lifeless on the ground, and Reat. Reat was being held up by two men. It is so vivid in my mind. I am seeing it over and over. I can't shake the image.

Even today, I can visualize myself in that parking lot. The rush of nausea associated with the scene is still immediate. I understand now that the sick feeling that day came from a rush of cortisol. When we experience a traumatic event, cortisol rises in our system and can make us nauseous. My body was pulsing with cortisol.

Guilt has been overtaking my mind. I should have been the one driving Reat. It should have been me parking the car. Maybe I would have parked in a different area or maybe I would have been just a couple minutes earlier or later. Maybe I would be dead instead of my dad. Maybe I would have saved Reat.

My dad was an avid hunter. He taught Reat how to hunt and they were both members of the NRA. Dad had two guns in his truck that day. He was licensed to carry and spent a substantial amount of time teaching me, my mom and his grandkids how to properly shoot a gun. I know he would have defended himself, and certainly Reat, if he had had the opportunity. It didn't appear that he had any time to defend anyone. He must have been ambushed.

As we approach the lighted "Emergency" sign, my world is surreal. My dad has been an ER doctor for the past nine years. When he left his 30-year medical practice in Duncan, Oklahoma, he didn't want to start a new practice, so he shifted his career to the ER. Dad and Mom began their journey to relocate to Kansas City in 2003, motivated by a desire for close proximity to their grandkids. Dad lost his maternal grandfather when he was just 4 years old. He had fond memories of his time with his grandfather and talked often about how devastating it was to lose him, at such a young age. I think this played into his decision to relocate to Kansas City. Other factors prompted my dad to close his beloved medical practice, so that he could maximize his time with his grandkids.

Reat and I moved in with my parents shortly after his birth. At 4 weeks of age, Reat was unaware that his parents were divorcing. He only felt a deep love from each adult who had the opportunity to cuddle and care for him. Reat was physically held by my dad, almost more than me, during the 10 months we were wrapped in what I refer to as "the cradle of love." Nutrition, exercise and sleep were not simply made available, they were mandatory and instructed by Dad. He made me smoothie concoctions each morning, filled with protein and vegetables, hoping they would add some much needed weight to my depleted body. Every day after work, Dad would don his back-pack carrier, place Reat inside the infant pouch and off they would go! The two of them traversed our 40 acres often, finding snakes, picking blackberries and loving the nature around them. This was a piece of heaven for my dad.

When I moved back to the Kansas City area with his "baby Reat," depression set in for both my parents, but Dad verbalized his longing to be with Reat more loudly. My phone call to Dad, shortly after Lukas' birth, asking for a higher level of grandparental assistance prompted the relocation discussion.

It wasn't easy for Dad to find a job in Kansas City, so he took a circuitous route. Mom and Dad moved to two different towns after leaving Marlow, before eventually settling in Overland Park, Kansas, a suburb of Kansas City, Missouri. First, Dad found a job in Nevada, Missouri, and then eventually landed in Pittsburg, Kansas, before finally securing a job nearby. That season wasn't for the faint of heart. Dad and Mom made huge sacrifices in order to slowly make their way to be near their grandchildren. A sacrifice of his life was not something anyone had intended.

We typically enter the ER as "family of the doc," but that is not the case today. On our way in, we find an ambulance, recently emptied, with the doors still wide open. I feel hopeful as this points to the fact they were obviously in a hurry. I approach the window and speak to the young man, "I am the mother of the young boy who was brought in with the head trauma from the gunshot wound."

These are horribly painful words to say. As they leave my mouth, I feel faint from the haunting reality that my father is dead. My concerns shift to Reat and I pray, with everything still left in me, that he is still alive.

Within a minute, a woman enters the hallway from a side door and takes me gently by the arm. Len, Lukas, Mom and Tony all surround me as we follow this woman, a nurse, into a small room. My sister-in-law Dana has arrived and walks in with us.

The nurse turns to leave the room and explains that someone will come get us shortly. I have heard enough ER stories from my dad to know that being led to a small room is not a good sign. Our nervous energy teeters back and forth between hope and fear. I pray for good news. I try to imagine the scenario that we get to see Reat before they take him into surgery of some kind, but I also have a sinking suspicion that this is not likely the case. I wonder how disabled Reat might be. My mind races frantically with questions. What kind of care will he need us to provide for him? Will he be able to sing again? Will he remember seeing his grandfather murdered?

I walk circles around the room because the only way I know how to cope is to keep moving. I am pacing frantically. Len is sitting completely still, with his head in his hands. Mom is in such deep shock that she is barely lucid. Lukas is near me, quiet with his tormenting thoughts. Only the night before, Lukas and Reat had argued to the point of some physical pushing and many hurtful words were shouted in anger. Tony and Dana sat with one another, conversing quietly about their young kiddos and what damage needed to be repaired from today's experience.

A man walks in, wearing scrubs and a mask, his mid-length gray hair pulled back in a ponytail. Not sure whom to address, he addresses all of us at once. All the questions that are pulsing through each of our minds are answered, quickly and bluntly.

"The young man, who was brought in with a gunshot wound, did not survive. We lost his heartbeat in the ambulance."

Two years passed before I made a lunch appointment with Mickey Blount, my stranger who cared for me, helped me unite with Len and Lukas at the scene and made our vehicle available without news reporters or rain interfering. Len and I met Mickey at a local restaurant in Overland Park, Kansas for lunch. I was not aware that Mickey had any guilt for actions he took on the fateful day of hate when my father and Reat were murdered. He was visibly nervous as we sat at the table and immediately apologized for taking me away from Reat during what were some of his last minutes of life. Following this lunch we hugged and exchanged addresses. Now, we exchange Christmas cards each year, which keeps me up to date on his three boys. As I was finalizing this chapter, I felt a nudge to call Mickey for some clarification. The following is an excerpt of his day, recorded during our phone call in July 2020.

When Mickey initially heard shots fired, he took cover with many others inside the Jewish Community Center. This didn't sit well with him, so the sitting and not helping aspect lasted only a few minutes, at most. Knowing there was likely a nursery full of children belonging to parents in the gymnasium, he ran to their location and "I moved many kids from the nursery room to the locker room, ensuring their safety." Next, brandishing a baseball bat from the lost and found box, he followed two other men into the parking lot. Moving in the direction of the gunfire, he could see someone tending to Reat in a small grassy area, next to a pickup truck. "As I approached the area where your father's truck was parked, I saw your dad and stopped. I knew that he had passed and didn't want to get too close. As I turned around to check on the other victim, who was your son, I ran right into you."

Mickey tells me, "Mindy, you were a ray of sunshine during a crisis. You repeated a few times 'I know my father is gone.' Mindy, you started praying as I held you close to me." It was comforting to me to be told that I prayed in this moment. Because I don't recall doing so. Mickey continues, "You wanted to be near Reat, but the guys working on him would not wave you over. In fact, they held their hands up in the stop position, so I kept holding you." Evidently, I stated that Reat might have died, too. Mickey recalls, "I stopped you from saying that Reat was dead. I asked you to not give up on him. You prayed out loud several times while we stood watching the men care for Reat."

Concluding his conversation with me, Mickey tells me what I know to be true, "On any other given day, the Jewish Community

Center would have been filled to capacity with families and children of all ages. There would have been more targets for this hate-filled, evil murderer."

I am grateful there were no more people murdered than three. It is also normal of me to wish that two of them had not been mine. The reality is, they were mine and the shooter picked the wrong family.

Top Left: Sharing cupcakes with his local grandchildren, Andrew and Katy Corporon, Lukas and Reat; Popeye agreed to celebrate what we would never have imagined to be his final birthday. A bowling alley in Overland Park, Kansas. January 2014

Bottom Left: A typical occurrence in our lives, Popeye and Mindy visiting Reat at Blue Valley Elementary School to ewww and ahhh over one of his projects. Stilwell, Kansas. 2005

Top Right: Our family unit of six, enjoying the Oklahoma vs. Texas football game. Another cherished memory. Dallas, Texas. 2013

9

Shattered

April 13, 2014, Palm Sunday.

Overland Park Regional Hospital—Overland Park, Kansas

"The young boy, who was brought in with a gunshot wound, did not survive. We lost his heartbeat in the ambulance."

As these words came out of his mouth, the room erupted in cries, wailing and cursing.

Someone fell on the floor.

Screaming is happening.

There is no air.

I can't breathe.

My mind races. I hear ringing and feel foggy.

The shrieks of anguish continue. It was my mom. My mother has crumpled.

He is talking. The doctor with the gray ponytail is continuing. I am struggling to hear him. I am trying to curl into the tiniest of balls ... I want to disappear.

It is difficult to hear him as the cries of distress and sorrow bellow, echoing around that small room. They tried to resuscitate him numerous times in the ambulance and again when he arrived at the hospital—these are his words. I hear them but don't want to know or understand them. They should not be for me, for us or for this room full of tormented people.

He tells us he is very sorry for our loss.

Our loss? Our loss is monumental. Does he realize my father was murdered only hours before this now devastating news?

His words mark the beginning of a daunting sentiment that I will hear thousands of times in the coming days and weeks. "I am sorry for your loss." I am shattered.

My chest feels as if a building fell on me. I struggle to breathe. The attempts I am making force me to focus on what it means to take in a breath. This focus now allows me to see the room full of misery. Somehow I become aware that I should reach out to another human for consolation. Standing up and walking toward Len, tears streaming down my face, I begin to shake uncontrollably.

The despair is so heavy that I don't know if my heart can physiologically withstand the pressure.

Falling into Len, he is holding me so tightly that he is actually holding me up. We hold each other for several minutes. Everyone in the small room is sobbing, hugging and trying desperately to wrap their minds around this heartbreaking reality. My brother Tony holds Lukas in an unrelenting bear hug. Together, they help my mom up. She had fallen to the floor after hearing the news. It feels impossible to believe we have lost two of our beloved family members. Through tears, the questions begin, "How did this happen to us? Why did this happen to them? Who shot them? Why, on earth, did someone do this?"

As the room rocks with loud tormenting cries of sadness, a calm settles over me. I just learned that I lost my firstborn son, and I feel the deep realization sink in that I am still a mother. I kiss Lukas on the cheek and hug him tightly. I tell him I love him very much.

He is 12 years old and has just become an only child.

I am still struggling to breathe as thousands of tears run down my face. It's as if they are racing to reach the ground first. The smallness of the room somehow becomes even smaller. I turn to Lukas, hug him and say, "We will survive this."

He responds with, "I don't know how we will, Mom. I don't know how we will."

Len and I embrace again and he says, "I am so sorry. I am so sorry. I know how much Reat means to you. I know how special he is to you."

Suddenly, I find myself defending my love for Lukas aloud. Although I am engulfed in a thick fog of fear and disbelief, I want Lukas to understand—with crystal clarity—that Len would be saying the same words about him if he would have been gunned down with Dad at the Jewish Community Center today.

"Yes, Reat is special to all of us. The same kind of special as Lukas," is all I can think of to say. Lukas seems immediately distant. Already, our new normal feels incredibly complicated and difficult.

Am I making this feeling up? Am I creating something that isn't real? We just heard this horrific news and now I am already imploding. The "momma bear" in me has awakened and I feel a desperate sense of urgency for my living son to know I love him as much as I love the son who was murdered.

I try to comfort him and repeat sentiments of how much we love him. I tell him that we know, without a doubt, that Popeye and Reat are in Heaven and that we will survive … somehow.

I wish I actually felt the confidence my words are portraying. To myself I think, "Are they in Heaven? Yes. Will we survive? I'm not so sure."

There is so much movement and chaos in the small room. The walls feel as if they are closing in as more relatives and friends arrive. Each time a new person enters, I wonder to myself and sometimes aloud, "How did you know?" Tears flow down their cheeks as each one recounts the name of the person who called them to share the horrible news.

Now, sitting again for steadiness as much as anything, the feeling of a warm blanket covers my arms and back. No one has touched me, other than my mom, who is patting my leg and squeezing it randomly. It seems as if an angel has arms around me and hugs me tightly.

As if I am back in the parking lot, I hear the words, "Your father's in Heaven. Go find Reat."

"I found him," I whisper to myself. "He is dead."

Gary Underwood, Reat's biological father, should be called. Immediately, the nausea comes up in my throat. Reat is all he had.

Reaching for my phone, I remember it's still in the parking lot of the Jewish Community Center. It is still in my father's truck. Now, it is part of a "crime scene." Two words I would never have imagined to be part of my life story.

My mom tries calling Gary from her phone, but he doesn't answer. Mom leaves a message for him to please call us back. "Gary, this is Melinda. There has been an accident in Overland Park. We need to reach you. Mindy does not have her phone. We need you to call me back, please. Thank you." She is polite, as usual, and incredibly calm.

Just a month ago, Reat spent four days with Gary in Houston during spring break. They had a wonderful time together. When I met Reat at the airport upon his return, I noticed he looked even more mature and handsome than he did when he left. I was grateful he experienced some quality time with Gary.

Everyone in the room seems to be talking in hushed tones. More and more people show up. Our room is getting smaller.

The gray-ponytailed doctor comes back in to gently explain, "Because the young man did not have any identification on him when he arrived, we need to identify him."

Of course, I want to identify him. He's mine. The gray-ponytailed doctor begins asking additional questions about Reat's identity. What clothes and shoes was he wearing? I feel frustrated because my brain is so foggy and I can't remember.

I sit quietly and take deep breaths. I think I can recall his clothing, "He is wearing his new black suit and a white shirt? Or maybe there was something that was purple. I think he had on his black shirt and his purple tie." My memory is hazy and I still feel faint.

Reat's shoe size has to be directed to Len. Len had been with him for that purchase. I had been with Reat for the suit, shirt and tie purchases. Memories come flooding back as I think about the day we bought his suit. Envisioning Reat standing with me at the store counter while I was paying for the suit, the salesman told us that when Reat grew out of this one or when it needed alterations, to please come back for free alterations.

Reat will never need to have his suit altered. Len speaks up about Reat's shoes.

After providing what I thought would be a sufficient explanation pertaining to Reat, the gray-ponytailed doctor asks if someone will actually come identify the body.

Quickly my answer is, "I will identify him. I can do it." The doctor stands completely still and shifts his gaze from me to Len. "Are you sure?" they ask in unison.

"We would rather someone else do this for you. Is there someone else who could identify him?" the doctor asks.

"Why can't I do it?" I ask. "I am his mom."

A young police officer, who introduces himself as Detective Reeder, slides in and positions himself in front of me. He is squatting down just a couple feet from me with a very serious look on his face. He speaks slowly and intentionally. "I am Detective Reeder. I will be working on this case. I am so very sorry for your loss."

As if this is a normal introduction, I respond with, "I am Mindy. My dad and son were murdered."

"Detective Reeder," I whisper through tears, "I want to see my son. I can identify him."

Reeder pauses, as if contemplating how to effectively communicate what he wants me to understand. "Mindy, this is a huge tragedy for your family and much is being asked of you right now. It would be best if you didn't see your son, as he is now."

"Reat," I tell him. "His name is Reat."

"Mindy," Reeder explains, "It would be best if … I feel it would be best if you remembered Reat as you last saw him and not in the emergency room."

"I last saw him lying unconscious in the arms of two men whom I don't know. He had red spots on his face." I was beginning to feel like these people were taking Reat from me again.

He pauses before he answers, "I understand that you saw him in the parking lot. I feel strongly that you would not want to see him in this way, as lifeless as he is now."

My mom and Tony are listening intently to our conversation. Tony asks if he can please identify Reat for me. "Let me do this for you. Please let me take this for you," Tony pleads. I am torn but I nod my head in agreement. I feel like this should be my job. I feel like they are taking more from me. I also know I am foggy; and I have never been in this situation before, so perhaps they know something I don't.

We have no idea how difficult this job would be to identify Reat. Not only was it incredibly difficult that fateful day, but it has also been an ongoing struggle for Tony. He wrestled with deep grief and sorrow, as well as palpable hatred and anger in regard to visions of Reat's lifeless body. The paradox of Reat's wonderful life stripped from him by a senseless hate crime, combined with the gunman's unwavering belief that he did the "right thing," was too much for Tony to resolve on his own. A few years later, Tony sought professional counseling, discovering he had post-traumatic stress disorder (PTSD).

When the doctor and nurse escort Tony back from identifying Reat, he found us moved into a larger room down the hall. We had outgrown the small room and needed more space to breathe. The Rev. Steve Langhofer, a minister from our church, as well as Rabbi Jonathan Rudnick have joined us. We aren't Jewish, but that doesn't matter. We need prayers of every kind.

My business partner, Rich, and his family have also arrived. More family and friends continue to show up. Who called them? How did they know it was our Popeye and our Reat? Questions continue to race through my mind. How can this be true? And why? Why? Why?

A woman approaches and introduces herself. She explains that her name is Christine and will oversee all communication from the hospital. She tells me that we know each other from our "Women Who Mean Business" group. "I am so very sorry for your loss," she says. There it is again.

"I will never forget that day. I know exactly what I was wearing and where I was driving." These were the first words I heard from Christine Hamele, assistant vice president of public relations and community affairs at HCA Midwest Health System, when I interviewed her for this book.

Christine received a call from her trauma medical director that a potential mass shooting had occurred and one of the victims was on the way to their hospital. Her trauma medical director was informed by Johnson County MED-ACT, the emergency care service.

Christine was on her way to the mall with her two teenage daughters. She hung up from that conversation and quietly called her husband to arrange for him to take the girls from her because of this emergent situation.

My Reat was arriving in the ambulance shortly after Christine. Her trauma team was ready to receive him.

She was receiving calls from the media and was waiting to talk to our family before responding. Her responsibility was to protect our family and her hospital before talking to the media. "At this time, none of us were aware of the whereabouts of the shooter and the hospital was on alert to potentially receive more shooting victims," Christine tells me as we talk on the phone.

In the hospital, Christine is explaining to me that the news media is beginning to gather. She wonders if we are ready to release the names of the deceased. The deceased. Release the names of the deceased. The sick feeling overwhelms my stomach and my throat. I am shattered. I am pieces on the floor.

Looking around the room, I am seeking help in answering this horrible question. I seem to be given authority because I am Reat's mom and Bill's daughter. Thank God, Tony steps in and begins answering and asking questions. "What does the press know? Have the police made any statements yet?"

Christine and Tony leave the room to find a quiet place to talk through questions they both have. They begin to explore what the press release should entail.

When Tony reenters the room, he tells me that our older brother, Will, is on his way to us via Tulsa, Oklahoma and then their home in northwest Arkansas. Len and my mom had called him and informed him of the shooting and now of both deaths. Will requested we delay releasing the names until he is closer in proximity to his own son Travis, who lives in the area.

As I was receiving messages from Tony, crying on someone's shoulder and angry about our new life situation, the police, the Federal Bureau of Investigation and the Bureau of Alcohol, Tobacco, Firearms and Explosives were creating their own command center somewhere else in the hospital.

The crime scene investigation at the Jewish Community Center had moved to the Overland Park Regional Medical Center with Reat's living and then deceased body. We were sick that my father's body was left in the parking lot for hours, with rain pouring down on the blue tarp that covered him based on my one, specific request. In my mind, the crime scene had stayed at the Jewish Community Center with the red truck and the secrets it would hold about the final minutes of my dad's and Reat's lives.

The police wanted to release the names of the victims. Pressure was mounting. The White House had called. Christine told me, "We had a lot of back and forth on giving out the names." She felt strongly and was supportive that our "family should be the one to offer the names." The Overland Park Police Chief, the mayor of Overland Park and the city's public information office all discussed "what is the right thing to do." An agreement was made to wait until our oldest brother was as close as he felt he needed to be to Overland Park and allow him to make the final decision. The family would decide when the names would be released, not the police, the city or the hospital.

"God was looking out for us that day. It was so well orchestrated with care and concern for the family. We didn't want nor did we allow the media to become storm chasers during your crisis," Christine explained to me.

At some point, I tell a medical professional that I want Reat to be an organ donor. A nurse appears, informing me that because his heart had stopped, he can't be an organ donor.

If it is possible to be any more devastated, I am. "What a waste," I think to myself. "What a complete waste." My feelings transition from shock and sadness to anger and despondence. I am shattered, again.

My thoughts are interrupted as my business partner, Richard, his wife, Gail, and Richard's daughter Laura (also my coworker) approach. When I see them, my mind races back to questioning: Is this real? Are we really in a hospital beginning to process and grieve the deaths of both my son and my dad?

The three of them sit with us for a while and then ask if they can take Lukas with them. They suggest it might be good for Lukas to get out of this environment. They ask Len and me if that is OK with us.

Suddenly, my parenting skills feel suspect. I let my firstborn die in an ambulance without me. I don't feel equipped to comfort Lukas or make good decisions about where he should or should not be.

Len and I have not left each other's side. We stand side by side, but we are constantly managing different conversations with various people simultaneously. We look at each other for a moment and try to grasp enough clarity to make a sound choice. Do we let our living son leave our presence right now?

After questioning ourselves and double-checking on a seemingly simple request, yet at a monumental time, we agree to allow Lukas to leave with trusted friends. I feel sick about this decision. I feel like any decision I make should now be in question. Lukas walks out of the hospital and I begin to cry.

My friend and coworker, Cindy, has joined us in the room. Leaning on her shoulder, my tears are flowing as she keeps repeating, "This should not have happened," she says. "I am so sorry."

The Rev. Kirby Gould is my father's first cousin and I know her well. Her arrival at the hospital is as surprising as all the others. And yet, I think to myself, "Of course she would be here." Kirby takes control of the information and communication flow for the Corporon family. I remember being grateful, in that moment, that we were a tight-knit crew. Over 40 Corporon family members, from all over the country, would arrive for the funeral.

On my feet, in a chair, on my feet, in a chair, talking with someone and then another, I am close to Len at every moment. A subtle fear lingers inside me. If I could lose two family members in one day, what else could happen to me? My mind was with me and then it wasn't. It was in the parking lot.

The hospital chaplain and social workers had turned the waiting room into a gathering place with food, as Christine was overseeing our family, calling in more security and determining how to respond to the mounting media presence.

The Rev. Karen Lampe from the Church of the Resurrection was present soon after we moved from that small room to the larger space. She was thoughtful and gracious as she hugged each of us with loving arms. Pastor Steve had prayed with us and now Pastor Karen laid her hands on each of us, with God's word asking for peace to find its way into our hearts.

Christine told me she will never forget the compassion Pastor Karen showed everyone, including her staff. Pastor Karen asked Christine, "How are you? How is your team?" She seemingly had the right words at the right time. The hospital staff were devastated for our family. Their job is to triage and save patients. The fact that they couldn't offer us a living Reat upon arrival weighed heavily on them. Pastor Karen's attentiveness was welcomed then and now, remembered annually.

A nurse, whom I have not yet met, asks Len and me to join her in a separate small room. Christine joins us in the room. This is the first, almost-private moment that Len and I have had since we heard Reat did not survive.

This nurse, Stacie Kelly, slowly and carefully sits me down in a chair and then squats down in front of me. Placing her hands on my knees, she locks eyes with me and I worry about what other terrible news she could possibly have. I fear I can't take any more. I begin to sob uncontrollably and the shaking begins. Len has his arm around me. My legs are shaking uncontrollably again. The nurse asks if I need a blanket. No, I'm not cold. I am in deep distress.

Nurse Stacie begins to talk in a soothing voice. She says she is so very sorry for our loss. She goes on to explain that the original reports we had been given, regarding Reat's inability to become an organ donor, are inaccurate. She explains how very sorry she is about that.

A glimmer of hope enters my heart.

My tears slow their trickle down my cheeks as I focus intently on her words. She explains to us that Reat's body can be used for tissue and ligament procurement. They need to start the process to prepare his body as soon as possible. She just needs my signature. She explains that Reat's large organs are not able to be used because his heart was stopped for too long, but she says the team will take anything they can for the benefit of others during the procurement.

The glimmer of hope grows. Reat will be able to help others.

It sounds absurd to think I could grasp any joy on this day. The day I found my dad and son murdered in a parking lot. Honestly, from 1:08 p.m. until this moment, I have experienced nothing but trauma and deep distress. But knowing that my baby boy will be able to help one or more families feels gratifying. I am able to muster a smile through my tears and with shaky hands sign the forms.

Nurse Stacie explains that I will receive a phone call the following morning, and I will need to offer more consent and answer some questions about Reat. This interview is required to take place before the procurement team can begin. "There is a finite time between his death and when his body becomes unusable," she explains, "so the interview will be key."

I hear those words again. "Your father's in Heaven. Go find Reat." I have heard an audible voice several times now. There is no mistaking what I am being told. I just don't understand what it means.

This message is beginning to frighten me. Why do I keep hearing these words? Who is saying them to me? It scares me to think these words might be coming from God. I feel reluctant to tell anybody else about them and concerned about what my family might think if I tell them God might be speaking to me.

Already I have questioned my abilities in various areas. I don't trust my own judgment and still feel like this might all be my fault. Now, I'm hearing voices. What is happening? The vision of my dad lying on the ground, his head and shoulders surrounded by a pool of blood, haunts me. I still feel the cool breeze from the storm that moved on my cheeks while the memory of finding Reat being held up by the two men on the lawn grabs me tightly. Now, the pressure of answering questions to ensure Reat can enter procurement is my responsibility.

After our discussion with Nurse Stacie and Christine about the procurement of Reat's body, we are finally told we can leave the hospital.

We are assured there is no sign of the media present as we exit, so we are able to leave without the pressure of giving a statement. Len and I stayed within a foot of each other the entire time we were in the hospital. Mom has been sobbing quietly throughout our hospital stay. Although she is surrounded by family, she seems alone in her thoughts. She has lost her husband of 49 years and her beloved grandson. Rabbi Rudnick, who was with us in that small room and prayed for our family during this crisis, had taken my mom for a walk through the halls to help calm her mind.

Len, my mom and I, gather our shattered selves and walk sadly, soberly and slowly to the car for our drive home. Home? We needed to take Mom to her home. There was no way I would leave her alone at this time and I wasn't ready to see my own home. Len followed instructions to drive us to my parents' home.

As my interview with Christine was concluding, she was forthright in saying how grateful she was that Reat had been brought to her hospital. For the first time, I heard from Christine that the four core people working together for the benefit of our family represented different faith traditions: Catholic, Baptist, Episcopal and Judaism. "It is amazing that a man filled with hate actually brought the four of us together, and we love one another because of that day."

Christine went on to say that because of the love that her team shows patients, "they also care for one another and have continued to do so." As a team, they attended the funeral and remain close friends today. They were impacted by Reat. The anniversary of their deaths, April 13, is a day of remembrance for the hospital team who worked to save Reat's life. Either by phone call or in person, connections are made, the stories from that day are shared again and my father and son are remembered.

From one mother to another, Christine sensed that even after six and a half years, my heart carried guilt for their deaths.

"Reat was not alone. He did not suffer. He was never alone. Mindy, you should not feel guilty. There was nothing anyone could do after his injuries were sustained. His life goes on through the procurement that you made possible. He lives on in all of us, in our hearts. Between what God and your family have done to change the face of kindness in Kansas City, we are so thankful for your incredible efforts to find the good."

She offered me as much solace as she could, to which I refer for comfort.

On the day of the murders and for several years after, I didn't fathom how completely shattered my soul was. There was no way for me to comprehend the continued cuts and bruises I would endure to pick up the pieces.

Top: Reat, about the age when he lost
the grape up his nose and a valiant
rescue was underway. This boy loved his
sippy cup. Stilwell, Kansas. 2000

Left: Thomas Bates on location
with the United States Army. Photo
courtesy of Thomas Bates. 2011

10

Treat the Wound

After becoming a mother, I found myself thinking through emergency scenarios with my babies. As a first-time mom to Reat, I was hypervigilant, from hiring Nanny Carrol to paying attention to what we listened to in the car to and from anywhere. My own mom was my first source of all things regarding timing … in what month do I start baby cereal, in what month might he begin teething and in what month should he be sleeping through the night. My ever-beloved girlfriends were my much-needed source for current nutrition and intellectual stimulation choices. Surprisingly, my maternal and paternal grandmothers were not shy about sharing their intellect when it came to current news for my health and that of my baby boys. Each of these loving, caring and sassy grandmothers would provide me their take on what might be trending in newborn and toddler health and then sprinkle with a dash of "this is how we used to do it."

Try as I did, I made mistakes in my care of Reat. For instance, we learned he loved pasta. For a quick dinner, I would make pasta with parmesan cheese and add some soy sauce. Reat LOVED this meal and ate it well every time I made it. For good measure, I would add boiled broccoli and he enjoyed eating the "trees" along with his pasta. When his skin started to get bumpy and rough, I spent many hours looking for the best bath and body products … not realizing that what I was feeding him was causing the skin irritation. We discovered he did not have celiac disease, but he was sensitive to gluten at age 10. Yep—I fed him all things gluten for 10 years without realizing my lack of knowledge was part of the problem.

Then there was the time I gave him a handful of grapes and time with Barney while I prepped our dinner. During our meal, his nose started to drip. Drip, drip, drip. His nose had a liquid flowing from one nostril. Being two at the time, he was using words well, "Mom-Mom, it's on my nose. Mom-Mom, it's on my nose," using his baby fingers to point and touch his nose. There was nothing ON his nose. I could see a liquid flowing from one nostril. For better exploration, with a flashlight in hand, I laid him on his back with his head between my legs for leverage. He was 2. He knew something wasn't right but he still wiggled. We were alone in our home and a storm was just passing through. The grape was pushed so far up his nostril there was no way my fingers could get to it. Tweezers would be the best and only way to grab that damned grape. After so many attempts, with sweat beading on my forehead and my sweet wiggly child turning red in the face, the storm broke—providing a clearing in my mind, too.

I was frightening myself with thoughts of his breathing getting labored and the grape causing lasting damage to his sinuses. Stuffing my tweezers in my pocket and lifting Reat to my hip, we scampered through wet grass and some lingering rain showers over to our neighbors, the Maxwells. To hear them tell the story now still brings tears of laughter. Their dinner dishes were cleared from the kitchen table and our patient was put in place on his back. Someone held his head, and someone held his baby legs and feet. My tweezers and I took one grab and pulled. The grape lost.

Growing up the daughter of a physician, my experiences provided me an aptitude for medical intervention. In all the scenarios I would imagine myself or my boys to be in, there would always be someone with the proper amount of knowledge and skill to be the hero and save the day. I could not have asked for a better man to be on duty at the Jewish Community Center on that fateful day. The tragedy I had never allowed myself to imagine. Who would?

As a combat medic in the Army, Thomas Bates lost other soldiers ... friends even from his own units. During tours in Iraq and Afghanistan, his duty was to put people back together, save them wholly if he could and move on. His military training taught him to be a robot. Treat the wound. He was not ever treating a Sergeant Smith, per se. He was treating an amputation. "You treat the wound; you are a robot," Thomas said to me. "There is no thinking of the person, the human, because you still have 12 months of deployment."

As a man and his son ran through the entrance door to the gym of the Jewish Community Center, the echo of a gunshot could be heard before the door had time to close. Thomas, who was working the counter at the fitness center, wasted no time in barking orders to those around him. One person was assigned to call 911. Thomas' younger brother, also employed by the JCC, was assigned to the locker room and was told to keep everyone inside.

He may not be in combat, but he still kept his A-bag, a medic bag like the one he carried on his person when deployed in Afghanistan, in his vehicle.

An Army combat medic specialist is primarily responsible for providing emergency medical treatment at the point of wounding on the battlefield, limited primary care, health protection and evacuation from a point of injury or illness.

Enlisting in the Army in 2006 and leaving in 2013, as a sergeant with two deployments—one in Iraq and one in Afghanistan—Thomas didn't hesitate to run toward the gunfire that he heard coming from the parking lot in suburban Overland Park, Kansas.

Immediately thinking to himself that his training could conceivably make him the only person with his background on location, he felt as though he would be the best person to make a difference. He might be needed to eliminate the threat and could do so with the pistol he kept in his truck.

After placing everyone in a role, he left the building to assess the situation. As an employee of the JCC, Thomas carried a handheld radio. There was no response when he called security.

Walking to the exit of this building and calling 911 simultaneously, Thomas saw a car pull into what we will call the lower parking lot. This is not the same parking lot where I found my father's truck, my father and Reat. This parking lot is on a lower level of the campus and has access to the entrance of the fitness center.

Looking for the direction of the gunshots, calling 911 and walking into a potentially dangerous situation himself, Thomas spots a family of four getting out of their car in plain sight. Running toward them, Thomas yells that there is a shooter in the area and to take cover. Scrambling the kids back into the car, the dad quickly drives offsite.

Thomas can't recall if he spoke to someone on the other end of the 911 call. He never heard anyone talking. They may have placed him on hold or perhaps he never got through to anyone.

With the family of four out of the way, Thomas runs to his own vehicle to get his A-bag and retrieve his pistol from the glove compartment. His pistol is not in the glove compartment. Pausing, Thomas considers the situation. Should he continue searching for a gunman without a gun himself? 2 Corinthians 5:7 is in Thomas' mind. As a Christian, Thomas knows this verse. He has lived this verse and chooses to hold it close once again in this moment, "For we walk by faith, not by sight."

Running toward the location from which he heard the gunshots, Thomas uses other vehicles as cover.

As he ran across the parking lot, he saw my father's truck.

The shooter had already left.

Thomas recalls that the driver's side door was open. Seeing a man on the ground, Thomas assessed the situation and knew the man, my father, was deceased.

"There is someone else," was all he heard them say. Another person had joined Thomas in the parking lot. Opening the passenger door to my father's truck, Thomas found Reat.

Reat made some movements.

When Reat made movements, Thomas thought to himself, "This one could be saved." His training had taught him to treat the wound, not the person, so he laser focused on finding the wound.

A few more men had made their way to the scene from where the gunshots occurred. Thomas asked someone for help. They carefully pulled Reat from the passenger seat of my father's truck.

Reat was in Thomas' arms and his head was elevated when Thomas heard a woman scream. This is when I found the two men caring for Reat.

The other men involved were Jason and Trey. Jason was trained as a paramedic and Trey is now a police officer. God had sent three wise men to be with Reat on that grassy space.

Hearing my screams startled Thomas. He knew my stranger to be Mickey Blount, the sports supervisor with the Jewish Community Center. Thomas said to Mickey, "Get her out of here."

Treat the wound, not the person.

He finished up with, "It's not safe here; make sure everyone is inside and safe."

Thomas heard me say, "This is my father." He then surmised that the boy in his arms was my son.

The fact that Reat had been shot and the severity of his wounds became apparent as Thomas assessed his injuries. The damage from the gunshot made obtaining an airway for Reat to breathe impossible, even with the tools inside his A-bag.

For the first time in his career, Thomas felt helpless.

He had stopped bad guys before. He had saved numerous limbs and lives on the battlefields of Iraq and Afghanistan, yet he was now helpless on this grassy spot in Overland Park, Kansas.

There was no way to obtain an airway; the gunshot wounds were too severe. Cursing out loud, he felt like he was failing Reat and everyone else. The fact that the injuries were too critical angered Thomas even more. Guilt came over him as he realized these might be Reat's final movements—the final moments of his life; and Thomas felt anger, not compassion.

Ten weeks of Basic Combat Training and 16 weeks of Advanced Individual Training, including in-patient care, were all part of Thomas' training to become a combat medic.

Patient-care techniques, emergency medical techniques, advanced medical care and plaster-casting techniques learned in training and all used on the battlefield would not heal the wound today.

Reat made no purposeful movements. He had no pulse in his wrist. The only pulse Thomas could find was in his neck. Shock was upon my baby boy. Making a few non-purposeful attempts to oxygenate himself, Reat was in the final minutes of his life.

Thomas stayed with Reat until the ambulance arrived. When he saw enough paramedics move in and take over care, he stepped out of the way.

At the time of this tragedy, Thomas was engaged to his current wife, Ashley. Thomas reached out to me after he and Ashley had their first child, a boy. When his son was 3 months old, Thomas had a medical emergency. He had an abscess behind his tonsil and his airway occluded. Thomas found himself not able to breathe. Fear. He thought he had about 60 seconds to make his life right. The idea of his son growing up without a dad was tormenting. In the ambulance ride and then at the hospital, he was fearing his death; but he was fearing even more the idea of leaving his wife and young son. His wife, Ashley, walked into the emergency room with their baby boy.

At that moment, Thomas realized nothing in the world matters more than your children. He remembered Reat and he remembered, Reat's mom, me.

Changing his perception of what happened to Reat, Thomas saw me as a victim of the murder and death of my son and dad. He said to me, "When I realized you, Mindy, were a victim, I became human." Knowing the love a parent has for one's children made him human. He thought about how he treated the wound and not the person, meaning how he treated me. Reat's injuries were too severe to survive. But I survived. I was the victim that Thomas didn't treat that day.

Thomas shared with me, "The whole community saw how strong you were. You turned tragedy into faith. You leaned on God. This is what faith brings us. I didn't have compassion on that grassy strip with Reat. Now, I think about the person, the humans involved, when I treat them."

I asked Thomas if he felt like compassion was transferred to him that day. "Yes, I guess so," he replied. I said, "Thomas, Reat was giving you his compassion. If nothing else, my baby boy was compassionate."

Thomas considers himself blessed. He doesn't have post-traumatic stress disorder, although he does have occasional nightmares about the battlefield. He also admitted to thinking about Reat more often than he thought he would.

As a memorial to the soldiers who Thomas knew who were killed in action, he wears a black bracelet with the following inscriptions, "6 died in Iraq. 21 died in Afghanistan."

One week each year, Thomas dons another bracelet. This one is silver with a cross and the Jewish star on it, along with the names, William and Reat.

I know Reat transferred his compassion to Thomas. I can hear it in Thomas' voice as we end our conversation. He is kind, caring and faithful, a wonderful husband to Ashley and no doubt a fantastic father to his two children, ages 5 and 2.

Now, a physician's assistant, Thomas shares his compassion with those he cares for, every day.

Top: Mindy asked Reat for a quick pose to show off his new look now including corrective glasses. Photo taken at the family home. Stilwell, Kansas. March 2014.

Top Left: Dan Stringfield (middle) and other first responders were recognized at the Kansas City Royals baseball game which featured a recording of Reat singing the National Anthem. Courtesy Dan Stringfield. June 7, 2014.

Middle Left: Collaborating for the best possible outcome for our families are Signature Group employees and employees of the Johnson County Funeral Home and Memorial Chapel. Holding one of the caskets is Mat Forastiere far left, Jay Dodds far right forward and Kati Farney far right away. Photograph by Joe Shalmoni Photojournalist, © April 18, 2014.

Mindy Corporon with Pastor Adam Hamilton placing Bill and Reat's ashes in the Jordan River, Israel. Reat and Bill are 'scoop and go' so they can travel the world. February 2016.

11

Where I Was Supposed to Be

As burial and funeral arrangements were made for both my father and Reat, one of our decisions was to cremate their bodies.

I was aware my father intended to be cremated at his death. The conversations he and I had were deep and honest. He trusted me and I expect my brothers, too, with knowing how he wanted to be cared for, including after his death. Because his death came too quickly, so suddenly and with violence, you might think that burial decisions would be difficult, or perhaps more difficult, under the circumstances. However, knowing that his final seconds on Earth were not his own, we took even more care and put even more thought into how we should best lay him to rest. We wrangled over a few details, but the question of a burial versus cremation was no discussion. We knew his intentions.

Reat, however, was a different situation. At 14, he had received his learner's permit on May 21, his birthday. Straight A's, reflected in his school portal, were part of our agreement for me to pick him up from school on his birthday and allow him to take his first driver's license exam. We had talked at the counter about his choice to be an organ donor. This was the only end-of-life discussion we had had to date, in 2013.

Days after their murders, sitting in the Johnson County Funeral Chapel & Memorial Gardens, contemplating how to best bury my baby boy, these words found a place in my foggy brain, "Mom, I'm not ready to die." They lingered longer than I liked. When did he say this to me? I could hear him saying them. I could recall the sensation my body had when he said these words out loud. It had not been that long ago. Why could I not recall the exact time and place Reat made this statement?

I know, baby … I am so sorry, is all I could feel my heart saying in response to this memory.

It was when I sat down to draft this chapter that the full memory appeared in my mind.

In 2014, only weeks prior to his murder, he and I were on one of many practice drives. As he was driving us across some railroad tracks near our home, I felt prompted to parent him, I am sure again, about the need to NEVER try to beat a train.

He said, "Mom, I'm not ready to die."

"Of course not," I recall, responding as quickly as he had blurted out these scary words.

Our dialogue was about his driving and my concern that he might possibly want to beat a train to make it to school on time, a debate competition (which he relished) or a future date. I was only stating what any parent of a new driver would say, more than once, about the need to be careful around train tracks. His response was bold and sharp. It also flitted away in my brain, until April 13, 2014.

The windows were open, a breeze was flowing through the car, it was cool and it was March. Reat was driving my car, which I loved, and he was learning to love. This would be his car, soon. When he could legally drive without an adult with him, we would pass my beloved Sooner Crimson Hyundai Santa Fe to Reat. The memory of him wearing his new glasses, his face beginning to sharpen in features and leaving his babyish face behind, became clear in my mind. I loved him in that moment. I loved who he was becoming, for himself. We were on our way to a shop to purchase dance pants and shoes. Reat's high school choir director, Marsha Moeller, mandated that in order to be in Chambers—the top-notch choral and dance group—he would need to take dance lessons at a local dance academy, Miller Marley. Reat was driving us to make the needed purchases for this class. A simple, yet important, errand that we were able to share in our lives.

The railroad tracks, my parenting statement about never trying to beat a train … this all occurred only weeks prior to losing him forever. His quick response to me, "Mom, I'm not ready to die," was made during this effortless errand. Reat was murdered before he got to wear the black dance pants. He never made it to one of these classes that would propel him into musical theatre. The school shows would go on without him on stage.

The mounting feeling of all that Reat would not do and the places he would not go filled my entire being and yet, I sat steady and still while family members opened the discussion about funeral and burial arrangements.

Mathew (Mat) Forastiere, currently the vice president of operations with Park Lawn Corporation, was weeks away from assuming this same position with The Signature Memorial Group. He would be overseeing four funeral homes in the Kansas and Missouri region, including the Johnson County Funeral Chapel & Memorial Gardens at the time our family was forced into this undesirable and unwanted conversation. With a hefty amount of empathy and compassion, Mat led our discussion, prompted us for responses and answered all questions we presented. During correspondence with Mat regarding this manuscript, he provided fresh eyes and his recollection of this same encounter.

"Those first few moments, as we sat together in the arrangement room, were tense. I could see and feel in all of you, the extreme devastation and shock. After some introductions and condolences were exchanged, I recall asking you and your mother, 'What do you want to do?' You both looked at me with equally blank expressions, so I repeated the question. I could tell you were each searching for an answer and finally someone in the room said 'We would like to have them both cremated,'" Mat shared.

Considering how to help myself and perhaps Len and Lukas in years to come, I had contemplated the following … with regard to burying a body: There is little to no way of retrieving a part of them and taking them with you. This thought gave me significant pause. Curious what happens to the ashes after cremation, I joined the conversation. Mat explained how the ashes would be placed in an urn of our choosing, a memorial case, so to speak, so they would be safely secured. "How secured would they be?" I asked.

After a brief explanation, I understood that Reat's ashes would be sealed in an inner plastic vessel and then placed in the memorial case selected by the family, I interpreted this to mean "locked away and not easy to reach." Reat's laughter, smile and hugs were already not easy to reach. I wanted some control, some 'reach' with respect to his ashes.

I can recall where Mat was sitting and the look on his face when I spoke these next words. "Is there any way to make Reat available to me, like a 'scoop and go' from the vessel?" Feeling all eyes turn toward me, I kept my eyes focused on Mat.

Fearing that everyone present, my mother, brothers, Shelly Miller (my driver) and other chapel employees would see me desperately grasping for Reat, I quickly continued. "Len and I enjoy traveling. We took the boys to many places, but Reat died at such a young age. There are so many more travel destinations for us, I think. I want to take him with me, us."

I could see Mat considering my question and now this key piece of information. I had volleyed to him to help me finalize my decision. He said something like, "I have never heard the term 'scoop and go,' could you explain a bit further, Mindy?" Feeling my heart in my throat and struggling to indulge in conversation about everything Reat would never do, never see or visit, I took a drink of water to clear my throat, allowing a few moments to pass. Shelly, sitting next to me, placed her hand on my arm, offering me her own empathy. "I want to be able to scoop a bit of Reat from the vessel and take him with us when we travel, say to a place with flowing water. I could place some of his ashes in our favorite locations and those we have yet to visit. If he is secured in the vessel, if he is buried in the ground, I can't do this. Could the vessel be opened?" A concerned look that had settled on Mat's face now cleared and he presented calmly to me and all of us at the table, "Yes, the vessel could be opened. The ashes would be inside a bag, inside the vessel, inside the urn or memorial case."

Mat remembers our conversation in this way, "When the time came to make an urn selection, I recall you wanting access to Reat's ashes. That you, Len and Lukas would take a piece of Reat on every trip you would take from that day forth, so he could be with you and you could leave a piece of him behind. I remember thinking how beautiful that was and ensuring you that you would be able to do that."

Reat is 'scoop and go' when travel plans are made.

I knew their cremation would take place after their funeral, which was, sadly, a double funeral. Not understanding the timing of cremations, I was surprised to receive a call from Kati Farney, employed by the Johnson County Chapel & Memorial Gardens, a few days after the funeral, asking if we would like to see the caskets one more time. In the whirlwind of activity after the funeral service, I stepped back into the sanctuary to see the two caskets, now completely covered in phrases of love, endearment, Scriptures and memories from those who chose to take up a Sharpie. Len and my mother had not had the opportunity to do so.

Kati was right, we would like to see the caskets one more time. Len drove the three of us to the chapel. We found their caskets lying side by side in a small, innocuous room, waiting for the finality of cremation. I knew where their souls were. Logically, my brain knew that only their lifeless bodies were in these brown caskets. Of course, I wanted them back, their humanness, their touches, laughter and smiles. All that they brought to my life, our lives … why had this happened to us? What would I do without them? Len, Mom and I touched their caskets lovingly, as if to caress them while we read each and every heartfelt sentiment, drafted with love and blessings for their sendoff to Heaven.

Besides the decision to bury or cremate Dad and Reat, we had also ordered death certificates during our initial visit and planning session at the Johnson County Chapel & Memorial Gardens. Anxiety gripped me after our time alone with Dad and Reat in their caskets, as I wondered when and how I would receive their ashes. On the phone again with Kati from the chapel, tears found my cheeks as I asked her the question, "When will we receive their ashes?"

There was no one to call about the death certificates, or at least no one I had already been in conversation with, like Mat or Kati. The

State of Kansas would send Reat's death certificate to me and my father's to my mom on whatever they deemed their normal issuing timeline. When the envelope arrived, I wasn't ready. Is any parent ever "ready" to receive such a final document? We had been receiving oodles of mail every day. Boxes, letters, framed photos, large envelopes and books were beginning to fill our dining room table from well-wishers around the world who wanted to express their sympathy. We received nine copies of author Sarah Young's book, *Jesus Calling: Enjoying Peace in His Presence*. A woman from Louisiana, who I didn't know and still don't, painted a picture of Reat leaning on Jesus as if they were best buddies. Human empathy was oozing into our home helping to repaint what life should look like.

My hand was on the document, pulling it out of the large manila envelope, before my brain registered what it was. I sank to the floor in a heap of tears and anger as the death certificate floated to the floor beside me. Still new to the effects of grief and the emotional and physical toll it takes on our humanness, I lay on the kitchen tile floor, sobbing, as Len came to comfort me. Not understanding what had taken me down, but clearly understanding this was becoming commonplace, he lay next to me, pulling me close to his warm body on the cold tile. The mixture of the cold and warm temperatures were as clear to me as the mixture of emotions swirling through my soul. I was sad, angry and distraught. I was tired, no, exhausted. I was beginning to lose control of myself, my sobbing wouldn't stop and then ... "I am with you," was in my head. As if a boulder had been dropped on my river of tears to dam the flow, the words "I am with you," dried them up as quickly as they had burst onto the scene.

"Len?"

His response was, "Hmmm?" still with his head cupped over mine.

"Len, did you say 'I am with you?'"

"No," he said, followed by, "But I am with you. I love you."

Adjusting my position with Len but staying on the floor, I moved back enough to look at him. "Reat, or God, just talked to me." I don't remember how Len responded, but I expect it was with another 'hmmm,' or perhaps a conciliatory "That's nice." Neither of us knew that Reat or God would continue to talk to me, or that I would continue to hear words such as these in the coming months and years. We were both simply thankful that my uncontrollable sobbing had found a pause.

Now sitting at our round wooden table, large enough and meant for a family of four and friends, in our kitchen, I studied each typed letter and number as if they would tell me something I didn't already know. Unlike an adult who might have insurance on their life, a bank account, a career or at a minimum, a job ... Reat was a teenager. He was a freshman at Blue Valley High School. They were at his funeral, almost all the staff and teachers and hundreds of students. They knew he was dead. The certificate was not for them. His life had not been insured. He had no debts to pay. He was not employed and there was no human relations department to contact about his 401(k). This damned certificate was just for me and I didn't want it, either. I wanted my son back. His smile, his laugh, his songs ... oh, as I sat staring at the certificate, I ached fully for what I had was lost.

Reat's date of birth, which I simply adore, May 21, 1999, typed on the certificate, and his place of birth, where I attended college— Norman, Oklahoma, caught my eye. I choked back tears as I saw the words "9TH–12 GRADE, NO DIPLOMA" in the box for Decedent's Education. Could you "effing" believe this? My intelligent, genius son will not get a diploma. What a God-forsaken waste of a brain.

Marital Status: NEVER MARRIED. This was causing me so much distress. Why don't they just yell at me with a megaphone: no high school graduation, no college graduation, no wedding, no wife OR children. The list was mounting and I was falling into a deeper despair, albeit sitting calmly at the table, looking like I was reading a good novel.

My name was listed as Mother and Gary Underwood was listed as Reat's father.

In the Cause of Death section:
IMMEDIATE CAUSE (Final disease OR Condition Resulting in Death)—there were up to four lines that could be used for this answer. Only one line was needed:

CLOSE RANGE SHOTGUN WOUND OF THE HEAD

My eyes were darting from one space to the next, aching for something to stop the mounting pain inside my chest. I was sweating now and feeling clammy; a nauseous feeling was rising in my throat.

Manner of Death
HOMICIDE

How Injury Occurred
SHOT IN THE HEAD

Good God, when would this end? And then, my eyes found box 34b.

Time Pronounced Dead
2:57 P.M.

Wait a second ... 2:57? Why is the time 2:57? I saw him, I found them in the parking lot at 1:08! Maybe, it was 1:10. He was taken by ambulance within 30 minutes, or so. This would place the time at 1:45, if I stretch the time a bit. Maybe 2:00 or 2:15 if I really allow for more time to go by, but 2:57? Where was I? Why was I not with Reat during this time? Why didn't someone come get me, pull me into, invite me into or carry me into the ambulance with my son? How was I not with him for such a long period of time before he actually died? What kind of mother am I?

These questions haunted me like nothing else from the day I received the death certificate in the last week of April, until June 7.

Not only were gifts arriving daily at our home, but also friends and those who had previously been only acquaintances were finding any thread they could to help us stitch up the hurt. One such thread was the knowledge that Reat had sung the National Anthem in front of over 1,000 people in the first weeks of his freshman year of high school at the Blue Valley Education Foundation breakfast. His performance had been recorded, which was of great importance to me. One of Reat's aspirations, among many others, was to sing the National Anthem at a Kansas City Royals baseball game or a Kansas City Chiefs football game. Jo Anne Gabbert phoned me in late April to let me know she had already spoken with "people at the Royals," and it was under discussion to play the audio and video of Reat's National Anthem performance at a game.

I wanted to be happy about this and I dug deep inside to tell her thank you. Thank you for caring so much for our family that you would even try to make phone calls asking for this to happen, is something I managed to say to her. In another week, she called me back, asking me if we could be at the Royals vs. New York Yankees game on June 7. And, would we like to be given 200 tickets for free to family and friends? Jo Anne Gabbert had coordinated Reat's performance of the National Anthem to be played before the home opener of the Kansas City Royals vs. the New York Yankees on June 7. I was elated.

We created a logo to memorialize Dad, Reat and Terri. A #heart, their names hugging the top of the heart, the date 4.13.14 and in all capital letters, "FAITH WINS!" was inside the heart. Stephanie Tillman, a creative genius, donated her time and talent, crafted the logo, printed the shirts and supported me as I took my first step to organize an event created by our family for the benefit of what would become Faith Always Wins Foundation. We sold all 200 shirts, each with one ticket to the game. Our message was clear, Faith Wins!

"Bring my people together," a message I heard clearly from God in late 2014, was somehow stirring early in my heart. I knew the value of bringing humans together for purposes of shining a light on peace even without fully understanding that in a few years the mantra "Bring my people together" would apply to faith traditions, and then to people of color and whites.

Len, Lukas, my mother and I, along with Terri LaManno's family, her husband, Jim, and children, Alissa and Gian, were in the green press room underneath the Royals' stadium prior to the game. This was the holding place for anyone who would be part of the pregame festivities. The Royals' communication team had decided to also honor the first responders who assisted during and after the chaos of the murders. My mother and I recognized a blonde police woman and spoke with her briefly. It was uncomfortable for us, and I expected for her, as well. They were first responders, they had caught the bad guy and yet, we were three sorrowful families who lost loved ones before their help could arrive. Just before we were all to depart the room, someone decided we should stop ignoring one another and actually meet. The first responders lined up, or maybe we, as family, lined up. Either way, there was a line of family standing still and a line of responders walking past us, shaking our hands.

A young, handsome man reached for my hand. I held it out and as they connected, we felt a shock. I say we because I looked at him when I felt it and he looked at me. "Were you there?" I asked. Some of the police and firefighters who had already passed through the line had been on the scene at Village Shalom, not the Jewish Community Center. Or they had been part of the team who arrested the shooter. This young man responded, "I was with Reat in the ambulance." He called him Reat, like he knew him. Still holding his hand in mine, I stated, "I have questions." He replied, "You can call me any time. I would be happy to try and help answer some questions for you." As our hands released, I ended that brief but electric moment by saying, "May I call you tomorrow?" I worked to hold back tears as he provided me with his work number and told me the hours he would be there.

When firefighter and paramedic Dan Stringfield arrived on the scene at the Jewish Community Center on Sunday, April 13, 2014, he found a young man being held in a seated position with a bandage wrapped around his head. A member of the Overland Park Fire Department for over 18 years, Dan understood standard procedures when a shooting occurred. He and his team were dispatched from Station 4, off 119th Street, to the Jewish Community Center for a shooting. Following protocol, they staged in a safe place, due to the violence of the crime scene, several blocks away at 115th Street. As they were waiting, another shooting occurred at Village Shalom. This was when Teresa LaManno (Terri) was murdered by the same evil man who had just taken my dad's life and left Reat in a perilous situation.

Informed by the Overland Park Police Department that their scene was secure, which meant the Jewish Community Center was now considered safe for their entry, they drove onto the campus, knowing a second ambulance was on the way.

Dan recalls seeing a pickup truck near a grassy space in the parking lot. He saw an adult male lying near the driver's side of the vehicle and noted there was no care needed. My father had died immediately from the gunshot to his chest.

Upon assessing the situation, he took over the care of Reat from the two men who had originally taken Reat from the truck and were trying to save his life. Reat was still breathing, but not well. Dan called it agonal breathing. During his first vital sign check, Dan noticed Reat had a good pulse. This made sense because of his young age. Dan remembers taking off Reat's clothes, looking for injuries. "This young man was a decent-sized guy," Dan thought to himself. He figured Reat to be about 17 years old. His injuries had caused his face to swell rapidly and he had a bandage around his eyes and forehead. Dan was surprised to learn later that who he thought was an older teen was only 14. Although Dan thought Reat was older than 14 when he first laid eyes on him, he could tell the boy in his care was a teenager.

The father of two boys, himself, Dan was cognizant of the severity of the injuries he could see and detect from Reat's blood pressure and now dropping pulse. He briefly thought of his own children and how desperately he would want them to survive this situation.

Still breathing but not well, Reat was lifted onto a gurney and transported into the ambulance. Dan knew they needed to assist with ventilation quickly to help him breathe. "A breathing tube was placed in Reat to help control breathing that was coming at about one breath per minute," Dan informed me. "An intravenous drip was put in place for purposes of a fluid and medication route. We started this medication route should his condition deteriorate," he continued. "All this was going on in the back of the ambulance as we were driving Reat to Overland Park Regional Medical Center," Dan said. Reat's vital signs were continuing to be read and they were telling the tale of a severe head injury. "His pulse was dropping and his blood pressure was going up. We were witnessing a Cushing's triad," Dan stated.

In other words, Dan explained, the trauma Reat received from the buckshot going into his face and through his skull caused his systolic blood pressure to increase, his heart rate and respiration to decrease, and resulted in irregular respiratory patterns. Dan knew this to be "Cushing's triad," a clear indication of severe intracranial pressure.

He continued, "Reat was only in transport for about four minutes when compressions were needed. His heart had stopped."

Reat's heart stopped beating while he was in the ambulance and it never recovered.

Dan and his team were on the scene at the Jewish Community Center for only 10 to 12 minutes. Transport time to Overland Park Regional Medical Center is eight minutes. They had called the hospital to alert them to assemble the trauma team. Upon arriving at the emergency room bay, they took him into the emergency room and transported him to their staff. The staff was waiting on Reat when the ambulance arrived.

At this point in our interview, Dan stopped talking about what he witnessed and felt when he was caring for Reat and asked me how I was. His compassion and empathy for his patient on this tragic day was still present and he was now offering it to me.

When Dan was informed of the plan for first responders to be honored at the KC Royals game on June 7, he wanted no part of it. His patient had died. He wanted to be done with the day, "Put it in a box and put the box away," was how he described to me his feelings about the day of the murders. Putting it away was difficult for anyone in our community, as the media attention and news about the violent crime was intense.

A white supremacist had come into a typical suburban town with a very low crime rate and murdered three innocent people, shooting at numerous others, on a quiet Palm Sunday in broad daylight. Antisemitism is real. It lives and breathes in our society. While only one man took it upon himself to murder my father, son and Terri LaManno, it seemed as if the entire world responded with an eruption of love, kindness, compassion, sorrow, empathy and prayer. Our local media covered all these aspects thoroughly and well.

Dan knew who I was when we were in the green press room before the KC Royals game. He debated with himself about whether to talk with me or let it go. "The Lord works in mysterious ways ... go introduce yourself and tell them you are sorry," were the words Dan was telling himself before we were positioned for just this.

As a responder, they want to help. In this situation, there wasn't anything they could do to change the outcome. "I felt defeated," Dan told me during each of our opportunities to discuss his time with Reat.

I asked Dan if there was anything in particular that had helped him process this loss. "The biggest thing was when I met you. I didn't want the recognition at the Royals game. I didn't deserve it and didn't want to go. But because I attended, I got to meet you. Mindy, you had questions that were unresolved and I could help you with this. I could take away the blanks and try to give you some closure ... I could take away some of the unknowns for you. This was healing for me."

Dan's experiences have taught him that family members who lose a loved one tend to need the details of the death, the scene and the last moments of their loved one's life. This was clearly me. Perhaps without realizing it, Dan told me what I had been doing ... telling myself stories of what happened or might have happened during the time I was not with Reat. Dan and other responders understand part of their job is to eliminate the stories in family members' heads and offer some clarity with peace instead. "Most people can handle the bad stuff. You can tell them their family member died. But when there are spaces of time that have blanks in them, people need answers to help them move forward."

"I wasn't able to help Reat, but I was able to help you."

Engaged again in our interview, Dan was ready to answer the question that had been haunting me and would haunt any parent of a child they were not with at the time of their final breath. I asked Dan if Reat had been conscious at any time after he was shot. He stated again the severity of the head injury and went on to say he and other responders performed all the checks on Reat to see if he would respond to them. Verbal and touch techniques were used; he was not responsive. Dan said they went to great lengths to check his responsiveness and there was none. Reat never regained consciousness.

Dan and his team stayed at the hospital for about 20 to 30 minutes. It was a busy day in the system and they were told to get back to their station for coverage. "After leaving the hospital, I returned to the station. While still engaged in writing and documenting the patient care report, I received a phone call from my dad who lives in Omaha, Nebraska. He was calling to check on me. I had had one patient and was in a bubble while at the scene of the crime. I wasn't thinking of how big the situation was at the time. My dad was able to put this into perspective for me. He told me that this crime was receiving international attention because of antisemitism."

Today, Dan and his wife are both in the medical field. They talk with one another about difficult and trying days to offer support. He also received mental resilience training; and his department has peer support groups, which were put in place about five years ago. Dan understands that all responders have some level of post-traumatic stress disorder (PTSD). His support network, including his wife, allow him to talk about their traumatic experiences in the field. He knows the importance of "letting other people know how you feel so you are not carrying the burden by yourself."

All these specifics were shared with me by Dan on June 8, 2014 and again on July 7, 2020. In our first private discussion, I shared my burden of guilt with Dan; and he valiantly gave me back the precious time I had felt so much guilt losing. Through many tears, I shared with Dan that I should have been with Reat in the ambulance. I should have held his hand as he took his last breath. Maybe my touch would have saved him. With such compassion, Dan said to me, "Mindy, Reat may have somehow known you were there. But the circumstances of his injuries were not reversible. He never had consciousness after the shooting. Breathing doesn't mean you are aware. You were where you were supposed to be. You were with your mom, your husband and your younger son."

Top: Mindy, Reat, Lukas and Jake Svilarich each made a 'vision board' as an afternoon activity. This photo is of the vision board Reat created during the session. There are messages on this board that have yet to be vetted and messages offering comfort, for instance, the Dove. In their home in Stilwell, Kansas, October 2013.

Bottom: Mindy asked Rabbi Arthur Nemitoff for a photo while attending a service at The Temple, Congregation B'Nai Jehudah in Overland Park, Kansas. 2016

12

Jews Don't Talk About Jesus

When I speak publicly, people often ask, "How are you so strong?" My answer is simple … *faith*. I truly believe Heaven is all around me, mostly because I *feel* it. My father and Reat are with me, often all around me. I have no doubt. Their presence is tangible. Miraculously, this realization allows me to put one foot in front of the other each day.

This belief and these feelings in my heart have not made my healing simple. On the contrary, for months after the tragedy, I wrestled painstakingly with God. I attacked his character—and his plan for my life—with a barrage of questions. Why? Why did this happen to us? Why *both* of them? Why?

My temper got shorter and I would fly into episodes of anger quickly, way more quickly than I had in the past. I required no one's permission to find or express anger at any time.

Struggling with the realization that I have had not only faith, but I have also been a good person, mom, daughter, sister, friend and business owner. Then why? Why me God? Why not the shooter's target—a Jewish person? Why not anyone else for that matter? Why are two of my family members dead from a violent hate crime?

My questions are all over the map. I question God about His capabilities. At times, I question my belief in Jesus, specifically who He is to me and what role He plays in my faith. As a young girl in church,

I was taught that Jesus is the only way to Heaven. I was told that, without a doubt, if you don't believe in Jesus Christ, you are going to Hell. This doctrine didn't come from my parents. It came to me during "playground" conversations as well as from our pastor in the pulpit on Sundays.

The specific Scripture used to portray this belief is John 14:6, "I am the way, the truth, and the life. No one comes to the Father except through me."

Grappling with the reality that we lost Reat and Dad to a religious hate crime, I am raw to all emotions. My heart feels bare to the world, as if it is bleeding incessantly.

My friend Gail Weinberg is arranging a dinner for our extended family at our home. Most of the people in attendance, she explains, will be our Jewish friends. She tells me that Rabbi Arthur Nemitoff, leader of The Temple, Congregation B'nai Jehudah, the largest Jewish congregation in Kansas City, would like to attend. He has expressed his desires to Gail that he would like to share his condolences and spend time with our family. Telling her I would be honored to meet him and would love for him to come to our dinner was a true statement and a lie.

The right thing to do is to welcome the rabbi into our home. The right thing to do is to be gracious to other Jews who want to help me and our family through this unthinkable tragedy that was aimed at them. They are helpful. Their sad eyes, their hugs and their food—even the fact that they are filling our home with life is helpful. Not one of them had the gun in their hands that murdered three people.

I could choose to be angry at them, and then what?

He is petite in stature and giant in grace. The moment he walks in, a tangible sense of peace settles into our home. He has come to offer his condolences for our losses. Rabbi Nemitoff explains that because the shootings were intended to be Jewish hate crimes, he feels compelled to walk with us through our grief.

Only minutes into our conversation, I am drawn to the rabbi. He takes my hands in his and says compassionately, "I'm so sorry." He speaks quietly and gently. It's clear he genuinely cares about our pain.

I know I'm in the presence of a very godly man. God's presence feels so tangible through the rabbi.

I love talking with Rabbi Nemitoff. His peaceful countenance makes me long for more time with him, for a deeper understanding of his faith and his life. When he stands up to leave, I ask him if we can meet again. "Of course," he answers, "Whenever you are ready. My home is your home."

I want to ask Rabbi Nemitoff so many questions about Judaism, as I am just beginning to understand some of the various facets of their religion. I am intrigued and hungry to learn more.

Deciding our next meeting, we agreed to meet at his office in the synagogue. I am already looking forward to another peaceful connection, conversation and perhaps my first tour of a synagogue.

By the time we meet, I have been reading incessantly and continuing to learn about the Jewish religion. I have also engaged in recent conversations with Jewish friends, in hopes of growing my familiarity with their beliefs and traditions. I'm researching out of desperation ... hoping to find something that will shed some light on the motive behind this horrible tragedy.

One such question burning in my mind is about Jesus and Jews. The murders have either given me license or emboldened me to ask questions about faith. Specifically, I inquire about their belief in Heaven and their belief in Jesus. Who is Jesus to them? Do they know about Heaven? How do they get to Heaven if not through Jesus?

I decide to ask my friend Irv Robinson, who is Jewish. Trepidation is brewing in me before I ask Irv the question. We have had a working relationship for over 20 years. I was a guest at his children's weddings, making them two of the five Jewish weddings that I have attended. Because of our working relationship, I am privy to private information about Irv. We have had hundreds of conversations about his wealth, family and business. We have laughed out loud, danced and dined together at benefits that he supported and benefits that I supported. He bought me gifts for my children when they were born. You could say we know one another well and yet, neither of us had ever, not one time, delved into a conversation about our respective religions, Judaism and Christianity.

I started in this way, "Irv, I would like to have a conversation with you about Judaism and most likely Christianity. Since the murders, I have some serious concerns about the dogma pertaining to Christianity." The first time I engaged Irv with this topic, we were on the phone; and I heard a breathy pause on the other end of the line. I proceeded. "Irv, do Jews talk about Jesus?"

"Hmm, not really," he replied.

Quickly, anxiously, I jumped all in with, "Are you aware that Christians believe Jesus is the only way to Heaven?"

Irv is thoughtful for a moment.

"Yes," he admits, "I am familiar that some Christians believe this." He continues, "As a Jew, I believe Jesus was a prophet and a great teacher; but I don't believe he was raised from the dead. Nor do I believe he was the living son of God."

"What about Heaven?" I ask. "How do Jews get to Heaven? Do you want to go to Heaven?"

As usual, Irv sits quietly to ponder his thoughtful response. Because I have engaged in conversations with this man for over 20 years, I'm familiar with his conversational technique, including reflective, delayed responses. Even over the phone, I can sense he is contemplating. He taps his fingers on the table, most likely places his hand on his chin, then rubs it and tilts his head to the side.

"I think I heard you ask, 'How do Jews get to Heaven?' Is this what you asked me?" A typical comeback to my question of him is a clarifying question of me.

"Yes," I answer. More waiting … I know from past experience that it is best to be quiet and allow him ample time to respond.

Irv begins, "I am not speaking for all Jews. I am only speaking on behalf of myself and what I practice in my own life. It is my belief—and I believe I learned this as part of my Jewish faith—that good deeds are the way to Heaven. I always want to leave people I meet in a better condition than they were in before we met. I want to do my part in leaving our community and our world in a better situation than I feel it is in now. Acts of good deeds are what I strive for to get to Heaven."

"Hmm, OK," I answer and ponder a bit. I appreciate his thoughtful response. It helps me better understand the Jewish perspective on Heaven.

Irv turns the tables on me and asks, "How do Christians get to Heaven?"

"Christians believe that Jesus *is* God," I explain, "Jesus, the son of God, actually was God in the flesh. We believe Jesus was born from a virgin, died on a cross and was raised from the dead three days later. Jesus died for our sins."

"So what do you have to *do* to get to Heaven?" Irv inquires.

This question has never been posed to me. Similar to Irv, I have to stop and deeply consider my own response. I realize that actually, *no*, you don't have to do good deeds to get to Heaven. Jesus died on the cross for our sins ... all we have to do is *believe*.

This feels like a weak answer. Because while believing can be difficult at times, it is just believing ... not actually actively doing something to better myself or anyone else. It seems like there should be more to it. Yet, I know this aspect of grace to be true based on my faith.

I offer Irv an example about a criminal. A criminal, a murderer, in fact, could state he gives his life to Jesus just before execution and could still be received into Heaven. I briefly recount the story of Jesus on the cross, specifically his offer for forgiveness and his invitation of Heaven to the criminal hanging next to him.

Caught off guard by the way I feel after spelling out my beliefs, I am dismayed. The Jewish way of helping others, leaving the world a better place, being a better person each and every day—I think I like the Jewish way better. I feel more comfortable with their way ... helping others, being kind and making a difference. Their currency seems much easier to measure and wrap my arms around. It feels tangible. Believing, having faith—this is not tangible.

Most recently, the tangible faith I had was yanked right out from under me. My faith didn't save my father or my son. I was still shattered, all the while, having faith.

As soon as I enter The Temple, Congregation B'nai Jehudah, that same profoundly peaceful feeling that I felt in my home starts to envelop me.

This feeling … I have felt it before in my life. When? A memory floats into my mind, softly and with kindness. I was about 13 years old. Mom and Dad had me stay the weekend with family friends while they went out of town. This family belonged to the First Baptist Church in Marlow. Evidently, a revival was taking place at the church during the time I stayed with them. Of course, this is where they were going to spend their time and I was with them. I attended the Baptist revival. At some point during and then after a sermon, my heart ached with this same peaceful feeling. Tears began to drop from my eyes. I had never cried in church before. Bowing my head, tears flowed. The preacher had asked for anyone to walk forward who was ready to dedicate their lives to Christ. Knowing I had already done so and in my own church, I wasn't inclined to take the walk. The peaceful feeling had brought tears, but not a feeling of needing to "take the walk."

However, this family saw my emotions through tears in the pew and gently encouraged me to take the walk. I took the walk. With a tear-stained face and now some embarrassment, I knelt at the altar. The peaceful feeling had left me as if to say, "You can take this walk on your own; I will wait in the pew." Going through the motions of "accepting Christ" and "being saved again" took place in the Baptist Church and my parents heard all about it.

I was 13 and felt this peaceful feeling. Now, I feel it again walking into The Temple, Congregation B'nai Jehudah.

In the synagogue with Rabbi Nemitoff, I can quite literally feel God's presence just by being near him. I'm amazed that I feel compelled to share so openly with this man I barely know. No question, God has intentionally placed him in my life.

The floodgates of tears open quickly. I begin to explain all the messages I have been receiving, as well as the fear I am experiencing. I try to formulate words around my new passion of learning about Judaism and my ultimate dream of banishing hate crimes. I barely take a breath in the first several minutes. Realizing I have been doing all the talking and crying, my cheeks flush as I wipe away tears.

The rabbi's gaze is intense and tender as he responds, "I can't wait to see who you become and what you've done 10 years from now."

He means this as a sincere compliment, but his comment invokes more pain, which leads to tears. "Ten years?" the words somehow escape as breathing becomes difficult. Unfortunately, this has become common for me. I said, "Most days I don't know how to make it through another day. I long to be in Heaven. I don't know that I can make it another 10 years."

When I lost Reat and Dad, I also lost part of my desire to live an earthly life. My focus, since that day, has transitioned from an earthly focus to a "somewhere-in-between" spot. I know Heaven is my real "home." And it feels so daunting to think about how long I have to wait to see them.

"Rabbi, if I'm honest, most days I long to leave this Earth and go be with Reat and Dad in Heaven. I've lost two major parts of my connection to this life."

He sits quietly as he ingests my words. When he finally looks up, his eyes are filled with empathy. "It hurts that badly?" he inquires.

I respond without hesitation, "It hurts that badly."

I admit to the rabbi that my personal devastation is still so heart-breaking that I often wish my life on Earth would end. The depth of my grief is so profound and disheartening that I often feel I literally can't go on without them. Although I wake up each day and muster the energy to go about some sort of routine, my heart and soul are tortured by the fact that I have to live without Reat and Dad. I'm honestly not sure how long I can live with my seemingly splayed open, heart and soul. My heart hurts, my body aches . . . this is the grief I feel every day.

Rabbi Nemitoff shares the Jewish legend of the Lamed Vavniks with me. He explains their belief that our world depends on 36 men (In Hebrew, the group could consist of both women and men and still be considered a group of "men.") who are in every generation for the existence of a peaceful world. He continues to explain, "Basically, there are 36 human beings in each generation, who exist with pro-found purpose, for our world's peaceful existence. A peaceful world hinges on their existence and their contribution to society."

I wonder why the rabbi is explaining this to me. Is he suggesting that Dad or Reat could have been one of these 36? He continues to explain, The Lamed Vavniks legend tells us that the 36 people don't know who they are and are not known by anybody else. They are simply in positions of such influence and importance that their presence keeps our world from the demise of evil."

It must be that one of these 36 was not working the day evil murdered my family.

Is the rabbi telling me this in fear of me taking my own life? Perhaps he believes I might actually take my own life. Therefore, I should know that I could be one of the needed 36. Never, have I thought I was or am one of the 36 referred to by the Lamed Vavniks legend. I am the ONE. I am Lukas' momma. His eyes, smile, hugs and his need for me, keep me from hurting myself.

When Rabbi Nemitoff finishes his explanation, I ask if he would be willing to look at a vision board that Reat had created in October 2013, six months prior to his death. The rabbi is happy to take a look at the board and I pull it from my bag. Sitting silently while he looks at each picture and searches for meaning, he takes his time and then begins to respond with his perception into what each picture might mean.

He begins with the picture of the dove. The dove, he explains, represents peace in Judaism. He shares with me a few other insights and observations about Reat's chosen pictures. He points out that he doesn't see any anger or pain in the photos. This statement warms my heart. I am so grateful this artistic expression of Reat's suggests he was healthy and happy.

Often, I wonder if Reat's vision board was a vision from God. The idea that God knew Reat's death was imminent frightens me. Of course, many Christians believe that God knew this would happen, that God expected it and that God planned it as part of our lives.

I am curious if their lives are shattered to the extent that mine is. Will they continue to believe a loving God chose death over life?

I wonder if God knew Reat's death would be connected to Judaism.

But if God knew these things, which I am fearful He did, why did He not stop the murders? If God is able to give us messages and be a part of our lives, why would He allow hate crimes like this one to occur? Why Reat? Why Dad? Why me? What is God's plan and God's will for my life—and do I really have to follow it?

All these questions swirled around in my mind that day and many others as I worked to process the murders, the violence and the new lives we are forced to live because of evil and frankly, ignorance.

One question I ask aloud is, "Rabbi Nemitoff, is your God my God even though we have different religions?" He assures me by saying, "Although we have some different beliefs, we share the same God."

Moving my questioning to Heaven, I ask, "Will you go to Heaven when you die?"

"I expect to be in a place of peace when I die," he replies.

"Do you believe Jesus was a real person?" I ask.

"Yes, we believe Jesus was a prophet," he explains.

I continue to seek understanding, "But, you don't believe Jesus died for our sins and was raised from the dead to save us?"

He continues, "No, we don't believe Jesus was our Messiah. We are still waiting on our Messiah. The Jews are still waiting on our Messiah."

"Well, when is the Messiah coming?"

He chuckles and tells me he will most likely see the Messiah at his death, not necessarily while he is on Earth. And until the time of his death, he will continue to strive to make the world a better place.

The rabbi explains that I am to know that God loves me. He says God knows I'm in deep pain and in search of healing. He tells me God will give me peace and I need to follow my heart.

I leave Rabbi Nemitoff's office with just as many new questions as answers. One such question is,

"Is God prompting me to stop believing that Jesus is my Messiah? Am I supposed to be Jewish?"

A family photo of Dana and Tony with Andrew and Katy Corporon in Overland Park, Kansas. Fall, 2020.

This photo depicts a typical family Easter weekend. Tony, Dana, Andrew and Katy Corporon with Len, Mindy, Reat and Lukas enjoying time with Popeye and Yea Yea on Easter Sunday. Photo taken in Lenexa, Kansas, April 2012.

Tony is leaving a message for his dad. Maggie Golden, Popeye's granddaughter, is close by. Photograph by Joe Shalmoni Photojournalist, © April 18, 2014.

14

Post-Traumatic Stress Disorder

When fun and exciting experiences happen to us, we retell them over and over. The energy we receive from these moments propel us forward and onward in our river of life, free and flowing. Consider the "high" you feel when your favorite team wins an important game and you saw it happen. We want this memory to last, to be indelibly etched in our brains and to provide us continuing joy for days, months and years. This is why at reunions of all types—family, high school, college, sorority and fraternity alike—we relive the personal and frequently shared moments of importance from our past.

Reliving traumatic events is not the same. However, reliving traumatic experiences can be just as or more important to our mental health. Talk therapy is an effective treatment and one of several promoted options for healing after a traumatic experience, per the U.S. Department for Veterans Affairs National Center for PTSD website.

This chapter is dedicated to my younger brother, Tony Corporon. Thank you, Tony, for stepping into a position of care in the midst of our shared pain. The following is an annotated excerpt from my podcast, *Real Grief—Real Healing with Mindy Corporon*, distributed on July 18, 2020, titled "Emotional Security is Mental Health Care." This is when I asked Tony to share with me his experience on Sunday, April 13, 2014.

My podcast recordings typically begin the same way each time. Dave Kropf, my producer provided by the Experience of the Soul Podcast Channel, has sent me and my guest a link to join him for a recording. I am sitting in my hopefully noise-free closet as I click the link. On May 13, 2020, I found Dave already in the session talking with Tony, my guest for this recording. They were chitchatting about our current dilemma with the COVID-19 pandemic and how cramped Tony was in his closet, sitting exactly where I asked him to be during his recording. Dave and I found that situating myself and my guests in our closets, filled with clothes, shoes, potentially a bed cover and pillows, too, makes for a wonderful makeshift studio.

I had asked Tony to be my guest for the purpose of recording his recollection of Sunday, April 13, 2014, the day our father and my son, his nephew, were murdered. If you could, for a second or two, consider a tornado. Being from Oklahoma, this came to me as an easy example. Essentially, we were all thrown into an F-5 tornado for a period of about two hours. When the eye of the storm passed, we were left with life-altering damage. Over the past six years, I have gleaned some of the details of Tony's experience, as compared to mine. However, he wasn't the person in our family to inform me of the lingering effects he was experiencing after this horrific day. Nearly two years after the murders, my mom shared with me the fact that Tony had sought counseling for depression, anxiety and post-traumatic stress disorder (PTSD). A wave of guilt washed over me. Images from our tragic day were not only mine … they were shared. Perhaps we didn't see, hear or feel the same things, but we were both experiencing the lasting effects of trauma.

Tony begins his explanation of the day in this way, "Sunday morning was a normal morning for us." His wife, Dana, informed him that she would be taking their two children for Easter bunny photos with our mom. It was interesting hearing Tony say that the morning was normal and relaying the information about Easter bunny photos in the same sentence. Clearly, taking Easter bunny photos is not part of a "normal day." Yet, during Easter season, we grew up with this almost mandatory expectation of "bunny photos." Tony continued, "Our mom, Melinda, really likes the Easter pictures and so we were playing the good family and getting the kids all dolled up to go. It was also the day before my birthday." Again, the day before his own birthday, Tony casually calls this morning normal for them. Perhaps growing up in the Midwest and being fed Methodist and Presbyterian doctrine took us on a path that said … no matter what happens to you, it is normal.

So much like my father and mother's relationship, Tony asked Dana what he needed to do to help her for the day. Dana is much more independent than my mother. I expect an entire generation of women who are a few years older than me, all the way to Dana, who is 10 years my junior, would attest to being more independent than their mothers and mothers-in-law. She was gainfully employed in a full-time corporate position with a bank and raising two children. Dana easily and gently responded to Tony, "Just do your thing today." At the time, it seemed innocuous, of course.

Tony continues, "So I went to the gym and was on a treadmill at one o'clock, or thereabouts, maybe five after. I got a call on my phone from Len Losen, your husband." Each person Len phoned—my mother, older brother, Will, and younger brother, Tony—told me that Len was yelling his comments into the phone, which startled each of them when they answered.

"Len yelled something about Popeye's shot. Dad went by any number of names: Doc, Bill and most recently, Popeye," Tony said. Popeye was the name Reat had chosen for our father, his grandfather. In fact, Reat named Popeye before he called me Mom-Mom. I was only jealous for a short time. Tony continues, "Len said there's been a shooting; Popeye's been shot. We don't know how bad, you need to get to the Jewish Community Center."

I was taken aback when I heard that this was how Len presented the message to Tony and presumably to my mother as well. I knew my father was dead and I had shared this with Len. Immediately, I felt he didn't trust me. Why had he not shared the same message with them? Len has since surmised he hoped I was wrong about Dad's death. He said that I sounded so frantic that he thought I could be wrong. Len is correct … I was frantic when I phoned him. He was the first phone call I made after I found them in the parking lot with my hands shaking so violently that I couldn't hold the phone that was just handed to me. My mind was clear, though. I knew what I saw. In fact, I carefully chose the words, "Dad has been shot and is dead," rather than describe how I knew he was dead. And I have never, nor will I ever, explain how my father looked when I found his body, injured so badly from the gunshot wound that took his life. The thought of not being trusted caused me an uncomfortable feeling, even as I consider it today. I have to process this feeling each time my family members explain what they heard Len say to them. I also have to forgive. So much forgiveness is needed for myself in each small, seemingly inoffensive step of the day.

Tony knew that our father had at least one firearm in his truck. A thought flashed through his mind as he was running from the gym to his car that any gunshots could have been from his own, legally owned firearm. "I really rushed out of the gym, grabbed my stuff and ran for my car. I probably exercised more between the locker room and my car than I actually did in the gym," Tony shared. "I needed to find out what was going on." Tony considered the location of his own family members, "I knew that Dana was with Mom having Easter pictures taken."

My husband, Len, had mostly followed my instructions to call my mom immediately about the shooting at the Jewish Community Center. Between the time of Tony driving to the photo studio where his wife and children were, my mother had received the call from Len. After hearing from Len about a shooting at the Jewish Community Center, my mom left the photo studio and drove the half mile to the Jewish Community Center, leaving Tony's wife and children.

Tony continued, "I went to pick Dana and the kids up from the studio and I still didn't know what was going on. I turned on the news, you know, to see if there'd been any reports. I was driving and not really focused on driving. I was trying to get a hold of family to find out if there was more going on … what was really happening? It was frustrating to not have a clue. I got to the photo studio and went inside." Finding Dana in the photo studio, she knew they needed to leave right away. "We drove from the photo studio to the Jewish Community Center, which luckily was just about a half a mile away." Tony and Dana, with their two young children in the car, arrived at the Jewish Community Center. It had already been blocked off by police.

Tony continued, "Specifically, there was a young lady highway patrol officer who was blocking the entrance that I was trying to access at the Jewish Community Center. I remember stopping and letting the woman know that I was a family member and was clear that I needed to get past the barricades they were placing. I was trying really hard to be calm and wanting her to understand the importance of letting me through without me saying 'my father has been shot' because we had my kids in the car and at the time they were 7 and 5." Tony did not convince the highway patrol officer that he should be allowed to drive onto the campus. He realized he would be better off on his own, with no vehicle or young children to contend with. In conversation with his wife, Dana, Tony said he would call her later and let her know what had happened as he was exiting his car. It was at this point when the highway patrol officer stated, "You can't stay here."

The deep concern and fear of what had transpired on the campus that led Len to call him and that led my mom to hurriedly leave for the same Jewish Community Center campus was boiling over in Tony's emotions. He blurted out, "Yes, I can because that's my father and that's my nephew who's been shot." Tony continues with his remembrance of that moment in time. "My kids heard what I said about Reat being shot and about their Popeye, their grandfather, being shot. I did not want my children to hear this in that way. They didn't know what was going on. They knew it was important. They knew this was an emergency but they didn't know what had happened yet. And I had to insist, in front of a police officer, that it was my family that was in there. One of my biggest regrets is not keeping my cool during that moment. My kids heard from me that their grandfather was shot, and I was stepping out of the car seemingly into the same space as where the crime had taken place. I was leaving them and their mom after just yelling at a police officer. Andrew (7) and Katy (5) knew that Reat was with Popeye. They knew, as we all did, that Reat had an important audition and that Popeye was taking him. It was a scary moment."

Tony has walked through the same scenario so many times in his mind, alone and with professional care, working to forgive himself for his actions and words during a tumultuous time.

With Tony now out of his car, Dana took the driver's seat and began to back their car away. Standing next to the highway patrol officer in a deluge of rain, Tony never truly received clearance that he could go on the property. Of course, there was a lot of chaos and the pouring rain helped to cover him as he ran to the east side entrance of the building. Tony continued, "I got inside from the east, not seeing the other side of the building—the crime scene. I found you, Mindy, you were distraught and in shock. You were very quiet and you had kind of gone into yourself. Mom felt sick and had to go to the restroom, so we followed her, you and I, into the women's restroom. My anger boiled over. I knew now that Dad had died from a gunshot. You informed me that Reat was seriously injured and had been taken in an ambulance but we didn't know which hospital. I had to get my anger out and used a bathroom stall as a punching bag."

We are certain the Jewish Community Center forgave him for breaking one of the bathroom stall doors in the women's restroom that day.

As Tony, Mom and I left the women's restroom, we saw Lukas running towards us in the hallway with Len behind him. My 12-year-old baby boy had terror, sheer terror on his face. I wish I could tell you exactly what happened next, but like some of the other aspects of this horrific day, I have to rely on the statements of others to assist me in piecing together the events. Undoubtedly, we embraced. I embraced Lukas. Len joined us. Tony and Mom joined in the full embrace. We needed one another. Our minds were racing and our hearts were fearful.

I stopped our interview for a few minutes, allowing each of us to breathe. Reliving the memory of racing through the parking lot, visualizing the hallway, the restroom, Lukas' face and that of my mother, Len and me, was a lot. It was time for a pause.

Tony recalls, as do I, that we stayed at the Jewish Community Center for a long time. It felt like forever and may have only been about 30 minutes, even from the time he arrived. It took longer than it should have for the police to inform us of where the ambulance had taken Reat. Reat didn't have any identification on him; and since most homicides in our county involve family members, one or more of us were actually thought to be potential suspects in the murder. This thought lasted for only a short time in the scheme of the day because the shooter murdered Terri LaManno at the Village Shalom and then gave himself up in the parking lot of a nearby elementary school.

Our interview begins again with Tony explaining his memory of our time in the hospital. "We went to the hospital and we were in a very small waiting room, the room you never want to be in. The doctor with the long gray hair came in and told us that Reat had died. His heart had stopped in the ambulance and they could not restart his heart. That was a very cold moment. I felt shivers. I felt any range of emotions that were heightened and certainly a significant sadness flowed over me." Tony continued, "The doctor with the ponytail allowed us a moment to grieve. Maybe he even left and came back to the room. They needed someone to identify the body. I heard the doctor say, 'He is a young man and didn't have any identification on him. We cannot identify him as who you say he is. We need someone to identify the body.'"

The ponytailed doctor has a name. None of us knew it at the time and I didn't try to learn his name either. Not out of anger, but out of sheer determination to not feel what I felt when he shared the news with us that my oldest child had also lost his life. Don Fishman, M.D., MBA, has been a practicing physician since 1988. He is an experienced, board-certified general surgeon with specialized expertise in trauma and surgical critical care. He currently serves as trauma medical director and surgical intensivist for Overland Park Regional Medical Center. Dr. Fishman is a diplomate of the American Board of Surgery and certified by the American Board of Surgery in critical care medicine. In addition to his extensive patient care experience, Dr. Fishman also served as an instructor at various medical teaching facilities in Chicago. Dr. Fishman also has a master's degree in business administration from Keller Graduate School of Business. His short biography presented here was retrieved from the HCA Overland Park Regional Medical Center website.

Ironically, I met Dr. Fishman one year later, face to face, as a guest speaker for Midwest Transplant Network. Our family has always valued the importance of organ and tissue donation. Because Reat was able to be a tissue and ligament donor at his death, we were asked to present our personal story on several occasions for the benefit of raising awareness from the perspective of the donor family. In May 2015, I stepped back into the Overland Park Regional Medical Center for the first time since I learned the news that Reat had not survived the gunshot wound to his head. Families were gathering and sitting in metal chairs, lined up theater style. A light brown wooden podium stood alone with a microphone set atop waiting for a presenter. Who I thought to be organizers of the event milled about talking amongst themselves and with people who looked to be medical personnel. While Midwest Transplant Network had invited me to speak, I wasn't sure of the roles everyone else would play. My role was to present our story of deciding to procure tissue and ligaments from Reat's deceased body, why we chose to do so and how this affected our family. As I contemplated how I would tell my story without crying through the entire message, I saw him.

Every time I speak about the exact moment that I heard "the young man who was brought in with the gunshot wound did not survive," I see Dr. Fishman, of Jewish faith, speaking these words. Now, I see him in person, standing only 10 feet away and in conversation with others. I didn't feel exactly the same sudden shock I felt when I shook the hand of firefighter Dan Stringfield. Now, I felt a flutter in my stomach about speaking to Dr. Fishman. Unsure of what to say, but brave enough to walk toward him, I stood up on my already shaking legs and found myself standing next to him before determining how I would introduce myself. There was no need to introduce myself. Dr. Fishman had been part of the committee who asked me to be present. He was thankful I had accepted the invitation to speak and was expecting me. I have no quotes to share about our conversation because my brain was so careful to protect itself and my soul from further potential damage. I chatted and listened, yet recall next to nothing of our conversation, other than feeling he had been the best person to receive Reat that day. Dr. Fishman was compassionately apologetic that they had lost their patient, my son. His team tried multiple times to coax Reat's heart to beat. The damage was too significant. I knew this already. I live it every day.

In my podcast interview with Tony, he went on to say, "After the doctor said they needed someone to identify the body, Mindy, you immediately said, 'I'll go.' I knew somehow, some way, that you did not need to see your son again in such a state. I mean, you'd already seen him at the Jewish Community Center. I told you that I would identify Reat so that you did not have to do that. I went back with the doctors (into the emergency room, where Reat lay) and I identified Reat's body."

Because we were sitting in our separate closets, miles apart, the tension I felt on my side of the computer could have all been my own. Realizing I had most likely never thanked Tony for lifting this task from my shoulders, I responded with, "Thank you." Even after one year of sinking into depression and feeling the effects of PTSD and one more year of careful work with a counselor, Tony did not hesitate with his response, "You're welcome."

Continuing to fill voids in the spaces that were fuzzy in my brain or those that I might not realize had taken place, I asked Tony to provide me with details of his involvement at the hospital after he identified Reat's body.

Tony proceeds with, "In any heightened public emergency or disaster, there is a certain level of public relations that needs to be managed." Tony wanted to be helpful and needed to be engaged. "The best way I saw to do that was to allow you, Mom, Len and Lukas to grieve with one another while I made myself available to the detectives from the scene of the crime. I did the first interview with the detectives who had arrived on scene. I also met with the hospital public relations team who were beginning to field calls from local news media about the shooting and requesting information about the victim. Initially, this was my role."

Isn't it interesting how he found a role for himself in the middle of the storm? Like my father and the Eagle Scout that Tony is, he found the work that needed to be done. Even as a griever, Tony provided assistance where and when it was needed out of the desire to care for his family and stabilize himself. Both of these are valuable traits to have when a shit-show crisis appears during your "typically normal day." Returning from his role as intermediary for our family, he found that we had been relocated to a larger room to accommodate a growing number of friends and family.

We were grateful and surprised to see so many friendly faces arrive at the hospital emergency area only a short time after we heard the news that Reat had not survived. Of course, as they were arriving, each of them knew of my father's death; but they were hopeful, as we had been, that Reat would be in surgery of some type, but living. As my eyes met theirs, each time, flowing tears continued and seemed to burst from a well that had no bottom. Fierce embraces lasted longer than normal, allowing each of us the opportunity to bury our heads in one another, trying to sob away the reality and pain.

One of several objectives for interviewing Tony was to elicit him sharing how he came to realize he had PTSD. This is what he told me:

"About a year after the shootings, I was having trouble controlling my emotions. I was distant. I was frustrated. I was not who I had been or who I wanted to be. So I sought help and went to a therapist that specializes in PTSD. It took about six months of therapy for me to come to grips with a lot of things, including the shooting and my role, and the things I saw and the things I had to do. But also I think trauma for an event like a shooting, like the sudden loss of a loved one, is not contained to the trauma of the loss or of the exact day. I can tell you to this day, I still feel trauma when I hear a song on the radio that our father liked to listen to or I hear a song on the radio that Reat liked to sing."

These are triggers for Tony.

"There is no day that goes by that I don't feel a sense of loss. But I have learned to cope and that coping mechanism that I worked through with my counselor has helped me to be me. You know, to deal with those pains, but also just to be a better, more well-rounded, more emotionally secure person."

I was appreciative of Tony for sharing so vulnerably with me and on a recording. He is not in the military. He did not suffer from trauma attributable to his own body. Yet, the traumatic situation, what he saw, heard and the emotions he felt during the events suspended Tony in this same space. Similar to my reliving of the entire parking lot scene over and over, Tony was doing the same. This suspension in time halted his healing. Professional consultations allowed Tony to process the emotions fully and flush them out of his psyche and literally release the toxins that were stirring up his anger. Living a typically normal life, Tony is a testament that this type of trauma can occur at any time, to anyone. We don't know how our bodies or emotions will react to any level of trauma. His story is now available for others to learn and realize they are not alone and, just as importantly, that help and healing is available.

Tony's final words for my podcast listeners and you are, "I'm glad that I was able to share this and I hope that other men, especially who feel trauma in their lives, recognize that it's not a sign of weakness to admit that you need some assistance to find yourself."

If you have suffered from trauma of any type and think you might have post-traumatic stress disorder (PTSD), please continue reading below for a clear definition and options for care.

The U.S. Department of Veterans Affairs is home to the National Center for Post-Traumatic Stress Disorder (PTSD). On the PTSD Basics section of their webpage is the following:

> PTSD is a mental health problem that some people develop after experiencing or witnessing a life-threatening event, like combat, a natural disaster, a car accident or sexual assault.
>
> It's normal to have upsetting memories, feel on edge or have trouble sleeping after a traumatic event. At first, it may be hard to do normal daily activities, like go to work, go to school or spend time with people you care about. But most people start to feel better after a few weeks or months.
>
> If it's been longer than a few months and you're still having symptoms, you may have PTSD. For some people, PTSD symptoms may start later or they may come and go over time.

Continuing with educational material from the U.S. Department of Veterans Affairs and now reviewing the history of diagnosing PTSD, I found this from Matthew J. Friedman, M.D., Ph.D.:

> In 1980, the American Psychiatric Association (APA) added PTSD to the third edition of its Diagnostic and Statistical Manual of Mental Disorders (DSM-III) nosologic classification scheme.[2]
>
> Although controversial when first introduced, the PTSD diagnosis has filled an important gap in psychiatric theory and practice. From an historical perspective, the significant change ushered in by the PTSD concept was the stipulation that the etiological agent was outside the individual (i.e., a traumatic event) rather than an inherent individual weakness (i.e., a traumatic neurosis). The key to understanding the scientific basis and clinical expression of PTSD is the concept of 'trauma.'

---

2 Diagnostic and Statistical Manual of Mental Disorders, 3rd ed. American Psychiatric Association (1980). Washington, D.C.

Top: Peacefully exclaiming that 'Love Wins' outside
the funerals of William and Reat. Photo courtesy
of Gloria Baker Feinstein. April 18, 2014.

Bottom: Mindy Corporon took this photo of Pastor Adam
Hamilton providing a message about hope in our community
as part of the ground breaking ceremony for the new
sanctuary, completed in 2017. Church of the Resurrection
in Overland Park, Kansas. February 23, 2014.

Top: Mindy is leaving a message to Reat. Photograph by
Joe Shalmoni Photojournalist, © April 18, 2014.

Bottom: Reat's casket is pictured here with numerous messages from family,
friends and well-wishers. Note that the message on the bottom of the photo
is from Josh Miller, a dear childhood friend of Reat's and now a mentor to
Lukas. Photograph by Joe Shalmoni Photojournalist, © April 18, 2014.

15

"Where is God Now?"

Len, Mom and I walk side by side slowly, in utter disbelief, to our car. We have lost so much. It will be the first of many rides for the three of us together as we begin this devastating journey of grieving.

Time stands still. The rain pummels our car. Nothing is what I feel, nothing. I am completely numb as Len drives Mom and me home. With no words to say or share, a haunting silence fills the space between us. Feeling alone, I begin an internal conversation with my father, which has continued to find a way into my self-talk even after six and half years. "Thank you, Dad, for showing beauty in this world. Thank you for taking Reat to the audition. I am so sorry. I am so sorry I didn't drive him. I might have parked in another spot. I might have been earlier or later than you. I am so sorry. I am so sorry."

I am blaming myself for this horrible day. Even today, when I feel devastating sadness descend upon me, I go back to this internal self-blame story. Could I have done anything differently to save them? This question haunts me in the deepest part of my soul.

Len, Mom and I walk into my parents' home. It feels the same. It smells the same. It looks the same. The furniture is arranged as it has always been. Mail is strewn across the kitchen counter, as usual. Their house appears as if today is just another normal, ordinary day.

Except ... it's not. There is no way to understand what our journey will look like during the next months and years. Seeing my father's chair sitting empty, I visualize how empty our lives will be. Crawling into his chair, wishing it were his lap, the numbness continues. Unbelievable is a good word to describe the immense loss; yet, I know now that I didn't feel the full loss of their lives until months later. Mom and Len walk in behind me, but I have no memory of where they sit or what they say. I can't feel or hear a thing. Fog envelops me.

"Lukas. Where is Lukas?" a shard of panic rips into me as I yell for someone to answer me.

"Rich and Laura have him," responds Len.

Oh, yes. I take a deep breath, knowing my friend and business part-ner and his daughter, Laura, will take good care of him. Richard Boyer came to the same hospital the day Lukas was born, 12 years prior. He wanted to be one of the first people to hold Lukas, who would join Reat—one of Rich's favorite chess opponents—in our family. The boys affectionately called Richard, Mr. Rich. He was like a "fun" uncle with the two of them. Pancakes on Saturday mornings after a Friday night sleepover, and often allowing them to ride in his lap and steer his car on our cul- de-sac road were some of Richard's favorite memories with them. Now, there is no more "the two of them." There is only one.

I reached for the phone number in my back pocket belonging to the man who protected me in the parking lot, the one who shielded me in case a shooter was still in the area. He had also run through the rain to fetch Len's vehicle at the Jewish Community Center. Above his number reads the name "Mickey Blount." He had been such an important figure in our tragic day. I am concerned he might not yet know that Reat died today.

Dialing his number from Len's cell phone, because mine was still in the truck dad was driving and is now part of the crime scene, my hands began to shake uncontrollably. A man answers. I ask if I am speaking to Mickey and he assures me I am. I stammer and stutter and say for the second time aloud, "My son, Reat—who you saw today—did not survive. I am sorry to tell you that he did not survive. He went to Heaven with my father. I thought you might want to know." Mickey thanks me for calling and says he is so very sorry. I press the end call button as deep heaving sobs overtake me.

Some of our family and friends who found us at the Overland Park Regional Medical Center begin to appear in the living room. The number of people begins to multiply and soon Mom's home is filled with low chatter and horribly sad faces.

As Tony has shared with me, I am inside myself. Everyone seems to be floating, or maybe I am the one floating, outside of our normal world. I feel detached from everyone present … all the while physical hugs are offered, one after the other. Five, 10, and then there were too many to count. People with sad faces and hugs continue to fill her home. How did they hear our horrible news? How do they know to come? And how do they know to come here—my mom's house?

The trauma I experienced was so great, much greater than I knew, while accepting each visitor. I have since learned how complicated trauma is. The fog in my brain was partly to protect my soul, or perhaps my soul was protecting my brain. Either way, the detachment I felt from reality stayed with me for weeks, maybe allowing the world around me to get in a position of support for my eventual fall.

My soul could feel an enormous pain, but my brain wouldn't allow this much pain at one time. My brain wanted to consider, and did consider, that this was all a nightmare and I would wake up. My brain wanted to go back to the hospital and grab Reat from the table, where I never saw his lifeless body, and hold him until he woke up. My brain wanted to go back into my kitchen when I was listening to Reat sing, "You're Gonna Miss Me When I'm Gone." They danced together, my brain and my soul. No one could see this, but I could feel it. The beginning of trauma-induced anxiety, depression and post-traumatic stress disorder were creeping into my body. Soon they would be part of my vernacular to explain to myself and others the journey, not simply the season of grief.

Each well-meaning friend appearing at my mom and dad's home told me with one look on their face that my brain would lose the imagination game of trying to keep Reat and Dad alive. The looks on their faces told me what I didn't want to believe but knew to be true. The nightmare was real.

Again, sitting in my father's chair, I see my pastor, Adam Hamilton, senior pastor of the United Methodist Church of the Resurrection, walk into the living space. Tears that had halted now found my cheeks, flowing freely. His presence flipped a switch in my soul, as if to say, this is safety. Not realizing I had not felt safe nor had I felt I could share all that I had seen or heard when I found my father's lifeless body, my heart and soul were screaming at me to tell "him." I can't control my tears. The same steady flow of tears that was upon me in the hospital is suddenly back.

Pastor Hamilton had met me on two previous occasions, none as memorable as this. Our most recent encounter was in the salad dressing aisle of the grocery store. Our church happens to be quite large. I wasn't on a church committee, or even more involved in church, other than attending. I knew who he was as I saw him carrying a small reusable grocery bag; and I said quickly, "Hello, Pastor Hamilton. I attend Church of the Resurrection." Politely, he asked my name, he said thank you, and we went our separate ways. One time before this, our family of four was leaving the church building and we practically ran into Pastor Hamilton. He saw our two cute boys and squatted down to ask Lukas what he thought of Sunday school. The exchange was embarrassing and, thankfully, quick. "Hey there young man, did you enjoy Sunday school today?" said our pastor to our youngest son. "No," responded Lukas.

Now, I am feeling extremely vulnerable as my heart beats openly, as if it is outside my chest. The words "Tell him, tell him … your father's in Heaven, go find Reat," were repeating like a drumming chant. He was kind, compassionate and held me in an empathetic hug as he said a few times, "I am so sorry. I am so sorry for your family and for your tremendous losses today."

Knowing Pastor Adam as I do now, six and a half years after our journey began, he would not want anyone to call him God, Jesus or place him in the same space with them or the Holy Spirit. I believe he considers himself in a position to deliver, educate and provide anecdotal evidence that the Trinity is real, Heaven is real and having faith is the path to both. Speaking to my mother and then Len with the same compassion and empathy, it is difficult to see him trying to soothe a wound that was so recently flayed open. Like me, Mom and Len are in another world, nodding their acceptance and gratitude for his visit with glassy, tear-filled eyes, doe-like and dreamy. My mind is jarred as a message is dictated to me, "God has been preparing you for this tragedy." This feeling, this dreadful, paralyzing feeling, comes over me.

"Your father's in Heaven. Go find Reat." Why were these words still in my head?

The Mindy most people know steps into the shoes of whoever was standing in the living room at that moment. From some place inside me, I had the audacity to ask Pastor Hamilton for a private conversation. He was there for me, yes; but he was present for Mom, Len, my brothers and all the friends now lining the walls, seats and floor in my mom's home. At this moment, it seems the right thing to do. I ask for him to join me in my parent's study, upstairs. It is as if God is tugging at my heart saying, "Tell him," and I feel like God is talking to my soul. The idea of telling my family is not plausible. They are burdened with the two losses of life; they don't need me heaping some personal "crazy lady" talk on them. I feel I should, and could, tell my pastor.

The thought of being known as the "crazy lady" by Pastor Hamilton crosses my mind as we walk upstairs. With some embarrassment, shaking legs and hands and more tears, I feel a powerful nudge from whom I will continue to call God. We each found a place to sit and without any hesitation, my mouth opened to speak. Words start to flow.

"For two years, I have felt like God has been preparing me for something. I have been overly devoted to attending church, helping others and listening to Christian music. I don't do these things because I have to. I do them because they fill my heart with tangible joy. The power I experience during these times is unmistakable. I feel passionately drawn to church and to my relationship with God. When I'm not able to attend service during a weekend, it's as if there's a deep hole in my heart." The words were flowing from an unknown source. None of this is what I had planned to tell him.

He is listening intently.

I continue to reveal to Pastor Hamilton that Christian music is a new source of great jubilation. I explain that I belt out the lyrics in my car, often singing through tears of joy. One day, recently, the feeling of

God's presence was so powerful that I pulled over, stopped and asked Him what was going on. "God, what is going on? What are You preparing me for? Am I going to get cancer? Am I going to die?" I didn't hear an audible answer, but I felt a physical sense of peace in my soul. That felt like my answer.

My tears continue falling as I dive deeper, disclosing this to Pastor Hamilton, with questions and statements, my discernment of God preparing me for this event. Frightened by the idea of being prepared and saying these words out loud, anger finds a channel in my tone. Without giving him time to respond, I am throwing angry questions his way. "Why on earth would God allow this to happen? Did God know that Reat and Dad were going to be murdered today? If people thought God could prepare them for tragedies, they would be afraid of God. I am scared, very scared. I am afraid of 'being prepared.' Now what? What does God want me to do with this? Is He angry that I wasn't prepared enough? Am I not a good enough Christian? Were they murdered because of me? Why didn't God save them?"

Fear is pulsing through my veins as my questions fly through the air and settle between me and a pastor who truly just met me. Fear of learning about some mysterious force that took their lives or fear of learning I could have stopped their deaths and didn't because I slacked in following instructions races around my insides. And then, I tell him how I found my father's body, lying on his left shoulder, a pool of blood still forming like an angel's halo. I tell him I heard a voice. So clearly, this voice spoke to me while I stood only feet from what was becoming a deeper and more feared nightmare. "I heard God speak to me today. He said, 'Your father's in Heaven. Go find Reat.'"

There, I said it. I said it out loud to a man of the cloth. Surely, he has an answer for me. I hope he tells me I am not crazy and this sort of interaction happens all the time. I desperately need him to tell me something that will ease my pain and fear. I need him to help keep my heart and soul from plunging into this terrible, gut-wrenching pain. I am only just beginning to embark upon this pain, and it already feels debilitating.

Pastor Hamilton has listened calmly and quietly. He seems to feel the pain and fear emitting from me because tears form in his eyes.

Taking a moment to gather his thoughts, he looks into my eyes and speaks to me with sensitivity. He explains that this was a horrible tragedy that was created by man. He assures me that God was with me before, during and now, as I begin to grieve. Pastor Hamilton says God will work through me as He needs to, but Pastor Hamilton admits he doesn't know what that will look like. He says he is so proud of me for even having faith at this moment and to be talking about God being with me and us. He assures me that my dad and Reat are, indeed, in Heaven. Our conversation ends with Pastor Hamilton's encouraging charge, "You will do great things with this knowledge, Mindy," he says. "And I will support you in your journey. Keep listening."

Can you conjure up a time when you asked your parents a question they weren't interested in or willing to answer? Perhaps they didn't feel you were ready to hear the answer. The famous quote "You can't handle the truth!" screamed by Jack Nicholson playing the role of Colonel Nathan Jessup in *A Few Good Men*, came to mind much later when I worked to understand how I felt, leaving this conversation. There were no loud voices or yelling and Pastor Hamilton told me what he could. He did have an interest in helping me grieve through the pain. He could only tell me the words he had available to him at the time. Pastor Hamilton answered me with the depth of knowledge he had; and yet, I felt cheated. Not by him, but in life. I had done all the right things. We believe in God, for one. Wasn't that the right thing to do? We gave to charity. We were philanthropic to a point of contention in my household. We cared for others as if they were our neighbor, the golden rule. Walking down only a few more stairs, I am confident in one thing—I am not content with his response. I want a miracle, dammit. They should be living. This should not have happened, not to us. I wanted him to stop the pain that is so palpable ... I can taste it. He is a pastor and has direct contact with God, right? Where is God, now? I want this nightmare to end. What am I to do with his recommendation to "keep listening"?

My thoughts of self-doubt, pity and sorrow are interrupted by the louder chatter now taking place on the main level of my mother's home. More people seem to be in the space; and I hear someone say, "Apparently, a student vigil is being planned for 8 p.m. tonight."

In cartoons, when a character feels love, the cartoonist might show their heart beating wildly outside their body. This is what I would have looked like if a cartoonist could have drawn my feelings in this moment. My heart leapt. While my brain was lingering in the foggy conversation with Pastor Hamilton, my heart heard where we are going next. My heart is listening. Without questioning or hesitating for a second, I announce to no one in particular and everyone within earshot that I will be going to this vigil.

My announcement is met with blank stares. No one knows how I feel at this moment, and I am adjusting to the quick pace of emotions myself. "I am supposed to be there. I need to be at this student vigil."

"Are you sure?" someone speaks up to pose the question everyone is thinking. Standing in front of Len and holding his hands, he hears me say, "I need to be at this student vigil," emphasizing the word *student* for myself.

With red, tearful eyes, he asks me not to go. He feels I should stay at Mom's. "I don't think it's a good idea for you to go," Len explains.

Disconnected from myself, I have a feeling of having my son Reat standing with me. He is gently present. Hearing what Len was asking of me, but listening to my heart, I knew I would be at the student vigil. Reat is with me. Reat is very much alive in me, and I have a message to pass on to his fellow students. God didn't kill my father and Reat. A man did. Reat's friends and any students hurting tonight need to hear this message. Not only do I know it to be true, but also I know I am the messenger.

Abandoning Len and Mom was not my intent. Caring for the students who I expected to be at the vigil was my mission. My baby boy had been torn from their lives, too. Their young, impressionable hearts and souls were aching. From a lifetime ago, an ache I knew well when I was 15, floated into my memory. The vigil would be necessary for the students, and I needed to be a bridge for them to move from horror to sadness to reflection to joy.

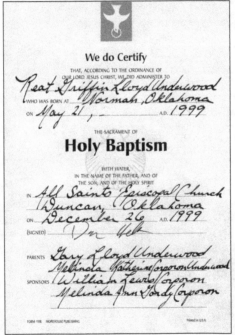

We do Certify

THAT, ACCORDING TO THE ORDINANCE OF
OUR LORD JESUS CHRIST, WE DID ADMINISTER TO

Reat Griffin Lloyd Underwood

WHO WAS BORN AT *Norman, Oklahoma*

ON *May 21,* A.D. *1999*

THE SACRAMENT OF

Holy Baptism

WITH WATER,
IN THE NAME OF THE FATHER, AND OF
THE SON, AND OF THE HOLY SPIRIT

IN *All Saints Episcopal Church*
Duncan, Oklahoma
ON *December 26* A.D. *1999*

(SIGNED) *Dn Helt*

PARENTS *Gary Lloyd Underwood*
Melinda Katherine Corporon Underwood
SPONSORS *William Lewis Corporon*
Melinda Ann Gordy Corporon

FORM 150E   MOREHOUSE PUBLISHING   Printed in U.S.A.

Top: Family was always near during Mindy's upbringing and now for
Reat's. From left: Travis Gordy, Jeff Fox, Barbara Fox, Rita Gordy, Reverend
Dwight Helt, Mindy Corporon (holding Reat), William Corporon, Melinda
Corporon, Tony Corporon—present for Reat's baptism held by All Saints
Episcopal Church in Duncan, Oklahoma. Family photo. December 26, 1999.

Bottom: Certificate of Baptism for Reat Griffin Lloyd Underwood
presented to Reat's mother, Mindy Corporon from All Saints Episcopal
Church in Duncan, Oklahoma. Family photo. December 26, 1999.

Encouraged by her Pastor, Adam Hamilton, to 'listen', Mindy Corporon found herself speaking at what she thought to be a 'student' vigil hosted by St. Thomas the Apostle Episcopal Church in Overland Park, Kansas, the night her world shattered. Standing beside Mindy is long-time friend, Tarra Freberg, offering emotional and physical support. © GettyImages.com/KansasCityStar, April 13, 2014.

16

"Keep Listening"

Of course, none of these words were what I used to try and convince Len, or anyone else in the crowded room, that I would be attending this student vigil. One of the amazing friends present that moment was K.K. She saw Len's concern and my resolute plan. Her ability to mediate a conversation came from years of success in real estate. You just never know when your day-to-day business skills will be put to use in a pivotal moment that has nothing to do with your actual line of work.

Len asks K.K. to stop me from going to the vigil. She encourages Len to allow me to grieve in the ways I feel are right for me. She reminds Len that nobody will be able to stop me if my heart is set on something. After a long, passionate conversation, he doesn't truly agree, but succumbs to my desire.

Another wonderfully dear friend, Jeri, assures me that she and her husband, Josh, will drive me to the student vigil. And she warns me that the weather has turned colder, so I need to bundle up. In the same jeans, T-shirt and sandals I donned so many hours ago when our world was on a normal path—a known trajectory—I looked down at my almost bare feet, not understanding how our lives changed as quickly as the Kansas weather. Comfortably walking into my parents' closet, I open Mom's sock drawer, taking a pair. Now, as if in slow motion, I sit on the floor, pull them on one at a time and look for her tennis shoes ... one shoe, then the other. Tying them just like I had taught Reat and Lukas to tie their shoes.

I pause.

Every movement I make is thoughtful and carefully considered, as this is the "first time" I am tying shoes without Reat living. Standing in their two-person, walk-in closet, I see sweatshirts hanging for me to take. Without regard for size, I grabbed my father's University of Oklahoma sweatshirt.

Each time I enter the living room or dining area, new people have arrived. The people are changing, but their faces are the same ... grief-stricken. Hugs and more hugs. "I am so sorry," is repeated over and over. I am saying it to myself and then hear it repeated by each friend. "I am so sorry." It dawns on me that the language we have is not sufficient to express the deep pain we are all experiencing.

People are scattered throughout the house. The conversations are in normal tones. I remember hearing the question, "Why?" multiple times. We don't yet know the facts about what happened, and we have no way of understanding the "why" behind this horrendous act of violence. Will we ever understand why? What makes someone want to murder ... a grandfather and his grandson, my father and son ... why?

Remnants of the lingering storm hold a chill in the air. The cold stings the warmth of love I had felt right out of me. And, for a moment, the chill holds me tightly, as if to say, you needed an escape from the sadness in there. The inconceivable events of the day are weighing heavily on me. Walking away from my parents' home and the despair it now held brought me a moment of relief. As I sit down in the front seat of Jeri and Josh's van, I feel grateful for their friendship. Their son, Dawson, is a good friend of Reat's, and we have experienced many Boy Scout adventures together.

Scouting weekends were a meaningful part of my role in Reat's life. Together, we traversed woods, rivers, the plains and snow. We have frightening memories of taking shelter from a tornado in a bunker and found some comedy in one of the women's "lollies," also known as a latrine. Most of our "overnights" included Josh and Dawson. Josh still teases me about my camping style. I carried my summer camp gear in giant plastic containers. It is well known that rain followed our Cub Scout and then Boy Scout troop to every campsite. I don't mind getting wet, but I want my stuff to stay dry. Josh finds it hilarious and loves to poke fun at me. Jeri and I have been in a moms' group together for many years. We started meeting monthly when our boys were in sixth grade. We discussed our kids' lives while drinking wine, in hopes of keeping a pulse on how they are doing and what shenanigans might be at hand. Similar to a few other friends of ours, we also have younger children of a similar age. Lukas, belonging to us, and Emma, to the Gardner's, were born two days apart.

A stream of consciousness is flowing from my mouth into the dark van. Jeri and Josh receive a moment-by-moment account of my morning with Reat and Dad. I keep reliving my dreadful experience from a few short hours ago. It feels as if this morning belongs to someone else, except that I keep reliving it … over and over. I keep thinking about the words Reat spoke to me this morning and the words I said to him. I replay the conversation with my dad, which I now realize was to be our final conversation. I never imagined that to be the case. I see myself waking Reat up that morning, how we laughed and how he warned me to steer clear of his drool. Classic Reat. He gave me a warm and loving hug, like he always did. It now registers as our final hug and will be remembered as one of my most memorable from him.

Reat was my awesome "hugger" of the family. He would come from anywhere to find me for a hug. He loved to drape himself on me as if we were one. We were so close.

After pausing to remember to breathe, I hear myself asking Jeri and Josh where the vigil is being held. I haven't been paying attention to where we are driving, and I don't recognize the area. Josh tells me that it is being held at St. Thomas the Apostle Episcopal Church. "Why, Josh? Why is this Episcopal church holding the vigil?" When I heard that this was a student vigil only a short while ago, I had envisioned a gymnasium opening for the students. Josh says, "I don't know darlin'. I'm sorry, I don't know."

The darkness of the van and their care for me prompts me to repeat my morning again. I continue to relive the day aloud with Jeri and Josh. Repeating the events of the day is a desperate attempt to wrap my head and heart around it. It feels as if repeating the day over and over might keep Dad and Reat alive. Reliving the story allows me to stay in the moment with the people I love. That feels much more comforting than the reality of the story I am living this evening without them. I want the day back. I want one minute back to warn them and to do anything to stop this harrowing tragedy, which will shift the trajectory of our lives forever.

In a childlike voice that doesn't sound like me, I ask Josh and Jeri again why the vigil is at St. Thomas the Apostle. Again, Josh says he doesn't know and apologizes for his lack of information. They extend grace as I rattle off more questions. "Who belongs to this church that would host a vigil? Why would this church host the vigil? Wouldn't a school host the student vigil?" They respond calmly and with compassion to my irrational questioning.

As we pull into the parking lot, the answer to why this vigil is being held at St. Thomas the Apostle Episcopal Church washes through me. Speaking like a child waking from a dreamlike state, as if being told a secret or reminded of a memory from years ago, I hear myself say out loud, "I know why it's at St. Thomas the Apostle." Without hesitation I continue, "Because Reat was baptized in an Episcopal church in Duncan, Oklahoma, when he was a baby."

I can feel God. His presence is palpable. I feel him speaking to me. I wonder to myself, "Can it be that God is actually communicating with me? Or has the trauma from today made me crazy?" My heart is all over the place. I am grappling with intense pain and deep sadness, but it feels balanced with comfort and peace. I oscillate back and forth. I'm wondering now with more confidence where God will lead me, if I listen.

The parking lot of St. Thomas the Apostle Episcopal Church is overflowing with cars. My hand is on the door handle as Josh mentions the rain I haven't even noticed. Walking toward the church, Josh and Jeri stay close to my side, protecting me. I feel their protectiveness. As we step inside, I realize the church is filled with people of all ages, not just students. "Where are the students?" I say out loud, but no one could hear me. A low hum of talking drowns out my small voice, "I thought this was a student vigil."

We cross paths with our good friends, Dom and Donna. They have two boys the same ages as Reat and Lukas. A brief conversation with them sparks an incredibly difficult realization. Wait, Reat won't age. That can't be true, can it? I begin another internal conversation. My mind is swirling. We hug and I lean in to talk to Dom. "Len will need you. Len will need you at our home," I whisper into his ear, bent low to my face. Len and Dom have had a close friendship since our oldest boys were 4 and in pre-kindergarten together. Both stay-at-home dads have been together on many adventures with our boys—to the zoo, the water park, the gym, the tennis courts, museums, etc. They all so enjoy their time together. Now, one of the boys—my boy—is no longer with us. Dom assures me with a gripping hug into his belly, which is as high as my head goes on his body, that he will be at our home soon.

I continue seeing familiar faces in the crowd. My girlfriend Tarra appears suddenly by my side. She slides a hand in mine. Feeling the warmth of our hands embraced gives me a strength I didn't realize I was missing. Her eyes are puffy, red and swollen. We have known one another since 1991, which was 23 years ago pre-marriage and children. Josh and Jeri disappear into the crowd now that I am with Tarra. My friend and coworker Laura emerges from the crowd. She had been at the emergency room and now is with me again. We are crowded together, the three of us, when Laura states she found three seats together in the sanctuary. Laura has since shared with me that intuitively she knew I would want to sit near the front and this is where she found the three open seats. We take them without hesitation.

Taking a quick look around and noticing the room full of people, I am thankful to be present. These are people already in position who will grieve alongside us. Someone is speaking in the front of the room, at the podium. I don't recognize him. The room is heavy with crying and sadness, similar to how my mom's home felt. I can feel the depth of sorrow in the room. The person talking doesn't know me, Reat or my dad. He is speaking in generalities of death and states that a third person, a woman, lost her life, too.

Selfishly, I consider, why did two of the three people have to be mine? Why did I lose two of my people today?

Someone else walks up to the podium. I can hear his words, but I am not listening. Nothing they say is penetrating the despair I have already reached. The trauma of finding my dad's body in the parking lot, watching two men care for Reat and the words "Your father's in Heaven, go find Reat," are with me. These words are sitting with me in the sanctuary, waiting to be released so the pain will ease. Instead, I am prompted to lean over to Tarra and tell her that I am supposed to speak. She looks back at me with a questioning stare. "Are you sure?" she whispers.

"Yes, I am very sure."

She walks to the front, on the left side of the room and joins a group of men and women who appear to be waiting for their turn to speak. I assume they have been asked to offer spoken messages of comfort. Why do I think I should speak? Because I am listening. God is nudging me to tell the students and now the adults *that a man murdered today*. This was not of God. Tarra bends down to talk with one of the men. This man and Tarra look my way as she points to me. The look of trepidation on his face is becoming familiar to me.

Tarra returns to her seat next to mine. The man that she had just spoken to follows her over and is now squatting at my feet. My body begins to shake. I am shaking like I did at the Jewish Community Center when I sat in the cool air and watched the men hold up my son and wrap his head in white cloths. The vision of my dad is also clear in my mind. The blood pooling around his head and the way his body was lying on the ground, I knew he wasn't aware of the gunman. He was ambushed.

The man, I learned much later, was the Rev. Gar Demo. He asks me my name and my relation to the victims. "I am Mindy Corporon. My son and dad were both murdered today," I explain. Tears come to my eyes, but I remain steady. He asks if I really want to speak at this vigil. I assure him that I do. There was no way for me to know, at the time, that God was speaking to Rev. Demo, too.

On two occasions, I gathered information from Rev. Demo asking him to explain his Palm Sunday. More than a year after this vigil, I sat to have lunch with Rev. Demo and his wife, Rev. Kelly Demo, at a local restaurant in Overland Park, Kansas. Our paths had crossed again because of the interfaith dialogue embraced by our Faith Always Wins Foundation. As if we had been friends for longer than one minute, we embraced and began remembering the vigil from our own perspectives. I engaged Rev. Demo a second time to provide details for this chapter in November 2020 via email.

The murders took place on Palm Sunday. Palm Sunday and the seven days leading up to Easter, let alone the 40 days of Lent that would have just passed, are a critical time in the life of clergy and their church. Rev. Demo had held services that Sunday morning and would do so again later in the evening. He told me it was common practice for him to turn off his phone between services and nap on any given Sunday because pouring himself into each church service for the benefit of his congregation held great importance. This middle-of-the-afternoon nap refreshed him for the evening service.

Rev. Demo shared with me, "That Palm Sunday was unlike any other I have experienced. In the morning we held multiple services with large crowds and had plans that evening for an intimate agape dinner for the congregation." This particular afternoon, he did not set his phone to silent, so he became aware of the situation as it was unfolding. More and more text messages came in that there was a shooting just blocks from his congregation.

He continues, "We scrambled to find out who had been shot, but little information was public. I knew this would impact our community greatly and took some time to pray and consult with leadership and family."

He didn't initially know the identity of the victims or number and was unsure if there was any congregational association with the three victims or their families. Rev. Demo's consultation and prayer included time with Rabbi Jacques Cukierkorn of Temple Israel, whom he knew well and had shared the space of St. Thomas on occasion. From the numerous text messages appearing in his phone, he began to surmise that his congregation and the rabbi's were connected in many ways to either the victims themselves or family members of the victims. The two congregations were reeling from this frightening crime.

It became clear to Rev. Demo and he stated to me, "I was led to open the church for a prayer vigil that evening and Rabbi Cukierkorn's temple would also be joining us. We figured at a minimum we would have a few dozen of our members come. We sent word out by email and via social media. Within an hour, what we thought would be a small gathering turned into a major community event."

Neighboring pastors, two city council members, the bishop, under whom Rev. Demo served, and the Kansas governor's office called, all of whom offered support and verified their willingness to assist. Television stations were quick to send crews for footage of our community caring for one another in the midst of fear.

Sitting in his church, alone, just before what would be an overwhelming amount of grieving, hurting yet caring people arriving, Rev. Demo prayed. "I prayed for God's guidance and peace."

The congregational leadership created the logistics of the vigil as if this was part of their everyday life. They were careful to include multiple faith traditions and religions. Immediately, each person involved understood they were called to care for and love their neighbor, which would overshadow the violence and hate that had only hours before sent sudden shock and panic into a typically quiet and calm suburb.

Call and they will come. Seek and you will find. Rev. Demo shared, "People started to pour into our church. The parking lot quickly overflowed into the neighborhood. We had reporters from all over the country including *The New York Times*, *Los Angeles Times*, *CNN* and *FOX News*. The community leaders were lining up to speak and multiple religious leaders came, including Muslim, Hindu, Jewish and Christian leaders. Community people were asking to speak, including a teenager who had been trapped in the community center during the shootings and lockdown that followed."

As speakers made their way to and from the podium, Rev. Demo noted, "The crowd was visibly shaken by the earthquake of hate striking our community earlier that day, and they were desperate for firm ground to find their footing. Everyone speaking, including myself, were inadequate in our words and struggling to articulate the peace and love we hoped to convey in the midst of hate and violence that tore through our peaceful community."

It was at this time in Rev. Demo's story that my dear friend Tarra appeared in front of him with the message that I wanted to speak. As I suspected, he rightfully thought to himself: 'There is such a crowd and so much attention. I don't know who this woman is. She could just be crazy and seeking attention.'

He tells me that it was when Tarra pointed me out in the crowd that he knew that I needed to speak. I can't speak to what he saw in me or around me, only that he knew I was supposed to speak. He said, "I looked at Mindy and felt a clear call to get out of the way of her speaking. I immediately went to her and we spoke for a few minutes, and she and her friend followed me to the pulpit."

Rev. Gar Demo spoke gently to me from his squatted position. "You will speak last, which is after the next person to go up to the podium."

Feeling grateful to Tarra and Laura for sitting with me and thankful for so many people mourning with us, I ponder the idea of them knowing how their presence is so helpful. Sniffling and crying reaches my ears. Dad and Reat would be thankful, too, for the outpouring of support. If Len, Lukas and Mom could see this, they would be filled with gratitude. I listen to each person speak. Their words don't bring me comfort. While I am not comforted by their words, I recognize that it's very difficult to know the right words to say at a time like this. Many months later, maybe a full year, I realized that the depth of pain I felt wasn't something easily reached. Thank God. This explains why, after the murders, typically sad movies, intent on creating tears and heartache, had little effect on me. Only another parent who has lost a child to a death in any form knows the same level of pain. When we meet one another, there is an immediate connection and bond between us … we know. Believe me, we wish we didn't know the extent of the heartache, life trajectory changes and the harsh reality life can throw at you in an instant.

It is almost my time to walk to the podium. What will I say? Why do I want to speak? To be honest, I question why I am standing up and walking toward the front of the room. Oh, yes, I feel my heart pulsing … it seems to know what is about to happen. I look over to Rev. Gar Demo, the man Tarra had spoken to, and he is nodding at me. I think he introduces me, but I'm not certain. Tarra asks if I want her to come with me. "Yes, definitely," I tell her. We hold hands as we walk to the front of the church. She is steadying me, as my legs have begun to shake uncontrollably.

Foggy. My brain is foggy, and I am still making my way to address this crying, tearful crowd, who I had mistakenly thought would only be students. Listen, feel, the words will come. I am not sure if I said this to myself, or if God was speaking again. I do know I reached the podium and my listening is what got me there. They need to know what I know. They need to hear that God didn't pull the trigger and shoot them. Dad and Reat are in Heaven. I know this and now they need to hear it from me.

Standing at the podium and peering out at the agonizing faces, it seems like every person looking back at me is crying. With my right hand gripping Tarra's hand tightly, my left hand tries to steady myself by grasping the opposite side of the podium. I whisper a prayer to myself, "God, what do I say?" And then, miraculously, the words begin.

"I'm in shock, but I want you to know that I appreciate all of you being here. My name is Mindy Corporon and I'm the daughter of the gentleman who was killed and I'm the mother of the son who was killed.

"And I want to tell you how much I appreciate you all being here. I heard there was going to be a vigil and we all grieve in different ways. *(Deep breath.)* And I just wanted to tell people thank you. I want you to know that I came upon the scene very, very quickly; I was there before the police; I was there before the ambulance and I knew immediately that they were in Heaven. And I know that they are in Heaven, together. My dad is Popeye and my son is Reat. And I just want to thank you; I don't have anything else to say. I just wanted to be here with all of you. I want you to know how much Reat loved school and theater. He loved acting and singing and he was at the Jewish Community Center to try out for a theater program for *KC SuperStar*. And, um, my dad got elected to take him because my mom was busy with other cousins and I was with my other son at a lacrosse game. We were in life; we were having life. And I want you all to know that we're going to have more life. And I want you all to have more life and just know he will be remembered and my dad will be remembered and love one another. I got to tell both of them today that I loved them. I was the last person in the family who saw them. And I can't tell you how much it helps to see other people. I'm sorry, I'm very sorry, I know there was another person killed and I don't know anything about that person. So I don't mean any disrespect at all to the other person. Um, so I know we should pray for that person and their family, as well. And I just appreciate you being here, it is very helpful to me. That is just how I grieve, thank you. God bless you."

Rev. Demo explained my speaking in this way, "She told us it was her son, Reat Underwood, and her father, William Corporon, who had been killed. The crowd let out a collective gasp of horror and sudden grief filled the air. In the moment I am clear that God spoke to the world through Mindy and her faith. She showed us love, forgiveness and clarity. The power of the moment was her calm demeanor, clarity and determination to share her faith, hope and love in the response to hate. As she concluded her thoughts, the emotions of the room and the collective grief had changed. Everything that had happened became real in Mindy's presence, and the pain all of us felt was overshadowed by the reality of what had been lost. Mindy had a light about her in the midst of the dark grief. Her walking in faith touched us all. She gave us solid ground upon which we could stand."

There is no question I was meant to speak at this vigil. I feel that in the absolute core of my soul. God had a message to share, and He chose to communicate it through me. His words funneled through me, one after another. And even though it was only the beginning of deep suffering and grief, following God's promptings brought me comfort. This marks the beginning of a powerful narrative which continues today.

Rev. Demo concluded his story in a similar way, "The next morning the national news reported on the shootings in Kansas City. There was an image of Mindy standing in front of the crowd and her message was being heard instead of the message of hate or anything about the one who had perpetrated the crime."

My heart was not just broken that tragic day ... it was shattered into a million pieces. Sometimes it feels as if my soul is trying to leap out of my body and join my loved ones in Heaven. But each time my heart yearns for this escape to be with Dad and Reat, I feel God holding me closely in His arms. He is using all the supportive and caring people in our circle to help me begin to pick up the pieces.

To this day, when I speak about my dad and Reat, a smile instinctively forms on my face. Their love is so deep in my heart and part of my being. When I talk about them, I feel connected to them. They are tangibly with me. It's profound.

Friends and strangers, who heard me speak in person or saw the video of me from the vigil held the same evening as the murders, shared with me that my strength that day was inspiring and amazing. They often ask how in the world I had the courage to speak that night. My only explanation is that I was moved by the Spirit of God and I simply followed implicitly. It was clear to me that following His direction that night immediately gave me strength and comfort. "Keep listening," my charge from Pastor Hamilton, paved the way for the days and weeks ahead.

Top Left: Kyle Loveless, a meaningful friend to Mindy and Will Corporon is pictured here in his yearbook, a student in Marlow High School, Marlow, Oklahoma. Photo courtesy of Janet Loveless. 1983

Top: Janet Loveless, aka "mom 2" to Mindy enjoyed catching up during one of Mindy's visits to her home town of Marlow, Oklahoma. Family photo. 2016

Middle, from left: Gabe, Brandy and Lynn (Loveless) Price, Janet and Leroy Loveless and Austin Price at home in Marlow, Oklahoma. Photo courtesy Janet Loveless. December 2020.

Bottom: Kyle Loveless and Will Corporon in front of the Loveless' home in Marlow, Oklahoma. The boys loved to fish! Photo courtesy of Will Corporon. 1980

17

What Is God's Will?

It is a sad truth that I have experience with funerals. My first experience with the death of a child was during my teenage years. My best friend, Lynn, lost her older brother Kyle in a devastating car accident. Our families lived just a few houses apart in Marlow when I was 7 and fresh in the neighborhood. Lynn and I spent most of our free time going back and forth between each other's houses, so Kyle felt like a brother to me.

Kyle, Will, Lynn and I were in and out of both of our houses many times daily and Kyle spent many hours fishing with my older brother, Will. At least one night a week, either Will or I would be at the Loveless' dinner table. My parents taught me table manners at our home, but they were implemented when visiting Lynn for dinner. Their table is where my love of fried okra was born and my understanding of praying before every meal was witnessed.

In 1984, on a foggy March 3 evening, I spotted Kyle circling our local Sonic Drive-In, the usual Saturday night entertainment in Marlow, Oklahoma. Honestly, that was the peak of our small-town entertainment on most nights. I stood next to Kyle's car and we talked for a few minutes. Mostly, he was questioning me about my choice in boyfriends. We chatted and razzed each other for a bit and then he drove off. As Kyle drove away, I had a feeling in the pit of my stomach that I couldn't explain.

At age 15, my curfew was 10 p.m.—no excuses. I was sound asleep when the hallway light woke me up in the middle of the night. I sat up in bed to see my dad standing in the doorway. Because the light was behind him, illuminating his frame, he looked like an angel standing in my doorway. He took a few slow steps into my room and I blurted out, "Kyle is dead."

He stopped in his tracks and asked who had called me to let me know. A feeling of sadness I had never known overtook me. I began crying and Dad was soon by my side, holding me in his arms. Cradling me, he was rocking me back and forth. He asked for a second time, "Who called you about Kyle?" This time I heard him and answered, "No one called me." Looking at my phone next to my bed, as if it might provide a better answer and then back at him, I said, "I just knew."

I may have had a premonition that Kyle had died, but I knew nothing of how it happened without my father's explanation. Through sobs, I asked how it happened. Dad explained that Kyle had been driving north of Marlow on Highway 81. He was headed to meet a friend and had a girl in his passenger's seat. Kyle turned left directly into a truck that was trying to pass him on the left. Kyle's neck was broken instantly.

An ambulance took him to the hospital in Duncan, Oklahoma, about 11 miles south of Marlow. Because my dad was the family's physician, he received a phone call. When Leroy and Janet arrived at the hospital, Leroy asked to go back to Kyle's room. Janet waited in the hallway. Leroy stood next to Dad as he announced the official time of his son's death. They walked out together to share the terrible news with Janet, that Kyle did not survive. Janet has told me she will never forget the look on Dad's and Leroy's faces. They didn't need to say a word.

We all broke into a million pieces that night.

And then, the next morning, the sun had the audacity to come back up. I couldn't believe it. I willed it not to. It felt like the sky should stay dark as we mourned. Although it was bright and sunny outside, the entire small town of Marlow was engulfed in darkness.

The day after Kyle died, my mom drove us to the Loveless' home to provide any comfort we could. Two years prior, we had moved several miles from town and my first home in Marlow on Ninth Street. As we drove over, I silently cursed the sun for shining. I was angry and distraught. My mom explained that we didn't have to have the right words; we just had to show up and be present. Sit with them in their pain. We offered our deepest condolences.

I still couldn't get over the sunshine. I wondered why it continued to shine on such a sad day. Why had the world not stopped completely? Why does everyone keep living when my best friend's world—as she knew it—was ending? I remember feeling completely overwhelmed by grief, but not having any words to explain the dark deep hole inside of me. The best I could offer Lynn was just to sit with her and hug her. I hurt with her as we tried to wrap our minds and hearts around why in the world this was happening.

Kyle's funeral was the first of many I would attend during my life and certainly the most painful one in my early years. Many more well wishers tried to attend the service than would fit in the United Methodist Church. ... standing room only, more outside on the church steps, and onto Main Street. As I was walking into the church, I was so distraught that I literally lost my footing. My brother, Will, and his friend, Gary Underwood, who became my first husband (1993) and Reat's father (1999), held me upright. My heart had never experienced such a deep, piercing pain. Once I regained my footing and composure, we made our way into the service. I saw the Loveless family was already seated in the front pews, so I quickly made my way up to them. Leroy has since told me, "We loved how you came straight to the family pews and snuggled next to Lynn. You knew where you belonged ... sitting with our family, holding Lynn (and us) together as best as you could."

I have asked God, thousands of times, who Kyle would have been if he had survived. How would my life be different if Kyle had survived? How would Lynn's life be different? And why did he have to die? Why? Why? Why?

For months, I was in a fog. I was constantly questioning why Kyle was taken from us. Nobody knew the depth of turmoil inside my soul, which I had no skills to navigate. My sadness was so heavy. I felt completely consumed by the question, "Why?" The cloud of grief was dense. My mind and body were honestly having a hard time even going through the motions each day.

I knew I needed help breaking free. Finally, in a moment of courage, I asked our interim pastor at the Cumberland Presbyterian Church why we lost Kyle ...why did God let it happen? I was desperate for some relief and hoped our pastor could provide an answer that would ease my burden.

It was after a Sunday service when I stopped him. With familiar tears lightly caressing my cheeks, I asked, "Why did this happen to Kyle? Why did Kyle die in a car accident?"

He waited for me to catch my breath and look him in the eye. He said very calmly and plainly, "It was God's will."

My heart dropped. I tried to understand, but the only feelings I could muster were defensiveness and anger. Surely, this was not the answer. But the pastor failed to offer any other alternative. He simply turned and walked away. I felt no ability to offer any dispute.

God's will? Seriously? Of course, we pray every Sunday that, "God's will be done," but this answer seemed so very wrong. It rocked me to my core. How could God want Kyle dead? How could God tear the fabric of our lives with his own hands? How could He allow such pain? How could He choose to wreak havoc on all the lives around me?

Unfortunately, the pastor's answer led me down a path of anger and deep uncertainty for years. My young soul did the only thing it knew to do in order to survive. It closed the door on God and faith in order to protect itself from further damage.

I was 15 at the time, and hearing the words, "It was God's will," might as well have been the words, "God wanted Kyle dead." As my immature brain desperately searched to make sense of it all, it felt like the pastor had said, "God was driving the truck that killed Kyle." I continued to wrestle. Why would God want Kyle dead?

I was not familiar with this God. This was not the God my family knew, loved and worshipped. I wrestled with God for many years as

I tried to sort all this out. In college, I ignored church and kept my distance from anyone claiming to follow God. Several times, I was invited to attend fellowship with friends, but I always left feeling dismayed. My friends were experiencing a God who no longer seemed available to me.

Hoping for the calmness and peacefulness that I could see in my friends, I attended a few different churches during my college years, all of which were Christian. Every sermon and young adult message I sat through sounded the same: God is reliable and I should be able to lean on Him. I felt like I trusted God until He took Kyle from us. Struggling to find any connection with God was trying. So I stopped concerning myself about the need for connecting.

Thankfully, my crisis of faith didn't take me down the road of addiction or anything terribly destructive. My journey became one of seeking personal achievement. I felt like I understood the path ahead of me; and while I walked obediently, there were blinders blocking the world around me. I charged on, full speed ahead. Don't look around, pain and suffering might be lurking.

My family and "extended family" (including Kyle's parents, Janet and Leroy) provided safe spaces and healthy examples of how to handle loss in their lives. They continued to go to church, praying for peace and grace. And my dear friends taught me that forgiveness overcomes hatred.

I respected how they were able to move forward. I longed for that, but somehow, I was not able to re-engage in a relationship with God after losing Kyle. I felt an emptiness. This emptiness lasted until I became a mother myself.

Top Left: Olivia Corporon's 8th birthday standing with her
oldest brother, Travis Corporon, in Bentonville, Arkansas.
Photo courtesy Will Corporon, their father. May 2020.

Top Right: Yea Yea and Popeye with Olivia Corporon at her
home in Bella Vista, Arkansas. Family photo. 2013

Bottom: Mindy Corporon, Hanna Golden, Will and Olivia Corporon signing
a casket. Photograph by Joe Shalmoni Photojournalist, © April 18, 2014.

18

The Eye of a Hurricane

"It was almost like being in the eye of a hurricane. Everything was swirling so wildly around us." Will Corporon, my older brother by three years, was speaking to me in May 2020, as I recorded his version of April 13, 2014, for my podcast: *Real Grief—Real Healing with Mindy Corporon.*

Will had received a phone call from my husband, Len, around 1 p.m. on April 13, 2014, Palm Sunday. Interestingly, Will was in the restroom when he saw the name Len Losen flash on his screen. He considered why Len would be calling him and because he was only standing at the urinal, he answered the call. Will heard Len tell him that Dad had been shot. Again, Len didn't give Will the information I had passed on to him, fearful that he would be providing bad information. Will then heard Len say that Reat had also been shot and we didn't know his physical state. Only 20 minutes later, Will received a call from our mother with the news that, indeed, our father had died from the gunshot. He had been murdered and we had no understanding of how this came to be.

Digesting this frightening information, Will and his wife, Heather, launched into an enormous amount of coordinating, rearranging and planning for five of their blended family's children. He credits Heather for synchronizing a plan they hadn't expected and providing added comfort to him during the chaos. She rearranged their travel and children while the enormity of what he had just heard worked its way through his consciousness. The next phone call only proved to heap on more sadness and despair as our mom called to tell him that Reat had lost his life, too.

Innate instincts began to kindle previously learned skills. He worked to think through the steps that he felt should take place. He said, "I think when tragedies happen, people kind of resort to what they are. Some people are good at cooking food and helping, and some people are great emotionally and supportive. Some people are planners and maybe can help with all the planning and things that go along with that."

Will studied broadcast journalism at the University of Oklahoma and worked for over 10 years in the industry. He held specific and helpful knowledge about the news media, their platforms, deadlines, expectations and working habits.

He continued, "I didn't realize that at the time. I just kind of reverted to my news days as we were driving." The drive from Tulsa, Oklahoma, to their home in Northwest Arkansas, packing and then driving another three and a half hours to Overland Park, Kansas, gave Will the opportunity to consider how best to control the narrative for our family. While in the midst of packing for a trip no one wants to take, Will turned on their television in hopes of retrieving information we were unable to provide.

"I turned on the TV and there was the Overland Park chief of police talking about what was going on. They had live video from the scene of the crime and were already hosting a news conference. They talked about the perpetrator, the murderer, briefly because they had arrested him. They actually showed him, already had video of him," Will told me. He heard from the news reporter that two were dead and one was in the hospital. Will, however, knew this to be false, based on the phone call from our mom. He continued, "I knew from covering stories like this and when I was in television that I wanted to control the narrative. I wanted to control what information they had, and really, my first thought was, they're going to need pictures of Dad and Reat; and they're going to want them very quickly."

His experience reminded him that a driver's license could be considered public information in some states. He didn't want the picture that the world sees of his father to be a driver's license photo. "This little grain of information got me thinking as we were driving," he recalled. He knew the media would retrieve photos however they could.

During the same drive from their home in Northwest Arkansas to Overland Park, Kansas, Will received a phone call from Christine Hamele, assistant vice president of public relations and community affairs at HCA Midwest Health System. "She was so good to work with, kind and caring," he shared. She told Will that a draft of a press release had been put together by the hospital and the family wanted him to review it.

After receiving and reviewing the press release via email, he commented, "I hated it." Will told me, "I just hated it. It was very nondescript and not personal at all. It wasn't her fault. But I hated it. That wasn't what I wanted." It was at this point Will knew we had to gather photos while he started to edit the press release. As our younger brother, Tony, sent him photos from his own phone and that of our mother's, Will continued to use his laptop and travel time to edit a few of the images, so they would appear well on a television and in a mobile format.

He also reworked the press release, providing as much personal information about our father and Reat that he felt would be comfortable for all of us, while also offering the media what they needed for the story. "If you don't give [the media] information, they're just going to keep pounding the streets for information and knocking on doors. If you're forthcoming with the information you want them to have, they don't have a need to go find it elsewhere," he said.

From the passenger side of their car, Will cut and pasted. He edited copy and photos, attaching the photos of Dad and Reat—the ones we wanted to use in portraying them for the news release. He and Christine were exchanging phone calls for many miles. Christine tells me she could feel so much love from Will for our father, Reat and the rest of the family. Together, they were working to protect our family from the wrong storyline, whatever that might be or could have been. The more detail they put into this initial press release, the better to help us and her with the media. While Will was crafting the press release, Christine was fielding calls from every major news station, nationally and internationally. The media had also planted themselves on the hospital property, waiting for an announcement about the life of the young man, now known as the grandson of the man who was murdered on site at the Jewish Community Center.

Several times, Will and Christine would be close to finalizing the press release and the phone coverage would falter. A crackling noise, and then the line would be silent. One of them would call the other back and they would begin their review again. Christine could tell that even though Will was emotional, he was on task and could accomplish what he planned. Since communication was spotty, it was best to provide Will with the list of media outlets already gathered and waiting for a nugget of information from the hospital or the family. From Will's perspective, "Somewhere between Joplin and Overland Park, I hit send and the initial press release hit the wire."

> It is with deep sadness that we confirm the tragic loss of Dr. William Lewis Corporon and Reat Griffin Underwood (Losen) who died as a result of the injuries they sustained in today's shooting at the Jewish Community Center. Dr. Corporon was Reat's grandfather, whom he loved very much.
>
> Dr. Corporon leaves behind his wife of 49 years and a loving and devoted family and extended family. Dr. Corporon practiced family medicine in Marlow and Duncan, Oklahoma, from 1976 through 2003, when he and his wife moved to the Kansas City area to be closer to their grandchildren. He was a well-loved physician in the Johnson County community, cherished his family and more than anything had a passion for caring for others.
>
> Reat was a 14-year-old freshman at Blue Valley High School—a school he loved. Reat participated in debate, theatre and had a beautiful voice. Reat had a passion for life and touched so many people in his young age. Reat was an Eagle Scout and loved spending time camping and

hunting with his grandfather, father and brother. Both Reat and Dr. Corporon were very proud supporters of the University of Oklahoma and its sports teams.

We would like to thank our friends, family and our church, the United Methodist Church of the Resurrection, and school community for the outpouring of love and support during this very difficult time. We take comfort knowing they are together in Heaven.

We ask for privacy as we mourn the loss of our beloved Dr. Corporon and Reat.

Thank you very much,

Will Corporon, son and uncle

The poor cell phone service, the trauma of knowing violent deaths have taken place, two of the deceased are your family and that this had never been needed prior to now are all good reasons for mistakes to be in the press release. There was only one. Reat was a Life Scout working on his Eagle Scout. Once this document was presented to every news station clamoring for a bit of information about the deceased, it was difficult to retract the mistake. Until I looked up the press release about six months after their deaths, I didn't understand why every news outlet, article and interviewer introduced Reat as an Eagle Scout. Will had been completely accurate about providing the media a narrative. Not only did the media need to tell the news, present the story to viewers and help them understand what had taken place, but they also never wavered from what we presented.

One of the photos used was of our father in his hunting hat with Reat beside him in a black and gold Blue Valley High School T-shirt. "Those were the photos; the ones that were used. Still to this day, they come up when the media discusses their murders and the hate crime that took their lives," Will recounted during our podcast interview.

Because Will sent the press release with his personal cell phone number for contact information, he was now in a position to field the media inquiries for our family. Recalling how the media took the initial press release and subsequent time for thoughtful interviews,

Will and our family were impressed with the respect we received from all the coverage, and specifically the local news outlets. His efforts to protect and help us while helping them was a win-win situation.

Our story would be about our family members and that of Terri LaManno, whom we didn't yet know. Our story would reflect their lives, all three of them, who they were to us and to the communities in which they lived. We would do our best to redirect any headlines or narrative about the shooter and the hateful atrocities he had committed. The hate he exploded on our families, shattering numerous lives, would always be part of our journey, but not part of our focus.

Will's former experience was put to use on several occasions in the first week of their deaths. Again, he was able to control the narrative he knew we wanted in the media. On April 15 at 6:28 a.m. Central time, not 48 hours from the moment I found our father dead in the parking lot and Reat struggling for his life, Will picked me up from my home and drove me to an interview for *The Today Show*. Savannah Guthrie interviewed me for just over four minutes, not once mentioning the shooter. She directed the interview with me with so much respect and honor for our father and Reat. In fact, the first time I had heard the shooter's name was through the earpiece I was wearing for the interview. Hearing his name rattled me and I was thankful she didn't mention his name while speaking with me. As soon as I completed the interview, I had concerns that I had sounded stupid to Ms. Guthrie.

Will offered me assurance that I sounded fine and reminded me he was thankful the story was coming from our family, rather than being crafted by someone in a newsroom who had never met Dad or Reat. He explained again the importance of us having the courage to share our story publicly, so that Dad's and Reat's lives would be shared in ways that reflect the depth of love we have for them.

Our next public appearance was also orchestrated by Will and hosted by the same place that would soon host a double funeral for us … the United Methodist Church of the Resurrection in Leawood, Kansas.

Several hours after my early morning interview, Tony joined Will and me at our church for a family press conference. Our mom was not well enough to be with us, so the three of us planned to speak about Dad and Reat for ourselves and on behalf of her.

While these interviews might seem planned or strategized, they were not. They were as impromptu as us losing our two family members. Other than Will providing direction to me about how we could tell their story, the story of Dad and Reat, we never practiced or rehearsed our comments. As Will stated in an interview with Jill Geisler of Poynter Institute for Media Studies, in May 2014, "We spoke from the heart."

Standing between my older and younger brothers and thinking about how I wanted to frame the story of Dad and Reat for anyone who was watching, I stated, "It was a horrible act of violence, my dad, our dad and my son were at the wrong place at the wrong time for a split second. We want something good to come out of this. We don't know what that's going to be. So we want people to let us know if they think that something good has come from [their tragic deaths]."

Will was the first of us to mention the shooter, and in a negative way, as it should have been. He told reporters, "It takes no character to do what was done. It takes no character, no strength of character, no backbone. It takes no morals. It takes no ethics. All it takes is an idiot with a gun. That idiot absolutely knocked a family to its knees for no reason."

Will's goal was to shine a light on our dad and Reat … he did so.

"We as a family have been dealt a huge, huge blow, as I am sure you can see and perhaps imagine. We will go on and we will get through this. There will always be a huge hole, two huge holes; they will never be filled. Every day will be a reminder. We do hope that if there is any way that a sliver of good, goodness, grace can come of this, then by the sheer grace of God, it will not have been just totally, totally for nothing."

Will's leadership in sharing our family narrative was crucial to the formation of our public voice in honoring Dad and Reat.

As Will stated early in our podcast interview, it was as if we were in the eye of a hurricane. For those left living, when the storm settles, is when the tough work begins.

I knew the hell that my family had experienced, but I didn't know how Will, Heather and their family had traversed the intimate daily living over the past six and half years. Yes, we saw one another during the holidays and kept in touch over Sooner sports! But I wanted to know if any aspects of his life had changed since the murders. Those aspects of him I couldn't see.

Will shared with me, "Well, I think from my standpoint, personally, I'm much more patient. I think I'm much more introspective. With all the kids, five kids in the house at the time, I mean, there wasn't a whole lot of time for any sort of major life changes. I'm not blessed with a lot of patience in certain aspects. But now, just enjoying a day and enjoying watching the kids do something mundane like Olivia drawing, painting something or playing tic-tac-toe with her cards or things like that are good for me." It's funny to me that Will didn't see himself as patient, because I saw him that way. This goes to show you that we don't know how someone feels about themselves unless we ask the question and listen.

Similar to our dad, Will is pragmatic. And why not, he was the firstborn son of an extremely pragmatic person. We ended our podcast with me thanking Will for how he stepped in to protect our family and in the meantime found a purpose for that week. A purpose he didn't realize at the time provided him a channel to process the initial shock of grief. Will closed with, "You're welcome. Everybody's different and I know some people don't get over [tragedies] and they collapse and it ruins their lives. I'll be damned if I'm gonna let this murderer, you know, take my life as well, and take our lives. We had been knocked off course, a lot, like I said, I mean 90 degrees off course, we were headed north when all of a sudden, wham, we headed east in an instant. But that doesn't necessarily mean that that wasn't the direction we were supposed to go. And that doesn't necessarily mean we need to struggle to try to go back north again. We're going east now. There's a lot of good stuff east; it's going to be what we make of it. I can't imagine how hard it was for you and still is; there's not even a comparison. But you know at some point, you're either moving forward or you're falling behind; and falling behind is not really enough for me."

Falling behind was not my intention either. The enormous magnitude of changes we have made in our lives to heal, to walk through the journey and to understand how someone hates to a point of murder … it is so much to bear. These words aren't even sufficiently large enough to define my intention.

How does one live through the eye of a hurricane and land standing? With faith.

Harrison cousins, Zsa Zsa, Hayden and Brandon with Lukas and Reat near Dallas, Texas at Cedar Creek Lake. Photo courtesy of Kim Harrison. 2012

Community support was offered just outside of the double funeral of William Corporon and his grandson, Reat Underwood. Photo courtesy of Matt Riossien. April 18, 2014.

Blue Valley High School Men's Combined Choir left a space for Reat as they sang "I Hear a Voice a Prayin'" during the double funeral for William Corporon and his grandson, Reat Underwood. Photograph by Joe Shalmoni Photojournalist, © April 18, 2014.

Pastor Steve Langhofer is observing Donna PaCicca, MD, Dominic DeCicco and Roxana Rogers Lemon (right side) with Francie Boyer and Laura (Boyer) Carley (left side), writing messages on the caskets of William Corporon and his grandson, Reat Underwood. They each cherished their friendships with William and Reat. Writing on the caskets offered these longtime friends an opportunity to begin their healing process. Photograph by Joe Shalmoni Photojournalist, © April 18, 2014.

19

A Production for Heaven

Divorcing in 2000 and as a single parent of Reat Underwood, I had a strong sense that something was missing in my soul. Tired and depleted, yes, from parenting alone and working full time, but a different type of depleted. I longed for the peace and calm I had seen in my grandparents' faces when they attended church. I wanted this. I was interested in finding contentment of my own. Still not realizing that God could fill this void, I happened to attend the Stanley Presbyterian Church on Mother's Day weekend in 2000. Reat was not quite 12 months old. Embarrassed to be a single mom of a newborn, especially with the spotlight specifically on moms that day, my courage won out over fear. Immediately, God's presence was upon me. My soul broke open a bit and a ray of light beamed from me. Tears fell down my cheeks and I named them, peace and fulfillment. It was as if He was reassuring me that He had been there all along.

Being a parent changed me in many ways. Being Reat's parent reignited my soul.

If Reat had been the only one murdered, family and friends would have gathered to grieve at our home. If my dad had been the only one murdered, family and friends would have gathered at my mom's home.

In a unique and terrible predicament, family and friends hopped from one home to the other, all moved at one time or spent much of their time in one home or the other. My side of the family, my brothers, aunts, uncles, and cousins spent most of their time at Mom's. Len's side of the family settled at our home.

Reat was close to the cousins on Len's side from the first time we met them. He was especially close to Len's cousin Kim. I originally met Kim at her home in Dallas over some spicy ranch dip and sliced crunchy red peppers. Len and I had just started dating. Len spoke of Kim like he would of his best guy friends. She was his confidant and the woman who handed out guidance and counsel about his girlfriends. The two of them can banter about anything, joke, tease, laugh and now cry. I find Kim to be hospitality in human form, a best friend to Len and someone who provides insight into family dynamics.

Our two boys and their three kids formed a "tribe" when they all got together. Kim had lovingly reached out to Lukas just after the murders. She asked Lukas how they could help. His request was that they come visit for a week.

On his own and without my knowledge, Lukas was in many conversations with adults during the weeks and months following the murders. Thankfully, each adult he chose as a mentor and counselor was whom I would have chosen, as well.

Kim and her family honored Lukas' request. She and her husband, Jon, and their three children, Hayden, Brandon and Zsa Zsa, drove from Dallas with full intent to rescue Lukas.

Like a breath of fresh air, our cousins the Harrisons arrived! Kathy, who played an integral role in breathing life back into our home and her husband, Ron Schikevitz, hosted Kim, Jon and Zsa Zsa while the boys stayed in our home. They set up a tent in the boys' playroom upstairs. Each evening, as I would try my best to put on a "normal" face and be routine with my goodnight hugs and kisses, I found all three of them snuggled in the tent, peering out just enough to see the Xbox. Lukas was in need of the security and love they offered.

These special cousin sleepovers would be the only nights in a four-month span when Lukas didn't sleep on our bedroom floor. The enormity of sadness Lukas was carrying could not be seen by anyone. While Len and I also felt the huge weight of loss from their murders, we were not aware that the evening prior to Reat's murder, our two boys had an argument. Lukas was not only distressed from losing his grandfather and brother, but he was also agonizing over losing his brother with anger between them. Having family and friends around him in our home and his ability to be with others and not alone in his own sadness was crucial during this week. Regrettably, we did not continue to surround Lukas in this same way, to the extent he needed it for emotional security.

Despite my best efforts to push it away, the day of the funeral was upon us ... April 18, six days after their murders, and another Christian holiday, Good Friday. Somehow, I am still living. Two of my dearest friends are within feet of me as I shower, dress and prepare for an event I could never have imagined would be mine to attend. Tandi Ball is in town from Arizona. We first met as Kansas City Chiefs cheerleaders in 1990. Oh, I have so many memories shared with her, surrounding our time on the squads, entering our own careers and dating. Tandi had been my lifeline when Reat was only four weeks old and now she was with me, physically walking in this new reality of pain. Rondi, her husband Steve and daughter, Samantha, are here from North Carolina. We met as neighbors on Hadley St. in Overland Park. Our oldest children, Reat and Samantha, brought us together; we bonded on our own as new working mommas. Neighborhood trick-or-treating and Easter Sunday were two of our mainstays that would find both families engaged with one another. With both women I shared laughter, sunscreen, silly stories, dinner, wine, the hard times in between the good ones and of course, the joy of life.

We had no desire to share this funeral.

As you grow older with friends, you expect to support them through the deaths of their parents. You expect to encourage them through potential rocky marriages and maybe a divorce. You expect to be there for their children's weddings. You don't expect to attend their children's memorial services. And yet, here they are. Along with so many other friends, who walked with us from the night of the unimaginable murders to this moment, we are lifted by them ... lifted with their love and hope for our future.

The cars arrive to transport our family and friends to the memorial service. We travel first to my mom's house, where my side of the family is waiting. I see my beautifully dressed cousins, aunts and uncles; and I desperately want to go back to times when we sat for hours playing Clue and cooking the Thanksgiving turkey in Muthie and GrandDaddy's home.

Much like at our home, it must have been sad and chaotic in Mom's home during these grief-ridden days. Reat loved chaotic family times. The thought of that brings a small curve to a smile that won't fully appear.

Loading into the vehicles, we are soon on our way to the church to offer the best public goodbyes we can muster for Reat and Dad. Approaching the church, it is difficult to not notice a large crowd lining the street on both sides. There are hundreds of people—all in white T-shirts. The sea of white feels like a beautiful illustration of being unified in God's peace and purity. They hold signs that read, "Remember Reat," "Remember Popeye" and "Love Wins!" Lukas rolls down his window to smile and wave at the strangers who are offering their kindness and compassion to us. My heart smiles but breaks a little more, at the same time.

The sun was shining. That damned sun … it knew what it was doing by providing the warmth I needed from somewhere. A slight breeze in the air could be felt on my bare neck and legs. I had chosen a black dress, but also wore a pin over my heart that Reat had made for me for an earlier Mother's Day. A wooden heart with buttons glued on the front with a glue gun. My recollection tells me this was made in kindergarten. Never had this heart pin held so much significance. Reat's favorite color at the time of his death was pink. I was lucky enough to have a three-stranded pink choker necklace. It popped with color against my black dress. Feeling sick to the point of nausea a few times, I didn't want to look green, too.

Len and I are holding hands as we walk into our church. Only one year ago, when Reat was in eighth grade, we had walked this same path for his confirmation celebration. I can't count the times we walked this same way over the previous eight years, with one hand in a smaller hand as our boys were on their way to Sunday school. Knowing the sanctuary could hold 3,200 people, we were completely overwhelmed to find every seat filled.

Caring for people is in the details. I knew this from my own experience from waiting tables to wealth management ... pay attention to your customer and client. Mat Forastiere and Kati Farney with the Johnson County Funeral Chapel & Memorial Gardens continued to touch all aspects of our double funeral with the utmost of care. My longtime friend Jay Dodds, currently chief operating officer of Park Lawn Corporation and then president of The Signature Memorial Group, was present and available to Len, Lukas and me while he watched with pride as Mat was instrumental in orchestrating our production for Heaven. One such detail was the color pink. Hearing me claim that Reat's favorite color was pink, Mat took notice and action. He shared with me, "Your eyes lit up when you told me pink was Reat's favorite color. I could not resist incorporating this somehow in our uniforms for the service. I had purchased pink ties and scarves for all the staff and I also threw on a pair of pink socks. When you arrived at church the first thing you said to me was, "Let me see the socks."

For a period of about 20 minutes, we waited while all the family from both sides of my family, Len's family and all those expected Corporon cousins were in a small vestibule inside the church, but outside the sanctuary. Some family members had literally just made it in time for the memorial service, while many others had flown in prior and joined us for a family gathering at a local restaurant only the night before.

From our shared space with family, we could hear Pastor Karen Lampe welcome the attendees, those who had already reached out to us and those who would at some time offer us the prayers that would keep breathing life into our sorrowful hearts. We had requested a Scout color guard to open their memorial service and it was magnificent. I peered down the path the Scouts were taking as they made their way to the stage for flag placement. Reat loved Scouting. He would miss the campouts, joking and razzing with his friends ... breathe, I had to tell myself to pay attention, breathe.

Walking into the sanctuary, the hymn "Holy Holy Holy" brought almost a full smile to my face. My mom had chosen this particular hymn because it was a favorite of hers and Dad's. Knowing this about them and knowing how much she and Dad loved this hymn, from somewhere in my soul I could hear Reat and Dad already singing, too … my smile felt real. My faith was holding me steady. I knew where they were. I knew they were together and by God, now they are singing to us.

Reat's biological father, my ex-husband Gary Underwood, was to be seated in the second row, behind where Len, Lukas, my mom and I would sit with Tony and Will. As we approached the front of the church, I noticed him immediately, with deep anguish on his face. We greet with an embrace that would never have been needed if Reat were living. "I am so sorry," Gary whispers into my ear.

Responding, I offer, "I am so sorry for you too, and I'm glad you guys spent time together in March." I am grateful Gary is there to honor Reat, his only child, and my father, of course. Finding my own seat, it is not lost on me the enormity of Reat's murder to Gary.

The murders occurred on Palm Sunday and today was Good Friday, a school day for Blue Valley High School. This was one of the main reasons we requested a 3 p.m. start time, allowing for so many students to participate and attend the memorial service of a friend and his grandfather. The Blue Valley High School Men's Combined Choir sang for us. In their positioning, they left a space for Reat. Front row, on the right side, is where my baby would be, if they were in competition. I wished they had been in competition and not singing, "I Hear a Voice a Prayin'" at his funeral. Their voices were sweet and soothing to my soul.

Psalm 130:1-2, Isaiah 61:1-3 and John 14:1-3 were all Scriptures selected by us in remembrance of our faith and the strength it provides when you can't find your legs for standing or your breath for breathing.

Our family is full of writers, talkers and storytellers. There was no shortage of content at the service. My older brother, Will, tells the story of Mom and Dad and life as he knew it. Being the firstborn to a young couple in medical school, Will shared that he didn't realize "we were poor," financially speaking. One of his closing statements was specifically directed to the audience. In hopes of something good coming from the tragedy that was now ours to bear, he asked them to "carry a piece of Dad and Reat's glorious humanity and sometimes put self second, or even third, behind family and community."

My younger brother, Tony, depicts life with Reat through Mom and Dad's eyes. A true love story, the story of Reat with his Yea Yea and Popeye, from beginning to end. Tony shares the following, "Together, Popeye and Yea Yea helped make Reat a star," when speaking about how involved they were with his theatrical performances. Also mentioning our father's passion for medicine and teaching, Tony shares, "His association with the young doctors, nurses and staff, kept him on his toes and allowed him to spread that wealth of knowledge to the next generation." This was a love we knew he had passed on to us. We were taught to help our fellow human beings.

Len took the stage after Tony and focused on compassionately thanking everyone for their love and support. He focused on four people in particular: Pastor Hamilton, Blue Valley High School Principal Scott Bacon, Blue Valley Middle School Principal Roxana Rogers Lemon and then Mickey Blount, as people who had and will miraculously help us survive. Poignantly, Len shared, "How truly blessed we are to live in such a wonderful community; the support and compassion has been overwhelming and humbling."

My baby boy, Lukas, now an only child, had written a statement with the help of our friends. He had not allowed me to see or read it prior to the memorial service. Knowing that I wanted Lukas to have this opportunity to speak publicly about his Popeye and brother and also not be potentially embarrassed by his comments, I inquired about the notes he had written. I was told that he wrote a great piece and I would have to wait to hear it with everyone else. Trust in others as I trust in God, came to mind. Lukas touched the hearts of every person in the room with, "I recently went with my grandfather turkey hunting. Funny thing, we didn't even hear a turkey." Laughter from the audience helped bolster Lukas' confidence, as I am sure he didn't think what he wrote was that funny. It was factual. Continuing, "We sat there for three hours doing nothing. But I told him I was having a wonderful time with him." The laughter from the audience allowed Lukas and all of us to take a breath; realizing that even in death, we must find laughter and joy from the memories that will sustain us. He told us about his brother, "Reat had big plans for his future. He was going to be a singing doctor and make a lot of money." As he finished, the audience applauded! A shining moment for Lukas, and as his parents, Len and I were so proud he wanted to share his love for his grandfather and brother, in such a public venue.

I was the last family member to speak, and presented a letter from me to Reat. I opened with how many moments we would now miss in his life. Of course, there were too many to mention, let alone say out loud, for fear of breaking down in a heap on the stage. Therefore, my piece moved quickly to the wonderfully full life Reat had for a 14-year-old. I am forever grateful for this. My speaking didn't include words or memories about my father. There was only so much I could bear, and speaking about my two people in the same space was not available to me. I knew that Dad understood.

The memorial service was filled with love, song, meaning and light. We were grateful to have a wonderful performance of "You Make Beautiful Things" by Gungor, sung by Lance Winkler, the current praise leader at the Church of the Resurrection. His music has filled my soul countless times in the past few years. The same years I started to feel a stirring in my heart for God that I didn't understand. Familiar with his smooth voice and tone, I hoped singing this particular ballad would be a bridge of peace and love to all those in attendance. "You make beautiful things out of dust. You make beautiful things out of us." I had heard and sung these lyrics since the song was released in 2010. "You make me new. You are making me new," was stirring in my heart. I wanted to be new; I wanted my life back, too ... a do-over.

I had no idea that my brain and heart were continuing to protect me. For weeks, I floated between Earth and Heaven. A lilting feeling of pleasure that my father and Reat were together in Heaven danced with the reality of my deep longing to have my two people living. This "in-between" space allowed me to function at what some might call a normal capacity. I knew I wasn't myself in any way, shape or form, but this "floating" and "in-between state" sheltered me from reality.

Romans 12:17-21. This Scripture instructs us to leave the retaliation to God and it ends with, "Do not be overcome by evil; overcome evil with good." My older brother, Will, appreciates the chapter of Romans and offered this as a Scripture he wanted to be read. Each family member was grasping for hope in our future and for a sliver of good to come from this tragedy.

When Pastor Hamilton took the pulpit, he addressed all of us by asking, "How do they have such strength?" He was speaking of us, my family. It was clear to him that our faith, the community and their willingness to be our stretcher bearers were what we needed to sustain us through this time.

The words "this time" washed over me. A funeral is but one piece of the grieving process. A memorial service is for the public to offer their well wishes, offer their stories, show you their love of those who passed and offer you hope for the future. Our memorial service for Dad and Reat was beautiful, amazing, heartfelt and one of the best damned services I have ever attended. They deserved this and much more. They deserved to live. "This time" is not over for us after the memorial service. "This time" for someone who loses a loved one is now truly, the "rest of time" as you know it.

I share with every person I know who loses a close loved one, a child, sibling or parent … the funeral is only one piece of a large tapestry, stained-glass window or puzzle. You will continue to cry, be sorrowful and be deeply disturbed by your loved one's death. Don't ever expect the funeral to move you back to joy. There is much work to be done … much healing to be encountered between a death and finding the elusive joy that we all consider belonging to someone else's life.

Pastor Hamilton continues, "How do we bring something beautiful from this? Tragedy is an opportunity for something so good, such possibility." He also spoke to my own message about God not being the shooter. The murderer was a human. As Will had stated, "an idiot with a gun." But Pastor Hamilton stopped short of using Will's quote, which seemed appropriate.

It has to be so difficult to come up with the message to offer mourners at a memorial service that just should not have been. Pastor Hamilton was thoughtful to weave in Passover, the defining story of Judaism. It is known now that Jews were the intended victims of the shooter. He planned to murder Jews at the Jewish Community Center and then at Village Shalom, a retirement community. He murdered three Christians. The defining story of Christians is Jesus' death and subsequent rise from the grave … hope above all else … loving and caring for others, specifically those less fortunate or marginalized by society.

What will be my defining story? I consider this as Pastor Hamilton is literally asking each of the audience members now. "What is your defining story that shapes everything else that you do?" he asks of us.

God doesn't cause evil, but he uses evil. The human condition in which we live causes pain, suffering and hurt. The possibility for good to come out of evil is inspiring.

Prior to the service starting and then as it ended, a video played a collection of photos gathered and produced by Mike Miller. The Scripture Romans 8:28 was featured in this video. Mike and Shelly's oldest son, Josh, was prompted to do something good within hours of Dad and Reat's murders. He created and ordered white bracelets with blue lettering that said "Romans 8:28," "Remember Reat" and "Remember Popeye" that he sold for $1. (The cash they raised was part of the seed money that opened our foundation, Faith Always Wins.) Josh knew and appreciated the verse, "And we know that in all things God works for the good of those who love him, who have been called according to his purpose."

Something good was already bubbling.

Pastor Hamilton's voice was powerful and encouraging to me as he stated, "God forces good to come from evil. God uses evil. Humans make bad decisions, accidentally and on purpose. God forces evil to accomplish His purposes in the end. PROFOUND things to happen in a good way."

Moving further into a message about overcoming evil, he incorporates the story of Emmett Till, a 14-year-old, who was lynched because of his race. While I knew the story, I didn't recall that Emmett was only 14. The same age as Reat. Immediately, I felt connected to Emmett's mother, Mamie Till, who wanted to send a message to everyone about the brutality of her son's murder. By doing so, she was shining a light on the hate that had taken him. In similarity to Dad's and Reat's deaths, they were murdered by someone because of hate.

Every Scripture, song, melody and word (at least those spoken by our family) were planned by each of us, intent on creating a final production for my dad and Reat. A production about them and for them that would swell pride in each of their already deeply missed hearts.

However, there was one aspect of the memorial service that was not of our making, at least not by initial consideration. The attendees of the service who entered from the north side of the building likely had the pleasure of being greeted by the Patriot Guard Riders. They are an online community who connect, gather and provide protection when a funeral, burial or a veteran in need requests their presence. While they ride motorcycles, they are not a motorcycle group as some would think. Yes, they help protect mourners from harassment. And you are thinking, why would Dad and Reat's funeral need protecting from harassment? Excuse me, they were murdered by someone filled with evil, vile and hate ... they did not hate. You are not alone; we wondered the same thing.

As soon as the date and time, Friday, April 18, at 3 p.m. was established for our funeral, Westboro Baptist Church, an organization well known in the Midwest, made claims on their social media that they would be picketing. I can't make this up. My dad and son are murdered by a white supremacist intent on murdering Jews on Palm Sunday. And on Good Friday, as we are celebrating their lives in our own church with community, family and friends, this extremist cult and hate group declares they will be present outside the church. My brother, Tony, was the first to hear of the potential picketing. He kept it from me until maybe the day before the funeral. By then, my head was so full of procurement, memorial service and cremation plans layered with my new and unwanted friend—the fog, I allowed this to flutter away like the wind rather than give it much consideration. I was too damned exhausted to give them any thought. Thankfully, Tony had the energy and took it upon himself and his friend group to reach out to the Patriot Guard Riders.

Something good was already bubbling.

There were no Black people or Jews involved in the murders of Dad and Reat. A white man, self-proclaimed as a white supremacist, murdered three white people he assumed to be Jewish.

The message that must be shouted is, "If this can happen to me, a white, Christian woman, it can happen to you!"

When hatred and evil such as this is allowed in our language, homes, schools, businesses and government, it will find you one day. This evil will find everyone, whether you are paying attention or not. Each of us can make a choice to stamp it OUT! It found me and my family. The hate of this one man, who was well known in the conversation surrounding his history of neo-Nazism, exploded in our lives.

Pastor Hamilton charged each of us to stand up for those who are teased, ridiculed and bullied. To be prepared to stand with those who are marginalized, specifically mentioning the Jewish and Black populations. "Stand up for those who need us to stand up for them," he proclaimed.

"To honor Bill and Reat, would we live our lives with LOVE as our defining story?"

If you are a member of the Church of the Resurrection or have ever listened to Pastor Hamilton deliver his Easter message, undoubtedly, you have heard his quote, "The worst thing is never the last thing." My brother, Tony, chooses good each day because of this quote in particular. And how does Pastor Hamilton explain his faith in Heaven? "I not only believe it, I am counting on it. This is what sustains us." No matter our faith or non-faith, what are we living for, if not for love?

As Pastor Hamilton finished in prayer, I watched the stage as my dear family friend Shirley Doyle made her way to the piano. Shirley is a longtime friend of my parents. I asked her to explain to me the relationship she had with them. "Bill and Melinda were an integral part of mine and my daughter's lives throughout years of church choir, Duncan Little Theater and OU football. He encouraged me to finish my education and thus, changed the trajectory of both our lives. To me he was a physician, 'older brother,' mentor and encourager." She considered him a rare soul. "He delivered my daughter during a very difficult birth that likely saved both our lives." Shirley brilliantly plays the piano and organ, and Tony suggested we ask her to play "The Lord's Prayer." Flying in from Washington, D.C., she was as heartbroken as the rest of us and said, "The manner in which he died traumatized me.

A man that put so much good into the world, yet taken in an act of hate, still astounds me."

Amazing, is all I can say … truly from Heaven. As I rewatched the video of their memorial service for this chapter, I could see a poignant moment Shirley had during her piece. She was nervous, of course, and wanted this to be perfect. She told us later that as she sat at the piano she wasn't sure she could play. But as a trained musician, the expectations of the audience and our family prompted her. Only moments into the piece, you can visually see her relax, with a smile. Her soul takes over from there; and we, along with thousands in attendance and online viewers, can hear the love, compassion and sorrow our family has been yearning to explain through words, Scriptures and songs. Shirley's talent and love of my dad, Reat and our family was exhibited in the most beautiful way. She played directly to them in Heaven. We saw her smile and the relaxing movement of her shoulders … she told us later that she felt comforting hands settle onto her shoulders. Dad was with her.

In each of the family funerals I had previously attended, the song "Amazing Grace" had always been part of it. We were thankful to the Blue Valley High School Men's Select Chorus for taking it upon themselves to learn, rehearse and sing this song eloquently to us, in a lovely tribute to their friend and fellow chorus member and his grandfather. Their young male voices, sweet and true, filled me with hope.

The caskets we purchased had room for messages to be written on them. An interesting twist on a memorial service, I know. This was not an easy agreement among us. In fact, it may have created the only slightly stilted conversation surrounding the service itself.

Mat shared this from our earliest planning session, "I remember discussing the impact your dad and Reat had had on so many and that it would be important for the community that had been rallying behind you, to have the opportunity to say goodbye. It was then, when I suggested matching caskets for the two of them and that following the service at the Church of the Resurrection we would invite all in attendance to pass by their caskets and use a Sharpie to sign the casket, leave a note or expression of love. I remember you thinking that was a pretty cool idea—the rest of your family was skeptical, but you pushed forward."

Sharpies were made available and Pastor Hamilton explained to the audience that after the family left the sanctuary, they were encouraged to write a message on one or both of the caskets. He had been skeptical of this when he learned of it, too. Our hope had been that this would provide an opportunity for healing for those who needed an outlet. We were all extremely surprised and exhilarated by the hundreds of messages guests had managed to squeeze onto each brown space of the caskets.

"Men and women of all ages participated, even some of the church's pastors and staff. Watching the teenagers write their memories and expressions of love on Dr. Corporon and Reat's caskets was something I will never forget. They gathered, crying, laughing and supporting each other. The healing and healthy expressions of grief your family allowed the community and those children to engage in that day was heroic."—Mat explained to me in a letter depicting his memories of our heartbreaking work together.

A photographer had flown in to cover the memorial service and subsequently took photos of family members and guests surrounding the caskets as the Sharpies were put to use for healing. These photos capture moments that would have never been seen by Len, Lukas, Mom and me, if we had not allowed such cascades of emotion from those in attendance. Writing a message on a casket is not typical but it achieved our intention.

I have left many memorial services feeling as badly as I did when it began. My personal goal was to assist all those in attendance, my own family members, including our loving cousins in attendance, and those watching online, to leave feeling uplifted and hopeful.

From a man who creates, implements and arranges burials and funerals for a living, I share with you Mat's depiction of our service, "The service was beautiful—remarkable even. From the lobby of the church covered in memorabilia, photographs and tributes to Dr. Corporon and Reat, to their matching caskets adorned with floral trib-utes in the sanctuary. Their tribute video, Pastor Hamilton's sermon, your father's eulogy and the eulogy you gave for Reat were uplifting and heartbreaking, at the same time. I remember being so emotional during the service that Jay had to put his hand on my shoulder to comfort me. To this day, I still have the photos and videos I took on my phone, while for two whole hours thousands of people in attendance waited patiently to write on their caskets and say their final goodbye."

A song released in 2011 that had become my recent favorite was played as we were all dismissed from the sanctuary. "Good Morning" by Mandisa picked up the pace considerably as we made our way out of the sanctuary from what had been at times heart wrenching, heart warming and a full-blown philosophical course in: "Bad things happen to good people," "Evil can be overcome with faith and love," and "The choice is yours; make it a good one."

"You give me strength. You give me just what I need. And I can feel the hope that's rising in me," are lyrics I love from this song. Reat listened to it with me, often as we drove together daily to school, to a practice he had or during his own driving sessions. I did have hope when I walked from the sanctuary to what is called the narthex. Standing for over two hours, taking tearful friends into my arms and thanking them for their shared sorrow, I was grasping for the ability to rise above the pain that would soon engulf me. Thankfully I had no idea of the tumultuous spiral of pain, fear of losing another child and life transitions ahead of me and our family.

Taking a lesson from Reat, one he left for all of us on his newly created Twitter account, "Live life to the fullest and never give up." I won't give up, baby. I won't ever give up on Lukas or the need to make good choices to overcome the hate that took you and Dad from our lives.

Top Left: Taking a step to heal herself, Yea Yea had one quilt made for each of her grandchildren with Bill's (Popeye's) shirts. Back row: Travis Corporon, Lukas Losen. Front row: Katy Corporon, Olivia Corporon and Andrew Corporon. Photo courtesy of Jordan Photography in Overland Park, Kansas. 2015

Top Right: Will Corporon, Mindy Corporon and Tony Corporon begin the celebrations of their mother's birthdays without their father, her husband Bill, present. At EBT Restaurant in Kansas City, Missouri. Family photo. August 24, 2014.

Bottom Left: Melinda and William Corporon in Ponca City, Oklahoma at the funeral for Rita Mae Gordy (Muthie). Family photo. 2009

Bottom Right: Popeye, Reat and Yea Yea after Reat's performance in *Guys & Dolls* with Blue Valley High School. February 2014.

20

Grief Journeys Are Individual

Melinda A. Corporon, my mother, is my namesake. Yes, we have almost the exact same name. She is Melinda Ann while I am Melinda Katherine. From birth, my parents called me Mindy. She gave me life, organizational skills and the willpower to do just about anything, even those things she hasn't and doesn't like. Her life was filled with helping others from the time her second sister, Jilda, was born. It was not Jilda's fault that she was born second and Melinda first, it just was. From an early age, she was instructed to help in any and every situation with cooking, cleaning and ironing (many stories about ironing sheets for "practice" have reached my ears). Mom would have made millions of dollars if these skills had not only been for her family, my father, her three children and now 10 grandchildren. She values being Bill's wife above all else, and a mom to Will, Mindy and Tony comes in a close third to each of her grandchildren, who, for the sake of keeping the peace, we will say are all equal in second place …. again, only to Bill.

She and my dad celebrated their 49th wedding anniversary on March 20, 2014, amongst discussions for how to celebrate their 50th. Unfortunately, we never know when our planning for the future will be snatched right out of our hands and our hearts. On April 12, 2014, Mom and Dad were over for dinner with Len, Reat, Lukas and me. Len and I had taken full advantage of my parents' willingness to keep our boys while we traveled for our own wedding anniversary in early April. This dinner was an opportunity to thank them and get caught back up on their lives and the time they spent with our boys. There were two topics of conversation at dinner.

The first topic included the words "50th anniversary," "Disney World" and "10 days." Mom's wishful, dreamy idea was for the two of them to vacation at Walt Disney World in Orlando, Florida, over a 10-day period, thus increasing their chances of each grandchild being brought to the same location by their respective parents for as many days as they would like. I can still see my father rolling his eyes when he heard what was most likely a repeat of an earlier request. Two people seated at our table were extremely excited about this topic and willing to participate. Len and I glanced at one another, noting that this was not the time for us to refute what my mom and perhaps my dad, to an extent, wanted for their anniversary. Listening to her request and watching my dad's response, even as I have recalled it to memory over the past six and half years, I am grateful. They loved one another. They led simple, not boring, but simple lives ... wanting family together above all else.

The second topic was our need to address a scheduling conflict the following day: Sunday, April 13, 2014—Lukas had a lacrosse game and Reat had an audition for *KC SuperStar*. While Lukas' game was to begin around 12:45 p.m., he was to report to the field by 12:15 p.m. or so. Reat's audition time was 1:30 p.m. The two locations sit about 20 minutes from each other, lacrosse being the farthest distance from our home by another 10 minutes, give or take a long stoplight. I had every intention of driving Reat to his audition and stated so. This would place Len with Lukas for the game. Reat picked up on a nuance I hadn't seen from Lukas. In turn, Reat said aloud to all of us, "Mom, I think you should go to Lukas' lacrosse game. You missed two of his games while you were out of town." Ouch! My 14-year-old was calling me out. Feeling uncomfortable about his true statement and the idea of missing his audition, I looked at Lukas for reassurance that I could, indeed, miss another game and still be a good mom. Hmmm, "not likely" is what I read on his baby 12-year-old face. His cute little half smile and quick response with a hug, with the thought of me being present at his game, told me where I needed to be.

My parent's oldest grandchild is Travis, firstborn to Will, my older brother. Travis named my parents Grammy and Grandpa. However, when Reat was born, Travis didn't live close enough to us to teach Reat that these were their names. Therefore, Reat named my mom "Yea Yea" and my dad "Popeye." We are fairly certain that "Yea Yea" came from the fact that she would sit in front of him and cheer him on with EVERYTHING he accomplished ... yeah, yeah! And thus, she is Yea Yea.

"Yea Yea," I affectionately called out to her from only across the round table holding all six of us, "would you be able to drive Reat to his audition?" She could not. Her plans included Andrew and Katy, my younger brother Tony's children, and an Easter bunny with a photographer.

In early 2020, my mom recounted her story of April 13, 2014 on a podcast interview with me. New to recording a podcast and interviewing anyone, she would be my second guest on episode 004, titled "You Have the Most Important Job Today." Her story begins with the expected plans she and my dad had for the day, "I had scheduled myself with Andrew and Katy, your niece and nephew, to go take Easter pictures. Bill was going to go take Reat to the audition for *KC SuperStar*. He had already been to swim. You know, he swam every day that he could."

Hearing her speak about this day was difficult. Of course, she lives with the outcome of the day, as I do, every single day. My dad's love for swimming was passed on to me. He would swim at least one mile, if not more, every day he could get to the gym. Often, he and I passed one another in the pool area or swim lanes. My father had taught my brothers and me how to swim. There was no swim club or team where I grew up in Oklahoma, which meant I only swam for fun. Once I was in college, the idea of waking early to swim laps was unfathomable. It was only after having my two boys and carrying a few pounds of baby weight that I decided a dip in the pool might be a healthy addition to my workout routine. Like my father, I am an early riser. It is common for me to wake with no alarm just before the crack of dawn in any given time zone. Mom, who is more nocturnal, rags on us by saying we are awake in time to see "dawn's early crack." There was a wonderful swim class starting at 6 a.m., which proved to help me train for a few sprint triathlons I completed in my 40s. The opportunity to see my father on many mornings passing in the swim lanes, by the side of the pool or walking in or out of the gym felt good. In fact, I didn't know how good this felt until it wasn't available to me any longer.

Mom continues, "After his swim, I fixed breakfast, scrambled eggs with fresh crab meat, which was kind of a special breakfast. And then we chatted a little bit. He was watching TV." I could hear her voice change in tone when she said, "which was kind of a special breakfast." The need to have created a special memory with my dad prior to his murder was important to her.

Meeting in high school, my parents had been in partnership for over 49 years, 20 of which saw her working alongside my dad to manage their medical practice. As a mom to Will, Tony and me, she was more than available as a leader in Scouting, several band parent organizations and highly involved as a cheerleading parent from my fifth grade year until high school graduation. Separate from my dad and the three of us, Mom made a name for herself as a woman of character and leadership in Duncan, Oklahoma. She created and directed the Duncan High School Leadership Program in 1995 after being a member of the Leadership Duncan Class of 1994-95. Her commitment to building a strong community was only second to building a strong family. Being honored by the Duncan Chamber of Commerce and Industry as their Woman of the Year in 1998 was a reward highlighting hours upon hours of her efforts. While these accolades were important to her in recognition of her accomplishments, she relished in the love of her husband, children and grandchildren.

She went over the schedule with my dad for what was probably the third time that morning. "I was getting ready to leave. I went over the schedule of the day one more time and told him when we'd meet back up at the house. After listing everything, I said to him, 'You have the most important job today.' He said, 'I know it.' And that's the last thing I said to him. I wish I'd ended it with, 'I love you.'"

The words, "You have the most important job today" were not meant to be the final words she would say to him. I can hear her sadness as she recalls leaving him with instructions rather than words of endearment. We can see the irony in what she said to him. We can recall these words and feel the power in them ... power she didn't intend.

Continuing with her explanation of the Easter bunny photo shoot, she said, "It was a lot of fun. Pictures were great. They were happy. We were having a wonderful time, we had finished the pictures and we were checking out when my phone started ringing. I didn't hear it for a little while and then I almost didn't pick it up. I thought to myself, I'll call back. But I did reach down and pick it up. It was Len, your husband, shouting, 'You have to get over to the J! You have to get over to the J! There's been a shooting! You have to get over to the J! You have to get over to the J.'"

Of course, hearing Len shouting at her through the phone about a shooting and the need for Mom to get to the J (Jewish Community Center) caused her to also shout, "What?" into the phone. Without truly having an understanding of what was transpiring but clearly realizing she needed to be somewhere other than where she was, Mom grabbed her purse and ran to her own car. As she was departing, she said to Dana, her daughter-in-law, "I've got to go! I've got to go! You call Tony to come get you."

The horror my mom found at the Jewish Community Center was only slightly different from my own discovery. Our beautiful Kansas morning, with a crisp cool breeze and brightly shining sun, had disappeared. She drove into the parking lot and somehow avoided being stopped by police officers or any sort of guard, who she recalls being present and then amazingly not stopping traffic. Perhaps there was an angel intervention at that moment. While she was driving the short distance from the Easter bunny photos to the Jewish Community Center, she dialed my father's phone number over and over. Because he was not answering, her thoughts were hopeful that he and Reat were in the basement somewhere, safely tucked away from any shooting. She also considered the guns in my father's truck and dashed the thought quickly out of her head that my father could have been a shooter if he had needed to protect Reat, himself or anyone else.

Thankfully, when my mom arrived, the scene had changed ever so slightly. Yellow crime scene tape was up, marking the space to be investigated. My father's body was covered by a tarp, upon my request. However, he was not fully covered. Her nightmare solidified when she saw my father's foot sticking out from beneath the tarp. Ominously, dark clouds formed over the Jewish Community Center and a chilly, now steady rain portrayed how swiftly our lives can change, and unknowingly at the time, the evil that changed them. She knew his shoe and his sock, both of which were visible. The realization that he was the body under the tarp sent her into screams.

Her screams in an otherwise quiet space quickly attracted a policewoman to her side. Continuing, my mom tells me, "I must have said something because she took hold of me. I wanted to go closer in and she took hold of me. She took me around into the Jewish Community Center and sat me down and really started grilling me, wanting to know who I was and why I was there. I kept telling her who that was under the tarp and I don't know how many times I had told her and then I kept asking her where Reat was. I said, 'Where's Reat? Where's the boy who was with him?' And she said something about the man who was in the truck with him. I screamed at her, I said, 'It wasn't a man. It's a boy. Where is he? Is he alive? Where is he?'" The policewoman was following her own protocol and, of course, not at all at my mother's level of distress. The policewoman was working to understand the situation—it was her job. Past experience told this policewoman that most murders in this county stem from a family member being the perpetrator. She was questioning my mom because my mom could have been a suspect.

After the policewoman surmised it was unlikely that my mom had pulled the trigger on the person under the tarp, she left my mom to go find more answers. Namely, she tried to find out which hospital the boy who was in the truck was taken to.

My mom, Len and I have shared with one another the odd sensation of time felt by each of us in the middle of our crisis. Personally, during the events themselves, finding their bodies in the parking lot of the Jewish Community Center, sitting in the back of the theater and then driving to the hospital all felt like the longest minutes of my life. However, the day after their murders, the clock began to move swiftly, as if I should be in a hurry. Len and I discussed this "fast movement of time" on more than one occasion. After the murders, we each felt as if we were chasing time and couldn't catch up with it.

Mom's experience of time during the events that uprooted our world offered a twist. She told me, "It's funny when I try to think back to that day. Time either seems like it went forever in between one little event or the other. It was like it was just dragging on forever. It was unreal. Or it seems like it was real fast ... it's kind of odd."

Because the time warp was happening inside my mother's brain, she wasn't sure if a short or a long time passed before a gentleman, unknown to me to this day, appeared in front of her and said, "Your daughter's here."

Taking my mom by the arm, he walked her into the White Theatre, where Reat should have been auditioning at likely that very minute. An audition for *KC SuperStar* had been Reat's dream for three years. We lived that dream together, including my parents. As a freshman in high school, Reat was now qualified to try out. In fact, we expected him to audition more than one year. Performing on a stage and in front of an audience was where he flourished. The rush of adrenaline he felt before stepping into the spotlight exhilarated him. Reat had a talent for memorizing lyrics, engaging an audience and melding these skills into an entertaining, fun performance. He had wanted this opportunity and we had wanted it for him. Instead my mother found me ... sobbing in the back of the theater where we had thought his dreams would begin to percolate.

Mom's recollection is that she knew my father had been the body under the tarp; and therefore, she didn't feel she needed to ask me who was under the tarp. The first panicky words I heard from her were "Was that your father?" as she burst into the dimly lit auditorium of the theater. Her concern quickly shifted to Reat and particularly about his whereabouts.

Like me, my mother had parked near enough to the location of the shooting and subsequent murders that her car was also part of the crime scene. Unlike me, she had a need for her purse. In the midst of chaos surrounding our desire to know the name of the hospital where Reat was taken by ambulance, my mom re-engaged in conversation with the same policewoman. She tells me, "My car was still out in the parking lot. I had, in the meantime, convinced the policewoman to go get my purse out of the car. I didn't have my purse and I had to really, really badger her about that. She finally did and went to get my purse." Mom's comment about "really, really badgering" the policewoman makes me giggle inside. Not to diminish the importance of the contents in her purse or her desire to have this one item to provide needed comfort, I have been badgered by my mom on many occasions and can't imagine how she came across to this policewoman under the circumstances of extreme stress. In a completely different situation, I would have liked to have been a witness to this interaction between the two of them.

Now, in the emergency room, Mom's recollection of the events is similar and different from mine. When recalling the emergency room doctor walking into the room, she tells me, "He told us that Reat hadn't made it. That was so hard to hear. I remember Len screaming and yelling and I yelled out. Our last hopes were dashed. Now, I feel so badly that I didn't immediately rush to Lukas or to Tony or to you. I just remember sitting there, almost falling over." Crushing. Finding her husband's body under a tarp in a parking lot, finding her daughter in a dimly lit theater sobbing and finding her grandson not living upon arrival at the hospital emergency room was such crushing news that it was debilitating.

Even in a state of disbelief and a wanting of denial, I knew Gary Underwood, my ex-husband and Reat's dad, needed to be informed. Mom recalls, "I know at one point you asked me to call Reat's dad because you didn't have a phone and I left a message for him." When Gary called back on my mom's phone, I took the call. Gary was the first person who heard me say the words out loud, "Reat was murdered." I explained as best I could from the mess of the chaos in my brain what had transpired. At the time, I was unaware that Terri LaManno had been gunned down also, losing her life and leaving a widower and three children in the same dismal situation as our little family. I was

unaware of the circumstances of the shooter, himself. A white supremacist touting antisemitism rhetoric his entire adult life had blown up
our family ... our simple, loving family.

Other phone calls were made to provide the unwanted, yet real,
news. "I called your brother, Will," Mom shared. "The room began
filling with people, one of whom was a rabbi. Rabbi Rudnick was
there, and he started walking with me. I think he decided I needed to
walk, or maybe I decided. We walked up and down the hall. We didn't
talk about anything. At least I don't remember talking about anything
with him. It was just a comfort to have somebody walking with me."

The fact that Rabbi Rudnick was present with us when we heard
that Reat had not survived a gunshot wound delivered by an antisem-
ite intent on killing Jews has not been lost on us.

Rabbi Jonathan Rudnick had plans to attend the play *To Kill a
Mockingbird* that same afternoon, at the White Theatre in the Jewish
Community Center. The same theater in which *KC SuperStar* was
holding auditions. The same theater in which my mother found me
sobbing. If the shooter had arrived 40 minutes later, he would have
found a full parking lot of theater-going patrons instead of two, my
two.

Rabbi Rudnick's position with Jewish Family Services as a Jewish
community chaplain is the reason he received a phone call from Fire
Emergency Services asking for his immediate arrival to the Jewish
Community Center shortly after the shooting. In his words, Rabbi
Rudnick explains, "I was briefed on the shootings and asked to come
as soon as possible to the Jewish Community Center. I arrived and
was allowed entry by the battalion chief. Entering the facility, I made
eye contact with the security guard—he was in tears. I found Jacob
Schreiber, then the chief executive officer of the Jewish Community
Center. I asked him what he needed and how could I best help. Jacob
asked me to go directly to Overland Park Regional Medical Center to
be there for you guys. He made it clear that your family is part of our
family and asked me to be with you."

Rabbi Rudnick found our family at the same time Dr. Fishman
was telling us that Reat had not survived. His formidable stature
and peaceful nature in the small room offered the opportunity for

stability in the turbulence of our storm. Rabbi Rudnick asked me about my faith community, to which I replied, "We attend Church of the Resurrection." He phoned the pastoral care team with our church and received a call back from Pastor Steve Langhofer, who quickly made his way to the same chaotic mess of our lives. Pastor Langhofer arrived at the emergency room at the same time as the Overland Park Regional Medical Center on-call chaplain, Rabbi Stuart Davis. These two clergy, from the Christian and Jewish faiths, led our family in a circle of prayer. My brain was not capable of comprehending the magnitude of this prayer circle and was oblivious to the interfaith connections being made in front and beside me.

Before walking with my mom up and down the halls of the hospital and leaving us for a necessary visit to Village Shalom, the location of the third shooting and murder of Terri LaManno, Rabbi Rudnick sat with Lukas. He shared with me, "As time, both chronos and kairos, unfolded, a 12-year-old boy was sitting in the middle of adult chaos. He was the only youth there. He was there, yet he was alone. I sat next to Lukas and tried to gently be with him." Offering Lukas compassion, the rabbi listened as Lukas explained the life events of our day. "Lukas told me about seeing and speaking with Reat earlier in the day. He told me what a big deal the audition was. He also told me about Reat helping to get the pool ready. Lukas cried as he slowly digested the terrible reality that his brother was dead, killed." Rabbi Rudnick exposed his own vulnerability during the conversation with Lukas when he told me, "I have a son who is now 20. Looking back at that day, I was unconsciously aware of the deep and strong connection to my son that was evoked in that encounter with Lukas."

There was no way for me to know at the time that his involvement, initially holding our family with care, was one step for me into interfaith understanding and dialogue. While I don't think that God is a puppeteer commanding our every move, I can confirm that God places us where we need to be. It is our job to listen and move in the direction we are nudged and sometimes shoved. As fall of 2014 approached, Rabbi Rudnick invited our family to Village Shalom for a Jewish spiritual care service to honor the memories of all those in the Jewish community who have died since the previous service. Of course, Dad and Reat weren't residents of Village Shalom, and neither was Terri LaManno, who was murdered by the same shooter and in their parking lot. Terri had been visiting her mother, who was a resident. Rabbi Rudnick invited us, saying, "It hit me that as your father, son and Terri were literally in our houses—our Jewish communal spaces—as part of our community, that of course there could never, unfortunately, be a more apt time to include your dad, Reat, and Terri as part of the House of Israel." The prayer gathering is the pre-High Holiday Service of Spiritual Renewal, Peace and Wholeness. As part of the service, a prayer called Kaddish is said to honor the memories of all in our community who have died since our last gathering. The "last gathering" for this prayer service had been pre-Passover, right before the shootings that took their lives.

In Aramaic, these words are recited:

> May God establish God's kingdom in your lifetime and during your days,
>
> and within the life of the entire House of Israel, speedily and soon; Amen.

Our paths crossed only a few times after the Kaddish prayer was offered for our family and the LaMannos. And then, in 2020, Rabbi Rudnick humbly accepted a position on an interfaith panel as our representative of Judaism during our LOVE Day during SevenDays® Make a Ripple, Change the World experience.

In our own little bubble of bewilderment and disbelief, we had no comprehension of the national and international attention these murders were receiving. "I don't know how they all knew about it," Mom stated, regarding the number of people who appeared in the Overland Park Regional Medical Center emergency room and at her home only hours later. We shared this sentiment. Family and friends flocked to us offering warm, deep hugs with the intention, I am sure, of taking some of the pain from our bodies into theirs.

Remembering the moments when she, Len, Lukas and I were loading into our car from the emergency room, Mom recalls her encounter with Detective Reeder, "He was very gentle. I remember him asking about releasing the names and it didn't even register. You know, why did he care?" Mom was sitting in the front seat having not yet closed her door, so Detective Reeder knelt down to speak with her. "He started talking to me about the fact that they would have somebody from the police department watching our home. They would beat the media away. We could call him for anything. He handed us his number and repeated the same offer of assistance. At the time it didn't register. I didn't question why; I just listened to him." Mom recalls.

I wasn't fearful for my life or that of the rest of our family until my mom explained in the car ride to her home that the police would be located on our streets, protecting our homes.

The shooter was caught quickly. He was cornered in the parking lot of an elementary school and gave himself up, but not without raising his hand in a Heil Hitler salute. This proved that his demented mind intent on murdering Jews came from a belief in neo-Nazism, white supremacy and antisemitism. They all smell of evil and their practice of hate leaves a pile of shattered lives aching to be whole. While he was detained soon after murdering my father, Reat and Terri LaManno, we had some concerns that there may be others like him interested in the same actions of hate. These concerns were for naught—thank God. The heaviness of death in our home did not also need an added layer of fear for the life of our only living child.

As people filled my parent's home, Mom recalls, "I think I was just vacant. Is that a good word to use? My mind was vacant. I recall you asking me for tennis shoes. Then I saw you walking out the front door wearing your father's Oklahoma Sooner sweatshirt. Len didn't want you to go to the vigil; and I couldn't even speak in full sentences, let alone try and stop you. Looking back, I wish I had gone with you. But, I was vacant."

The vacancy in my mother lasted for months, leading to several hospitalizations for fluid needs. Her mind was too vacant to care for herself physically, and she would become dehydrated to the point of nausea, vomiting and dizzy spells. Her health declined so rapidly that Tony, Dana, Len and I were actively involved in as much physical recovery as she would allow.

Her grief and healing journey is different from my own. While I pushed through grief and sadness to the point of creating opportunities to cry often or for long periods of time, she stayed away from any activity or potential memory that might inflict more pain. In trying to help her continue on a healing path, I asked her to explain how she has healed during our podcast interview in March 2020. This is her coming to terms with a path unlike mine:

"And you said something about healing and my immediate reaction to you was, I haven't healed. I've been thinking about that. I think maybe there's a little different definition of the word healing. Do I manage to get through every day now, mostly without tears or not being able to function? Yes, I've been able to do that for a while. I will say that the first year was disbelief. I kept waiting for them to come through the door. Every time I walked into the house, I expected Bill to be there; I expected to see Reat. The second year, reality set in and it was really difficult. The third year was a combination of the two." After almost six years, my mother can say, "In many ways, I am healing."

Loss is universal. The way we grieve, heal and move onward is individual.

I share in this aspect of her interpretation of healing, "Does that mean that when I hear a song, something that either Reat sang or something that Bill and I used to dance to, my heart doesn't hurt so badly? And tears don't come to my eyes? No, that still happens all the time."

"My heart hurts," she explains, a pain that I know well. "I didn't know what that meant until now, you know, your heart really does hurt. Your chest aches so badly sometimes that you don't think you're going to be able to catch your next breath. I love being with family, with the grandkids—the things I can do with them and for them— that's very healing for me. And also mixed with sadness because every time I'm at an event, a ball game, a concert, anything, one of my first thoughts is, 'Bill should be here. Reat should be here.' Will I ever get over that? No, I know I won't."

Continuing with her own definition of healing, which, in fact, is my point in this memoir and podcast, that we each heal differently and in our own time, "I love playing bridge, which you know, and I continue to do as much as I can. I want to say I work hard. I work very hard when I'm around my friends and when I'm around the family to be upbeat, to not be a downer. When I'm around other ladies, mostly my age, some of whom are married, divorced or widows, we might discuss husbands. I bring up humorous things about Bill and laugh. While many of my lady friends knew him, I keep it light. I know I'm doing that on purpose because I don't want them to think that it's not all right to be themselves around me. I think maybe that's part of healing. So I just keep putting one foot in front of the other; I keep doing and going."

It was heartwarming to hear my mom talk about what she knowingly is doing to make her way through life after losing the love of her life times two. Her life had been perfect. Her life trajectory had been bountiful, with the fulfilling challenge of assisting my father through medical school, overseeing their medical practice, raising three responsible adults, completing her beloved community service and having years upon years of fun at my father's side in theater productions … all had been in her grasp to enjoy.

And then we were shattered.

I would love to see her find pure joy during this last quarter of her life. To know that her heart could be filled to the brim with love and laughter, all the while knowing she wasn't replacing my father, would enrich me. But it's not about me. Her healing is not my healing.

When I revisit her final words to my father the morning of the murders, "You have the most important job today," their intensity leads me down a path of peace. Dad was to get Reat to the audition on time and be his chauffeur. My father did much more than this. My father was the first person to receive Reat in Heaven. They walked in, hand in hand, as they reached their savior, Jesus. As a Christian, I must lean on this … holding it tightly to my heart, willing it to be so. Having faith, believing in this image of Heaven receiving the two of them as one, provides the peace I need to wake up each day.

Top Left: Mahnaz Shabbir, with Mindy and Melinda Corporon, assisted with our interfaith panel during SevenDays® Make a Ripple, Change the World hosted by Cleveland University compliments of Dr. Carl and Elizabeth Cleveland, III. Photo courtesy of Mahnaz Shabbir. 2016

Top Right: Mindy is embracing Hafsa Hussein at a vigil held for her brother, Abdisamad Sheikh-Hussein. Hosted by the Masjid Al-Taqwa (Somali Center of Kansas City). Photo courtesy of Crescent Peace Society. 2014

Bottom Left: Friends attending the Candlelight Christmas Eve service at the United Methodist Church of the Resurrection in Leawood, Kansas. From left: Ruth Bigus (Jewish), Zaynab and her brother, Belal Jamil (Muslim), Lukas, Len and Mindy, Saúl Egido (Christian), Kelly and her mom Janea Long (Christian). Family photo. 2016

Bottom Right: Mindy and Mahnaz Shabbir continue fostering their friendship at the SevenDays® Make a Ripple, Change the World Patron Party hosted by The Museum at Prairiefire in Overland Park, Kansas compliments of Fred and Candy Merrill. Photo courtesy of Mahnaz Shabbir. 2016

21

Islam or Muslim

The first week of December 2014, Abdisamad Sheikh-Hussein was murdered outside his mosque in Kansas City, Missouri.[3]

A sophomore at Staley High School, Abdisamad was a brother to three siblings, well liked by his peers and had just finished leading the prayers for their Muslim youth group. Abdisamad and his family had emigrated from war-torn Somalia only a few years prior.

At the same time, the murders of Dad, Reat and Terri LaManno continued to be prominent news, locally and nationally. This is why I practice avoiding all news channels and most, if not all, television. Not knowing when a photo of one or all three of them would appear on the television made me edgy for months. With each announcement about the district attorney's case against the shooter, a photo of the shooter would also appear. For the sake of my mental health, I surmised it would be better to leave the television in the off position. For these reasons I haven't yet heard the devastating news about a Muslim boy, who was run down by a vehicle in front of his place of worship with his friends and two of his siblings present.

The email came from my pastor, Adam Hamilton, senior pastor of the Church of the Resurrection. His message informed me that a Muslim woman was interested in reaching me for a conversation.

3 *KC Star*, December 4, https://www.kansascity.com/article4299890.html

Hmmm? Not knowing the news, not knowing any Muslims, at least not thinking I know any Muslims, I am perplexed. This is interesting, I think to myself. What now?

Pastor Hamilton picks up the phone after a few rings. "Mindy, have you met Mahnaz Shabbir previously?" he begins. "No, I have not had the opportunity." Quickly, I am embarrassed to find out I did have the opportunity to meet her when Pastor Hamilton interviewed her about a year prior for a special series he hosted at the church.

Pastor Hamilton goes on to explain that he first interviewed Mahnaz, a Muslim woman, about a year ago during a sermon. He describes her as a lovely, articulate and peaceful person. He tells me she is a mother to four boys—and a widow. Her husband, a physician, died suddenly eight years prior. She is raising four boys on her own and has an extensive background in the health care field.

He continues to explain that Mahnaz would like to speak with me about a tragic event that happened only a few days ago. He said, "A young Muslim boy was brutally murdered. He was 15." As he continues to talk, my brain freezes in place on "he was 15." Reat should be 15.

While this brain freeze has happened to me before, I am still unaware of the power that trauma has on humans and, more importantly, the lasting effects. Somehow I have managed to live for eight months without my dad and son. Living doesn't equate to healing.

Immediately feeling connected to the story and the pain his family is feeling, I physically shake off the "freeze" and concentrate on paying attention. Pastor Hamilton continues to explain that yesterday evening the boy had been in his mosque, leading prayer services. Afterward, he and his friends were standing in the parking lot talking. Suddenly, a car raced into the parking lot and ran over the boy … not once, but twice. "The man proclaimed to be a Christian who had converted from Islam," he said. Based on my personal research of Abdisamad's murder I found that witnesses believed the suspect's conversion from Islam to Christianity was a significant piece of this tragedy because the suspect's vehicle was seen with language defaming Islam in the weeks and possibly only days ahead of this murder.

The suspect was well known in the Somali community, but not necessarily well liked.

"Another religious hate crime," is how I heard the message on the phone. Another promising teenager had his life brutally taken. A faithful boy, no doubt, after delivering prayers with his teenage friends. A loving family member, as he was with his own siblings at the mosque. His life taken from him, cut short by hate. Unfortunately, Abdisamad will be remembered for who he was, rather than for who he could have been.

Abdisamad's parents had to be sick to their stomachs. They had brought their son to the United States for safety, an education and a chance at a better-than-decent life. I was sick to *my* stomach. The nausea found its way into my throat as quickly as my brain took me to the parking lot at the Jewish Community Center. This was another brain freeze for me, a trigger.

Frequently in my mind, I found myself standing in the parking lot, wind blowing softly around me, no one present—except for my father's bleeding body. Shake it off. Shake it off, I have to say to myself. The physiological reaction I am having is noticeable. Having difficulty removing my thoughts from the scene of the parking lot, I stand up and try walking to clear my head.

"Young people witnessed the horrific death," I heard Pastor Hamilton say! Frankly, I wasn't sure if I had potentially missed any of his words while the dark memory was holding me captive in the parking lot. My own voice took over and said, "Of course, you can provide my number to the woman, Mahnaz, who is looking for me."

Later that afternoon, my phone receives a call from an unknown number. Ma (short "a" sound) – nahz (sounds like Oz) - Sha (short "a" sound) - beer. I am fairly certain she is the first Muslim with whom I have ever spoken personally.

However, in April 2015, I realize that Reat's friend Belal Jamil is Muslim. Really? How come I didn't know this? I think to myself, once I discover this, that I have known Muslims, had Muslims in my home and never thought about learning more about who they are.

Mahnaz is friendly and compassionate as she explains that she is very sorry for my loss. She is also sorry for the unspeakable crime that has been committed against this young man. She says Abdisamad's friends asked her to, "Reach out to Reat Underwood's mom." Prior to Reat's murder, when I was referred to as Reat's mom or Lukas' mom, my heart fluttered. I was happy to claim these as replacements to my own name from the time each boy had playmates or when a nurse tending to their care called for an insurance card or signature. It was a responsibility I not only cherished, I owned. After Reat's murder, when one of his classmates at a restaurant or grocery store recognizes me with a quizzical look and then a hesitant ... "Are you Reat Underwood's mom?" I am quick to smile and engage them in conversation and sometimes a full on hug. As the words from Mahnaz reached me, "reach out to Reat Underwood's mom," she had me.

Here is how Mahnaz reached out to Pastor Hamilton via email:

> Dec, 6, 2014, 8:46 a.m.
>
> From: Mahnaz Shabbir
>
> Hello Adam. I hope you and your family are doing well.
>
> I am helping with the Abid Samad Sheikh-Hussein (15 years of age) who was killed two days ago in front of the Somali Community Center's memorial service. We thought it would be helpful to have Reat Underwood's mother be at the vigil as well. Would you send me her contact information? Also, if you are available tomorrow at 1:40 (I know Sundays are busy for you)—that would be wonderful as well to say a few words of comfort and religious solidarity. This young man was the son of the Imam at Masjid Al Taqwa. The vigil will begin at 1:40 at Masjid Al Taqwa (Somali Center). Thank you.
>
> Mahnaz Shabbir

I am honored to hear that they want me to come to the vigil for their friend, as a representative of my own boy.

Again, I am struck by the irony of his age. He was 15. Reat would have been 15. That fact plays like a recording over and over in my head. It seems so simple, really. Reat should be alive and so should Abdisamad.

They were both murdered because of their faith (or in Reat's case, what was believed to be his faith).

This has to stop.

I agree to attend Abdisamad's vigil without asking any family members how they feel about this, namely my husband. Len has agreed to attend or watch me attend numerous vigils in the past eight months and hasn't balked at one. Today, he is not as harmonious. "Mindy, this boy was murdered because of his faith in plain sight of witnesses," Len warns. "There might be others like him who target the vigil." Len was fearful for my safety.

Fear. I hadn't thought about fearing for my own life. Len reminds me that we have a 12-year-old at home who needs his mom to stay alive. Yeah, I know this. I am still not fearful. I know I need to be there.

It's not that I felt bulletproof. I simply didn't think about dying myself or being a target for anyone. I was simply trying to live the best I could. If my attending this vigil could help Abdisamad's parents and family and other teenagers, I would attend.

Life can throw pretty much anything at me, and it cannot be any worse than what I've already experienced.

Honestly, if death comes knocking, I know it will transport me to be with Reat and Dad. That doesn't sound too bad.

Len isn't happy with me, but also doesn't have the energy to fight. Common for anyone experiencing a tragedy is exhaustion. I was taking advantage of his exhaustion, at this moment.

I call my mom and my younger brother, Tony, to let them know I will be attending the Muslim vigil. Not wanting me to attend alone, they offer to join me.

Now that I am planning to walk into a mosque for the first time in my life, the hairs on my neck prickle and my heart races. I wonder about the appropriate dress for a Muslim vigil. I'm not concerned about my appearance. I am at a loss as to what their religious and cultural standards are for a vigil, for a woman at a vigil.

So I do what anyone else would do, I Google. I Google, "What to wear to a mosque." Then I give Mahnaz a quick call to confirm I can

wear pants. Pretending to know more than I do, I let her know about
my plan to wear a head scarf and ask for confirmation. Mahnaz con-
curs with the expectation of me and all women entering the mosque
to have our heads covered. She explains that the Islamic faith instructs
men and women to dress modestly. Telling me that these scarves are
called hijabs ("hi" with a short "i" and "jobs"). She assures me it doesn't
matter what kind of scarf I wear, but that my mother and I should
cover our hair.

With this small amount of confirmation regarding my apparel, I
quickly become apprehensive about not understanding the difference
between Muslim and Islam. These two words were used by Pastor
Hamilton and now Mahnaz. Are they interchangeable?

In June 2014, language such as "Islamic State," could be heard on
the radio as a band of deviants were raising hell in another part of the
world. Islamic State of Iraq and Syria (ISIS) became more common in
our terminology when discussing all the bad, evil people and potentially places in the world. Hearing the words didn't pierce me until I
was now considering entering a mosque filled with people who called
themselves Muslim.

Yep, I Googled. What does Muslim mean?

Muslim—a follower of the religion Islam.

What does Islam mean?

Islam—the religion of Muslim people, a monotheistic faith regarded
as revealed through Muhammad as the Prophet of Allah. Islam is one
of the three Abrahamic faiths.

I felt stupid. I had never had a reason to know the meaning of these
words.

Mom is driving the three of us to the vigil. Seated in the front
passenger side of the car, with Tony in the back seat, fear creeps in as
I wonder how to appropriately and compassionately encounter this
family. The tables have turned on me. In this experience, I am the one
coming to offer my condolences. The death is still new to them. Hell,
the deaths we experienced are still new to me, almost eight months
after our fateful day. Right now, Abdisamad's family has foggy brain,
are in shock and are wandering through disbelief. How am I going to
help them? Perhaps it was a bad idea for me to be present.

Thinking of how people often appear and act when they encounter me, I pause. The uncertainty about what to say and what not to say regarding the tragedy is written all over them. Every person who has encountered me since the murders has never known exactly what to say. How could they? How could I know?

Feeling overwhelmed by these thoughts, I share my concerns with my mother by saying, "What do I say to his mourning parents and siblings?" My mom tries to reassure me with, "Mindy, you always know what to say. I am sure your presence alone will be helpful to them. That is all they are asking of you."

In an area of Kansas City we have not frequented, let alone ever driven, my anxiety finds me. The coldness I felt after I saw my dad's body in the parking lot and my heart racing have become more commonplace in my body since April 13, 2014. I am praying that Len was not correct about further retaliation at this location. His warning comes to the forefront of my mind, "You have a living son who needs his mom." Suddenly, I feel vulnerable.

From the outside, the building is much smaller than I expected. I had not thought about what a Somali Center or a mosque should look like; but if I had, this would not have been it. Immediately, I thought about the Christian churches I have visited from Oklahoma to California, to my current home in Kansas. The vast array of worship sanctuaries, chapels, and even outdoor revival tents did not prepare me for what is in my sight. A sadness came over me. A sadness I didn't have the capacity to understand. Where is God found? Is God in the cross hanging in a church? Is God to be found in a park with people gathered singing joyfully or perhaps, mournfully? The young boy murdered, Abdisamad, had his life taken after he said 'prayers,' in this building. Surely, God is here, too.

December in the heartland isn't helping my mood either. The day is chilly and gray. The clouds are covering any chance of sunshine to brighten our spirits and warm our faces. It is as if the weather is aware of our somber mood.

This is a vigil for a teenage boy, murdered in cold blood. I am saddened to see few people arriving. The trickle of cars and the lack of people exiting them angers me. My mind takes me to the hundreds or so people lining the street outside of Dad and Reat's funeral. Thirty-two hundred humans filled the Church of the Resurrection. We heard that over a thousand others watched the funeral online. Where is the outcry for this young man?

Initially, I am aware that we are the only white people filing into the mosque.

My exploration of how to dress for attending a mosque had not taught me that we would need to take off our shoes. Luckily, I wore socks and some flats with my pants. We watch as others take off their shoes and place them in the corner of the entryway. As I am slipping off my shoes, curiosity creeps in. How will we find our shoes when it is time to leave? There are no cubbies or other organizational system, just a pile of shoes. Sort of like being at a gym filled with trampolines and long ropes to swing back and forth until you drop into a pile of sponges ... this is how I feel right now. I feel vulnerable and out of place. Removing my shoes makes me feel defenseless. It seems wearing shoes allowed me to have the confidence to believe I can run away, if necessary. Now, without shoes, any escape is hampered.

Taking off our shoes and wearing a head covering: these two acts of respect are needed and meaningful to the Muslims around us. They are uncomfortable for me.

Proceeding through the small entryway, we are immediately in a large room. It reminds me of a living room. To our right, a group of men are standing. Nope, now they are on their knees praying. Paying no attention to the flow of people steadily streaming into what I would think is their "prayer space," the men are now in a prostrate position. They look as if a yoga class were ending and they all went into child's pose on command. Standing and kneeling on sheets and towels, they do not allow their feet to touch the carpet. Should my feet be touching the carpet? We keep walking, following the flow of women to a space that looks as if it is receiving us.

Metal chairs are set up in the middle of the room in a classroom setting. The chairs are facing a podium and a window is in the back wall behind the podium. We wonder where we are supposed to wait for the vigil. We slowly move toward the empty chairs. As we move in that direction, a beautiful woman approaches. She radiates beauty and kindness. Wearing her hijab, her face is pronounced and beautiful. Her eyes are sad.

As she walks toward us, I feel grateful that someone has spotted the clueless and uncomfortable white people. This woman is clearly coming to rescue us and offer us the correct place to sit. The entire space is too small for us to have sneaked in, found a seat and stayed incognito. As her eyes meet mine, she asks, "Are you Reat Underwood's mom?" There it is again. My ghostly badge of honor, 'Reat Underwood's mom.'

"Yes, I am," I answer with my best gentle smile.

When I hear Reat's name said by anyone, I smile to some extent. The love I have for him isn't only in my heart, it is all of me. Losing Reat, I lost part of myself. Hearing Reat's name is painful, real and helpful, all in the same moment.

A piece of paper is handed to me by this lovely, sad-eyed woman. As my eyes glance down at the sheet of paper, I notice it is a program for the vigil. "Do you know when you speak?" are her next words.

My name. I see it. There is my name on this piece of paper, this program. The words my mom said to me in the car, "I am sure your presence alone will be helpful to them. That is all they are asking of you," are like a drum beat in my ears. I am certain all the blood in my body rushes to my head. I begin to sweat and feel my face becoming flush. "Excuse me?" I ask, hoping somehow the lines of communication have been crossed.

"Do you know when you speak?" she repeats, "We have you speaking sixth, after a 'Message from the Islamic Community.' See, here is your name," she says as she points to the program.

She is correct. My name is listed as the sixth presenter in black ink.

Questions begin to circulate in my head. What happened to "the teenagers want Reat Underwood's mom to be present?" Where are those teenagers, anyway? What is Islam? What is Muslim? What is going on? My heart is racing. I feel insecure about my complete lack of knowledge regarding this family's faith. The chairs no longer feel like safe spots. I am staring at the podium and reeling at the idea of speaking to a completely unfamiliar crowd. My mom repeats a sentiment that is now familiar, "You always know what to say, Mindy. Whatever it is, it will be just fine."

My agenda for the vigil has just shifted significantly. And wouldn't you know it, more people have arrived. People of color, white people, I see someone with a white turban. From where did these people come? Were they all truly this quiet or was the pounding of my nervous heart beating too loudly to notice a full room of people from different backgrounds?

Quickly taking a seat, I begin my research. Hello again, Google. "What is Islam?" I dig deeper this time. I learn that there are five pillars of Islam. Who am I kidding? There is not one Bible verse that comes to mind without notable prompting. How do I expect to inhale five pillars of a religion I only recently felt the need to explore? I'm curious to understand if they believe in Heaven. That knowledge will be crucial in formulating whatever I might be able to say.

Another beautiful woman walks up to me while I am cursing my lack of awareness and knowledge. Mahnaz, who passed the "teenager invitation" to me, introduces herself. I feel as if I already know her from our phone call, but I am grateful to put a face with a name. We hug as if we're old friends. All vulnerability aside, I express my anxiety to Mahnaz.

"Mahnaz, did you know they're expecting me to speak?" I ask.

With wide eyes, she responds, "No! I didn't! Did somebody else contact you—other than me?"

No one else had contacted me. Only beautiful woman No. 1 with sad eyes, whose name I couldn't pronounce or remember, had handed me the program and announced that I was to speak sixth.

With a loving smile, she responds, "You will know the right thing to say." She sounds like my mom.

"Mahnaz, can you help me out?" I ask with urgency. "Do you believe that Abdisamad is in Heaven?"

Without hesitation, she confidently replies, "Yes, without a doubt." She explains, "He was strong in his faith, a good young man. I am sure that Allah, *subhanahu wa ta al*, would make sure he is in Heaven."

"OK," I say, feeling relieved. I can work with that. I know a lot about Heaven. However, I don't know much about Allah, and why did she insert the phrase *subhanahu wa ta al*? I know nothing. That's not true, I know that I know nothing about this religion, this faith.

(I have since learned that *subhanahu wa ta al* means 'Allah the most glorified, the most high.' In the moment I understood only the word Heaven in our conversation.)

The vigil is beginning. I take my seat next to my mom, bow my head and offer up a quiet prayer. In times of great stress, other than THE most stressful day of my life, I try to remember to recite the Lord's Prayer.

Once, on a trip to Mexico when our boys were ages 8 and 5, Reat got very ill. He vomited over and over during the night ... no fever, just vomit. After each bout of expulsion, I would wipe his face, neck and any other areas splattered with the muck and then pull his mostly naked body into mine and repeat the Lord's Prayer over and over. My memory tells me we did this about four times until I woke up, realizing that I woke up on my own, without his vomit-convulsing body waking me. The peace that came over me each time that I said the prayer calmed my nerves, which in turn calmed Reat.

Since the murders of Dad and Reat, I have been asked "to say a few words" here and there. I always think that I have nothing new to say, which causes my heart to race. Therefore, I take the time to recite the Lord's Prayer before I speak. In email conversation with Mahnaz about this chapter, she offered that the Lord's Prayer is very close to the first prayer in the Quran (sounds like 'kr-aan'), called Al Fat eha—The Opening. Mahnaz has been a source of wisdom and friendship for me since our initial phone call. I also learned from her that the Quran is the Islamic holy book. In similar fashion, the Torah holds the Jewish scriptures and the Bible is the holy book of Christians.

Reciting this prayer quiets my mind, allowing the Holy Spirit to give me something to say.

In this moment, in a mosque, I recite the Lord's Prayer in my mind.

> Our Father Who art in heaven, hallowed be thy name.
> Thy kingdom come, thy will be done, on earth as it is in
> heaven. Give us this day our daily bread, and forgive us
> our trespasses, as we forgive those who trespass against us.
> Lead us, not into temptation, but deliver us from evil. For

thine is the kingdom and the power and the glory for ever. Amen.

I say the prayer, wait a moment and continue with an open heart to God and another request of Him.

Here I am, Lord. Help me be the servant you need me to be. Thank you for giving my heart peace when it needs peace. Please guide my words tonight because they aren't really mine. They're Yours. In other words, help me get through this and not screw something up that You would like to have happen. Amen.

My armpits are sweaty and my neck is hot. I don't recall many details about what is said by the other speakers, but I remember a service filled with the unknown. Our classroom-style chairs had filled to capacity, which made me feel good for Abdisamad's family. Mom, Tony and I are no longer the only white faces, although white faces are the minority. It was still too small of a gathering for the heinous crime, but it was a vigil and vigils are needed.

Someone read from the Quran. Sometimes I hear this pronounced "Kr-aan." Other times I hear it pronounced without the hard K, sounding like "Hr-aan." My previous recollection with the Quran was draped in bombings and shootings from the news. The news that told me Muslims want me dead. I wonder to myself what we, clueless Christians, are doing, sitting in a mosque in these metal chairs with no shoes. Why were the Muslims trusting of us? I suppose I know why they trust me. I'm Reat Underwood's mom. How did these relationships between the other white people and the Muslims who opened their community center doors, spark?

A group of people now make their way to the front of the room. A diverse racial, gender and seemingly religious group walk to the front of the classroom chairs, forming a semicircle. The diversity catches my eye while my heart begins to calm itself, allowing my brain to pay attention. They explain to their audience that each of them represent a different faith. There are 12 of them. I'm struck by the fact that I'm not even aware of 12 different faiths.

They read Scriptures from various texts. They hold hands and pray. A beautiful display of unity. I wonder what group they represent. Looking in the same program that has my name listed as speaking sixth, I find that they are the Greater Kansas City Interfaith Council.

What does "interfaith" mean? If this is a council of people who represent different faiths, why are they together? What do they do? Do they help people? Did they come to our vigil when Reat and Dad died? Did they come to our funeral?

My mind is captured and my heart is racing as I yearn to understand more about this group. The insatiable anxiety becomes satiable as my attention transitions to figure out this group of people. My eyes are drawn to each of them as they depart, walking to the back of the room. Thinking about how I might get in contact with their leader, I hear my name announced from the microphone.

It's my turn to speak.

The podium is almost my height. On the bright side, since I didn't know I was speaking, I don't have any notes to place on it. I take the microphone off the podium, face the audience and stand with my left side next to the podium.

Introducing myself, I explain that, in April, I lost my father and son to "hate." I explain that I know Dad and Reat are in Heaven and that I find comfort in the expectation that I will see them again. I tell the audience I know Abdisamad is in Heaven, too. I tell them we all need to join together—regardless of race, religion and culture—to end this horrible violence.

As I walk back to my seat, I exchange glances with several people. They have tears in their eyes and empathetic smiles on their faces. When I sit back down, my mom and brother simultaneously reach to comfort me by patting me on the shoulder and knee. They assure me I offered relevant and meaningful words for the occasion.

My brain feels empty, like the slate of a whiteboard just cleaned. I can feel my heart pumping in my temples. I know I spoke from my heart, but I already can't remember what I said. I want to ask Tony to remind me what I had said; but the quiet vigil continues, so it's not an opportune time for me to think about me. More Scripture from the Quran is read and people continue to weep all around us. The room is enveloped in grief, a depth of sadness I am only learning to understand myself.

After the vigil ends, a beautiful young girl in a full burka approaches. Her face peeks through the opening. She introduces herself as Asha Sheikh-Hussein, Abdisamad's sister. She is completely surrounded by her family as we engage in conversation. Her mother, father, younger brother and grandmother are all standing at her sides. Her father holds the middle space, but she stands close to interpret.

As Abdisamad's father begins to speak, I reach out to shake his hand. Despite my reach, he continues to hold his hands, one over the other, close to his belly. I leave my hand extended, assuming he will eventually shake it. After an awkward pause settles over us, I realize this custom must not be appropriate. Slowly, I lower my hand.

Mahnaz appears on my left and interrupts the silence. She offers words of encouragement for Abdisamad's family and for my family. As others join our circle, Mahnaz quietly offers me some insight that Muslim men might not offer their hands to women who are not part of their immediate family. I am thankful for her explanation and am able to manage the rest of my interactions with a better understanding of how to properly greet any Muslim man in the room.

This vigil, and all that it entailed, increases the fragment of a desire I have been harboring to understand other faiths. I don't merely want to understand; there is a yearning in me to help bridge the gap between them. Never far from my thoughts is the fact that a man who hated Jews, enough to kill them, murdered my father and son. What, if anything, am I to do about this?

Intrigued and honored to have been invited to speak, I find myself greeting many of the attendees. Peaceful, gracious and thoughtful are words that come to mind as each person, most of them Muslim, introduces themselves. Stupid is how I feel as I struggle to pronounce the names I hear.

Several people from the Greater Kansas City Interfaith Council introduce themselves. They represent various faiths: Jewish, Buddhist, Hindu and Muslim. There is one Christian too. I realize we are definitely the minority in this setting.

A group of teenagers is huddled up in the center of the room. There they are. Those teens who wanted "Reat Underwood's mom" to be present. I assume they are the friends of Abdul, Abdisamad's brother, who had asked for my presence. I walk slowly to the group and thank them for inviting me. Their eyes are weary from little sleep and many tears. Empathy rises up as I remember the grief-stricken faces of Reat's friends on the days after his death. A mother's concern is on my face and most likely out of my mouth to Abdul, who has lost his brother. I'm fumbling, unsure of myself but clear that I would welcome a conversation with him if he so chooses. Considering my own precious pre-teen, Lukas, I am ready to leave. It is time for me to be with my own boy, embracing him with my love and caring for his broken heart.

One boy explains that they would like to host a walk in memory of Abdisamad. I ask them to please contact me as I would like to help and attend.

Mom, Tony and I walk toward the entryway and gather our shoes. I feel silly because there was no problem locating my flats. Quietly slipping them on, shame flutters in my heart. As we walk out the door, I find myself looking up and down the street for something. There were no police, no gunman or any others raising a ruckus at the idea of Muslims grieving. I suppose I was looking for a sign that this event truly took place. Once safely in our car, we all breathe a collective heavy sigh.

Looking at my shoes, now on my feet, I relive each moment from the time we exited our car to now, while Mom drives each of us home. Did this just happen? Did we just attend a vigil at a mosque? Did I speak to a group of grieving Muslims, who grieved in the same way as me and for the same reason? Did I recite the Lord's Prayer, albeit in my head, in a mosque? I wasn't harassed, targeted or threatened in any way. Our commonality of loss, tragic loss had brought us together. Our humanity was highlighted.

It all feels surreal.

I left feeling more filled up than I had felt when I arrived. This family and community had asked for my help and I had provided what I could. What if each of us provided help to another, when asked? Even as uncertainty, anxiety and trepidation swirled around me, I answered their request.

I offered of myself what they needed, with the grace of God. Or, with the grace of Allah? Yes and yes, I would soon learn.

Top Left: Lukas with his Harrison cousins, Brandon, Hayden and Zsa Zsa in Dallas, Texas. While not in the photograph, Stewie Griffin also made this trip. Family photo. July 14, 2014.

Top Right: A simple shopping excursion produced what has become a meaningful memory for Lukas. Bass Pro Shop in Olathe, Kansas with his Popeye. Family photo. 2013

Bottom: Mindy and her family, attempting to suppress their pain of a Thanksgiving holiday without Popeye and Reat, volunteered to serve others instead. From left: Melinda Corporon, Lukas Losen, Tony Corporon, Mindy Corporon, Len Losen, Barbara Fox, Dana Corporon with Andrew and Katy Corporon at a local food pantry and kitchen in downtown Kansas City, Missouri. Family photo. Thanksgiving Day, 2014.

Lukas leaving a message for his Popeye. Photograph by
Joe Shalmoni Photojournalist, © April 18, 2014.

22

Part One: Our Teen in Crisis

On November 28, 2020, my 18-year-old son, Lukas Losen, tells me during an interview for my December *Real Grief—Real Healing with Mindy Corporon* podcast, "Major grief events, major life events that happen definitely can alter you; but it's all about how you handle it. It's all about how you take it and it's a lot on the people around you. You really see who your friends are when stuff like that happens. If you have the right people around you, then you can get over it quicker. If you have the wrong people around you, you may never even move forward. And you always have to have support. I've had a really good support system, so I was able to get over it."

Immediately, I had mixed emotions. 'Oh baby', I want to interrupt him and say, 'You will never get over it'. But these are the words he used, they are not my words. This is Lukas' story, not mine. My heart began to overflow with love, mixed with a familiar sadness as I heard him use the words "If you have the right people around you."

In the Overland Park Regional Medical Center emergency room on April 13, 2014, Rabbi Jonathan Rudnick found Lukas. "Both chronos and kairos, unfolded. He was the only youth there in a room full of people. He was there, yet he was alone, alone in the middle of adult chaos," the rabbi shared with me. The ancient Greeks had two words for time, chronos and kairos. The former refers to chronological time, while the latter focuses on time as an opportune moment. The tick, tick, ticking of the clock sped up like a Bugatti Veyron Super Sport— the fastest car in the world. I'm told it can go from 0 to 60 in 2.4 seconds. As a Kansas City Chiefs' football fan, I am familiar with wide receiver Tyreek Hill who can run the 40-yard dash in 4.29 seconds. Considering these two examples hopefully makes your heart race and aligns you closely to how we felt after hearing that Reat, Lukas' older brother by two years and ten months, had also not survived.

The unimaginable had just been spoken.

Lukas remembers his childhood babysitter, Laura Carley, being at the hospital. Laura and her father, Richard (my business partner in Boyer Corporon Wealth Management), enveloped Lukas during the most vulnerable time in his life. We had not only lost Lukas' grandfather to a violent murder, we had also now lost Reat, his only sibling. Within hours, other family friends became part of a tribe caring for Lukas. "They basically took care of me for the next few days along with tons of friends and my mom's friends, my mom's clients, too, and the Women Who Mean Business, this fabulous organization that my mom was involved in, I mean, oh my goodness. It seemed as if 60 women were at our house every day just begging to take a preteen to lunch and dinner. Everyone took care of me for the next few days." Regarding April 13, in particular, Lukas shares, "I remember we wound up at my grandma's at some point. The head pastor of the church that we go to showed up. He was there talking to us, which I always thought that was a really big deal because he is a really big deal. He showed up to talk to us, like who were we to him? We are actually really good friends with him though, which is pretty cool. And that's honestly all that I remember of that day."

Only a few days after Dad and Reat were murdered, Lukas desperately wanted a few items from his school locker. Part of our family's caring tribe, our friend Kathy Schikevitz, drove him to school. This was the conversation she recalled. "One of my most vivid memories was helping Lukas. He really wanted to get his University of Oklahoma hoodie out of his locker at school. As we drove up to the school he said to me, 'My brother was always the popular one, and so confident. I was looking forward to being at the same school with him. I don't know what I'll do without him.' Walking into the school, Lukas' friends and other students were quick to surround him in hugs. Everyone in the school now knew who Lukas was."

Trauma can do a number on our brain chemistry and functioning. We can appear extremely operational and yet our brains are truly uninhabited for a period of time. Everyone's "time" in trauma triage differs. Lukas was loved and well liked from the beginning of school. The traumatic murders, coupled with fear, layered self-doubt and skepticism on his now fragile state of mind. There used to be information I knew, and now there are blank spaces or holes in the messaging. For a period of time, I lost the ability to compute mathematical equations, even simple addition and subtraction problems. This proved to be frustrating, considering I was the CEO of a wealth management firm.

In the week following the beautiful funeral for my father and Reat, I am sitting at our kitchen counter, desperately pleading for the world to just stop. "Please stand still. I don't think I can muster the strength to keep moving with you," is written in one of many journal entries in late April 2014. It is as if we have been placed in a pool of thick molasses and expected to walk normally through the same syrupy, heavy muck. I don't want to move, which of course makes moving in any direction all that much more difficult. Now, while in that pool of molasses, we need to figure out how to parent a 12-year-old who has just lost his brother and grandfather to murder by gunfire. Hopelessness comes to mind. Where will I find hope during this tumultuous storm of life?

Parenting is a tough job. Parenting after losing a child feels close to impossible. Learning to breathe on my own was only one step in thousands I had to take while I was parenting a hurting 12-year-old who had to be experiencing the same anguish. Losing my father and Reat was painful; parenting Lukas after their deaths had its own layered complications.

The conversation at hand is about Lukas. Len voices his desire for us to find our "new normal." He feels Lukas' "normal" is going back to school. My brain fog is heavy during these conversations about going back to school or staying home. Len had been watching me cry through each day, meandering from one room to the next like a ghost. He didn't want Lukas staying home to see more of this. Nor did he want Lukas holed up in his game room, drowning himself with car chases and scoring touchdowns on his favorite video games. I wasn't sharing my insecurity in parenting with anyone at this time. My own guilt and shame were just that, my own. Settling in my gut was the reality that Dad and Reat were at the Jewish Community Center because of my planning. I scheduled the audition for April 13. It was me who chose the 1:30 p.m. audition slot. The turmoil inside my body was excruciating and not shared with anyone for over a year. Having little mental strength or resolve, I agreed to send Lukas back to his sixth grade classes at Blue Valley Middle School.

As a preteen, Lukas didn't know how to manage the myriad of emotions that had been thrust upon him. While we had involved Lukas in Little League baseball, lacrosse, flag football and Scouting, we had not previously signed him up for "grief 101" or "how to cope with significant loss." There was no question that Lukas was so broken and sad that he could have benefitted from staying at home, snuggled next to me, watching a movie or two. Len believed school—and his friends there—might be the key to Lukas beginning to resume life as a normal kid. This sounds plausible. This sounds like good parenting and it places Lukas in someone else's care for several hours each day. Those someones were not as broken as his mom, who needed some space to collect herself.

In the evenings, Lukas worked to pull us together the best way he knew how ... through comedy. He wanted all three of us to sit together and watch movies ... but only comedies. He demanded only comedies because he was searching for our laughs. I am careful not to tell him that a smile was difficult for me to find, let alone a laugh. However, after sitting through pretty much every Will Ferrell movie together, it dawns on me that this is Lukas's path for personal healing; and he is helping to ease the pain for all three of us through laughter. His unconscious intuition is insightful.

Still wrestling with the deep fear that accompanies losing a child, I am seeking a physical connection with Lukas. The shooting robbed me of parenting my Reat. His life, taken in such a rapid and dramatic way ... I was left breathless, aching and desperately longing for more time to be his mom. This reality has caused me to want every moment with Lukas to constitute "quality time." I want to connect with him through closeness, snuggles, reading together, talking about anything and experiencing new memories together. Lukas wants none of this, at least from me. He had always gravitated towards Len, and this attraction to and desire for his dad's attention is noticeably increasing.

During this same time in our lives, our male friends provided a caring hedge of protection around Len. They were well meaning as they picked him up in the early evenings for dinner and drinking. I expect Len had shared with them the misery I portrayed daily at our kitchen table, reading one sympathy card after another until I reached 14 cards each day. Because we received hundreds of cards, this "pushing-through-grief" process went on for weeks. I can imagine he was looking for an escape. The escape came with red wine and late nights. While I so appreciated their loyalty and support for Len, I worried about how often he was numbing his sadness with alcohol. Again, having barely the strength for myself and placing Lukas second only to my basic physical needs, there was no complaining from me to Len about his chosen path for grieving. During the daytime, we slowly drifted into our own rooms of the home, outlining physically that we had chosen different paths for grieving the loss of our child.

Reat had been my person and I had been his. It was typical when the four of us went anywhere that Reat sat next to me and Lukas sat next to Len. There was hardly a question when we boarded a carnival ride as to who would sit with whom. Dinner tables found us doing the same. However, any time we flew on an airplane, I got both boys while Len sat in his own row. Hmmm. Was it only because Reat shared my hazel eyes and dimples that we were so close? No, my heart aches recalling the depth of our relationship and that of mine with my father and my father with Reat. We were each other's person, no questions asked. Now, with Lukas seeking Len's attention over mine and Len finding solace with friends, wine and Lukas in return, I am alone in my own home ... even when we are all there.

We breathe a sigh of relief when school let out for summer, only weeks after the murders and funeral of two family members we should not have lost. The final weeks of Lukas' sixth grade year were a nonevent for his brain. He showed up only physically, which—for the time being—we and his teachers were agreeable to.

Somehow, the summer months made their way through our calendar without us noticing much. We did leave our home for the July 4th weekend to see "the cousins:" Kim, Jon, Hayden, Brandon and Zsa Zsa Harrison, at their lake home near Dallas. Len basically packed our bags and gave us the date and time of departure. Lukas was more than willing to leave our sorrowful home, but unwilling to prepare himself in any way. I, on the other hand, allowed fear and a new trepidation of meeting people who didn't know our story, to convince me that I could live in our home and stay in our community of people we knew for the foreseeable future. The first panic attack I recall ever having in my life occurred as I buckled my seat belt to leave our home, for another state, knowing that the reason Reat wasn't with us had nothing to do with him being at summer camp. He was dead.

As quickly as I could, the buckle came off; and I shouted to Len and Lukas as I jumped out of the car, "I have to get something." Having no idea what I might be retrieving from our home, I was up the stairs and in Reat's bedroom, frantically looking for something to give me solace before my own brain could surmise what my heart was leading us to. Lukas needed to leave our home for a while. Len demanded we leave our home and drive to Texas. Frightened of this new reality of living with just the three of us, or the two of them and me, I stopped in the middle of my boy's bedroom and stood still. "Reat, I am so sorry. We are leaving for Texas without you. I am so sorry, honey. Please help me with this. Could you please help me take the next step?" And then, my eyes settled on a stuffed doll on Reat's bed. It was a doll from a popular cartoon that Reat watched. He had won the doll at an amusement park when he was with his dad, Gary. Grabbing the doll quickly, running back down the stairs and remembering to reset our alarm and lock our doors, my mind is noticeably clearer. Lukas watches me curiously while I buckle this doll into the backseat next to him. "Stewie!" Lukas says out loud. "So, that's what you needed to get, Stewie?" he asks. Now, realizing the doll has a name, I go with it and act as normal as possible. I responded, "Well, yes. I think it will help us all if Stewie takes this trip with us, since Reat can't be here."

Len says nothing during my entire escape and return. I buckle up and as we drive away from our home, I know the pain will follow me; but somehow I know Reat and perhaps Dad are with me, too.

Here is what I realized in 2020, as I was finalizing this paragraph about Stewie needing to come with us on this particular trip: Stewie's full "fictional" name is Stewie GRIFFIN. I didn't know this until I confirmed how to spell his first name ... yes, the name of the doll. Reat's name is Reat GRIFFIN. This is but one of over a thousand "messages" or God Winks I've received since April 13, 2014.

The first day of Lukas' seventh grade year (which should have marked the beginning of Reat's sophomore year) sends me into a deep depression. I didn't realize how difficult it would be to watch Lukas walk into school and not have the opportunity to watch Reat do the same. Caught completely off guard by the unexpected depth of grief that accompanied me that day after dropping Lukas off at his middle school, my car seemed to drive itself to our friends' home.

Jeri and Josh, who were my drivers to and from the vigil on the night of the murders, have provided steadfast support throughout the past several months. They welcomed me in and allowed me to sob as I desperately pleaded to have my son back. I know my unplanned visit is causing them to be late to work, but there is no mention of it. They sit with me as the pain pulses through my body. I'm familiar with this painful process of grief by now. The panic arrives initially and then followed by a fear that I can't place. My heart rate increases quickly, as if struggling to keep up with my frantic, racing thoughts. Breathing becomes difficult and gasping for air is common. My soul is shattered and ripped apart, and I have no choice but to break down in tears. Somehow, each river of tears paves a path for calm. Crying, and then laughing, through several camping memories that come to mind of Reat, Jeri and Josh help this particular episode find an ending. The sorrow will continue, but the panic and fear have subsided.

Because crying is still a daily ritual for me, I notice Lukas' lack of tears. He doesn't cry much anymore and I start to worry that he is shutting down emotionally in order to avoid the pain of grief. On the outside he appears to be fine, which is exactly how I tend to appear.

Six and half years into this journey I know that the outside is a farce. Knowing what is going on inside is key—it's crucial to our survival.

In August 2014, we received a warning, a "red flag," about how Lukas was processing his grief. At about the exact same time, one year prior, with Reat and Lukas in tow, we were visiting the George W. Bush Presidential Center on the Southern Methodist University campus in Dallas, Texas, when Lukas doubled over in enough pain that we rushed him to Children's Medical Center of Dallas. We suspected an angry appendix causing the problem, but a CT scan found Lukas had an obstructed bowel. He was in surgery within an hour. Lukas and I spent three nights under great care and when he was released, Len and Reat had decided our summer trip was over and we drove home.

Now, his mention of severe stomach pain takes the three of us to Children's Mercy Hospital in downtown Kansas City, Missouri. My journal notes from August 26, 2014, read, "Yesterday, Lukas had severe stomach pains like he did last summer. Len took him to the Children's Mercy ER. His urine and blood were normal and they processed a CAT scan. This scan revealed swollen or enlarged lymph nodes on the opposite side of where he is feeling pain." Due to his previous colon obstruction surgery, Lukas was admitted for observation. The doctors were considering a colonoscopy, but also were waiting for fluids and a special cocktail to rally his bowels into action. When a long-awaited bowel movement arrived, we were released with instructions for him to take Miralax as a daily regimen. My journal notes continue on August 29, "Lukas made it through the entire day of school!"

Thankfully, Lukas' teachers are supportive and patient with him as he becomes a daily fixture in the office of his school counselor, Candy Moore. And our dear friend and his principal, Roxana Rogers Lemon, welcomes Lukas into her office at any time with no questions asked. Lukas manages to spend more time with Candy and Roxana than in the classroom.

Lukas is not unruly; he has just decided not to be in class often, or at all. Engaged only in seventh grade football after quitting lacrosse and Scouting, Lukas floats through school.

My grieving process was to busy myself and pull others along with me. In late September, I joined my two friends Kathy and Lori for a sprint triathlon in Lost Pines, Texas. In early October, my mother accompanied me to a speaking presentation in front of the KC Medical Society. And late October found us spending money with wild abandon on tickets to attend several of the Kansas City Royals' home games, as they marched through the World Series playoffs against the San Francisco Giants. In between these two experiences we were honored in Washington, D.C., by the Anti-Defamation League at their 20th annual In Concert Against Hate. It was a marvelous trip. My mother, her sister (my aunt) Barbara Fox, a large gathering of the LaManno family, my cousin Cecelia Prewett and her husband, Will Nuckols, attended. Dear friends, Shirley Doyle and Sharon and Mike Davis, who have played key roles in our lives and in this memoir, were able to share with us in the magnitude of tragedy and celebration of life that was captured in in song, prose and music. The event itself was fabulous and heart wrenching at the same time.

My ability to live through memories, the stories of April 13 and all the details has always presented differently than any other family members. I can only surmise this to be so because I found Dad and Reat in the parking lot. Feeling as if I was with them when they lost their lives, I have placed a responsibility on myself to carry their story to others for purposes of clarity and education. In doing so and perhaps as often as I share the details of their murders, I can speak to the story without seeming as though it causes too much distress. As our story was being told in song and prose, Lukas became quite upset. I had hoped he would see the value in their story being told to this audience and forgot that his 12-year-old mind might shut down based on the trauma inflicted upon him. Lukas was rescued by Cecelia, as she leaned into our row offering to take him out of the auditorium for a walk.

Having Dad, Reat and Terri honored along with our families meant a great deal to us. We were thankful for the opportunity to meet other honorees, such as Jacqueline Murekatete, founder of the nonprofit Genocide Survivors Foundation. At the age of 9, she lost her entire immediate family and most of her extended family in the 1994 Rwandan genocide. She has since become a lawyer, married and is a mother of two. Meeting Jacqueline and her husband was a highlight for us all, especially for Lukas. We were in need of something or someone to help him engage in any planned activity. JB, Jacqueline's husband, was fond of Lukas. Over dinner, I could see Lukas coming out of his angered stance and opening up to their personal story. Lukas had lost his grandfather and brother, a horrible tragedy. He now listened to Jacqueline and JB tell of all the people they lost during the Rwandan genocide. Incomprehensible. Knowing he was not alone in grieving his own family members, Lukas connected with both of them immediately.

From the White House to the Crime and Punishment Museum (which now looks humorous in the same sentence), Lukas complained with each step. Hungry every hour, he would not allow anything to satisfy or calm him. He quieted only when we walked into the United States Holocaust Memorial Museum, almost as if the angels in the room summoned him to do so. Lukas raced through the museum with little interest, and we lost track of him for about 20 minutes. It was when he appeared in front of me with red cheeks and tears flowing down them that I focused on the pain inside his heart, the pain he refused to mention. Lukas had found the exhibit displaying the shoes of the victims. Grabbing me by the hand, he pulled me past exhibits I had yet to see and placed me in front of the shoe exhibit. "Were they all killed for the same reason as Popeye and Reat?" he whispered.

Finally, a discussion about their deaths presented itself. Our arguing about where and what to eat and about which is the next museum or tour all came to a stop. We sat on the floor next to the shoes and talked about how Popeye and Reat were murdered for similar reasons as the people who were murdered in the Holocaust.

As thankful as I was for the honor from the Anti-Defamation League and all the pomp and circumstance for Dad and Reat, I could not have known Lukas needed to see the Holocaust victims' shoes to break open the shell he had built around himself.

Thanksgiving brought on another panic attack for me. Fearful of sitting down to our Thanksgiving meal without the two of them, I explained over the phone to my sweet sister-in-law Dana, Tony's wife, that Reat and Dad each needed a seat at the table. Hearing my anxiety and caring for me deeply, they created a table setting, complete with a photo including both of our loved ones. They died together and would sit together at Thanksgiving, too.

We only made it through Christmas because seemingly the rest of society, as we knew it, forced us through each damned, stinking day. Honored to carry Christ's Light for one of the Church of the Resurrection Christmas Eve services, Len carried the candle leading Lukas, Yea Yea, Tony, Dana, Andrew, Katy and me down a dark path, through a significant portion of the congregants attending and up onto a darkened stage. Mind you, this is the exact same location of the funeral held eight months prior. Christ's Light is the only light in the entire space filled with 3,200 people seeking hope, inspiration and peace this holiday season. Our broken family, chosen to represent that survival from the unthinkable can be obtained. Physically, we looked the part. Christ's Light is used to light what is called the Advent Wreath, symbolizing the passage of the four weeks of Advent. Christ's Light is then used to light one, two, three or more candles, and in turn, each of these candles light the same number. Within only minutes, we can see faces glowing in the seats near the stage as Christ's Light is now beaming back at us from 3,200 gleaming candles. Our pastors and those in attendance may have thought we were there to show them what hope and inspiration look like. Each one of us, tearful and aching with now an all too familiar pain, were filled from their light, Christ's Light. From the stage, we could see hope and inspiration in front of us, beaming with love to continue with us on our journey.

As we rounded into 2015, my relationship with Lukas was shifting in alarming ways. He was becoming more combative. Quick to anger and verbally lash out at a target, he chose me as his mark. When he wasn't watching a funny movie, it was easy for him to become enraged. Lukas was also gaining weight quickly and had grown taller than me. I still had the upper hand, but only because of my confidence as an adult. Lukas never hit me nor did he make any attempts to do so. However, I feared his ability to take an action that he could not take back if we didn't find a way to soothe his temper. In and out of what seemed like a dozen or more local counseling sessions, Lukas was diagnosed with depression and post-traumatic stress disorder. Still, he wanted nothing to do with processing his anger or grief in a formal, traditional manner.

While we didn't believe he was "all right," this is how he described himself after slamming more than a few doors in my face.

A new version of fear came to fruition when we received a call from Candy Moore, the Blue Valley Middle School counselor, in late February of 2015. My world suddenly stopped all over again.

Candy explained to me over the phone that Lukas had confided in a friend that he was contemplating suicide over the weekend. His friend told her mother, who then called Candy. A feeling of disbelief washed over me. I feel like I was taken out at the knees, again. At the moment, it reminded me of how I felt when I arrived at the parking lot of the Jewish Community Center, when I found my father and Reat. I am in a panic with seemingly less control of my life and obviously none of Lukas'.

Len received a panicked phone call from me with the same message I had heard from Candy as I ran to my car. Because he is closer to Lukas' school than I am, we agree he will pick up Lukas from school and we will meet at the South Johnson County location of Children's Mercy Hospital. Having been there numerous times for ear infections, tubes in ears, a tonsillectomy, a broken foot and most recently in August for Lukas' clogged bowels, we were too familiar.

Len and I sat in a cold, stark room as a doctor evaluated Lukas. I feel my fear turning into a myriad of other all too familiar feelings: panic, sadness and seething anger. Len verbally jabs at me for being too busy in the evenings. He explains his desire for me to be home more often. Feeling his comment as an attack on my way of grieving, I am quick to retaliate with my own verbal assault. A bubbling anger about his indulgence with friends and red wine slaps him in the face as if it were my own hand.

From my perspective, he is staying out too late with his friends, which tends to manifest itself in a pretty worthless Len the following day. I, however, am in a self-righteous place as I continue to explain that my "busyness" is changing the world, while his time away from our family is a waste of time.

This back and forth volcanic eruption of sorrow, guilt, anger and blame is interrupted when the door swings open and the doctor walks in with his evaluation of Lukas. Without mincing words, he offers simply, "Lukas should be transported to the Research Psychiatric Center." We are overwhelmed with pain as we look at each other after hearing this incredibly difficult message. Immediately, setting aside our anger at one another, we join forces as Lukas' parents to get him the help he needs.

The enormity of the situation becomes even more clear when we hear the following, "Lukas can be transported by ambulance or you can drive him there. But if you choose to take him, it's imperative that you keep the doors locked and don't stop anywhere along the route."

The last time one of our children was in an ambulance, they died. Not placing blame on anyone but the shooter, we are still wary of considering this transportation. And since Len had just arrived with Lukas by our own car, we opted to transport Lukas to this new destination in the same manner. While we wait for the approval to leave Children's Mercy Hospital South and for the necessary admittance paperwork to arrive at the Research Psychiatric Center, Len drives to a gas station to fill the tank. This was a whole new world for us. This world involves words that fill our minds with angst and trepidation unlike we had known: suicide, depression, anxiety and mental illness.

Waiting in the observation room, still at Children's Mercy Hospital South with Lukas, mostly in silence, I peer over at his sweet almost-13 face. There is no question his sadness is manifesting itself in a deep depression. His bowel difficulties, anger outbursts, lack of attention in school and now considering taking his own life, these are all indications of deep distress. I know this to be true. But how do we heal him?

The three of us had never experienced a psychiatric hospital. Upon arrival, we encounter two young boys, about Lukas' age, being taken out of a police car and into the lobby with us. Our anxiety only increases.

We check in and fill out required paperwork. Lukas is taken into a separate room for an intake evaluation. Len and I are led into a different room for an interview. Len and I both feel compelled to point out that we would not be here if our family members hadn't been murdered. We would have a healthy and happy 12-year- old. And his older brother and grandfather would be alive too.

Eventually, Lukas is released to us as they find no indication that he intends to harm himself, or us, for that matter. He is admitted as an outpatient in the teen program. They explain to us that this particular program typically lasts about nine business days. He is admitted to attend their program during school hours.

During my podcast interview with Lukas, he describes being admitted and his initial time at Research Psychiatric Center in this way, "I was admitted into an outpatient program. I went to this outpatient program, which is basically group therapy for eight hours a day. It actually did help a lot and was very interesting. The first day I showed up, it was just the diversification of everyone, all the different backgrounds, like kids from all around the state of Kansas were there. I mean, you had your high school cheerleaders, you had your football stereotypes and you had, you know, the kids that thought that they were lowlifes. It was a very interesting mix of kids. I think seeing that just made me realize like, oh, you know, life's not so bad when you realize that other people are going through what you're going through. You think that you're by yourself and you don't think that anyone else is going through it. That's when you're at your darkest place. Then I went in there and I realized even on my first day that I'm not alone, other people feel the same. And so that gave me a lot of reassurance to keep going."

Lukas slept on the floor of our bedroom for another six weeks. There was never a time we didn't allow him to find his way into the nest of our room for safety and comfort.

Most days, Len drives Lukas to and from the hospital, which takes a toll on his mental health as well. I help out when I can find flexibility in my work schedule. The importance of a solid, consistent routine feels important. It's as if we are caring for an infant, a fragile teenager, just the same. We establish new rules and habits within our home. Instructed to remove all firearms and pocket knives, we deliver these items to other family members who can store them properly. We must also arrange our schedules so that Lukas is never home alone for longer than 15 minutes, until further notice from his attending physician.

Thankfully, we all survive Lukas' nine days as an outpatient at Research Psychiatric Center. We are all better off for it, too, most importantly, Lukas.

Top Left: Blue Valley High School Principal Scott Bacon posing with Lukas and Saúl Egido after the graduation ceremony in Kansas City, Missouri. Family photo. May 2017.

Top Right: Lukas bravely moves from Kansas to Florida, enrolling at Montverde Academy in Montverde, Florida for his second semester of his sophomore year of high school. Photo courtesy of Montverde Academy. 2018

Middle Left: Lukas is sharing his PHYSICAL transformation after nine months in the Hitch Fit Online Program with personal trainer, Micah LaCerte. On location at the Hitch Fit Gym in Kansas City, Missouri. 2019

Bottom Left: Mindy is using her triathlon gear to offer a message to those hurting for one reason or another. RU stands for Reat Underwood. The Faith Always Wins Foundation promotes dialogue for the betterment of our world through kindness, faith and healing. Family photo. 2014

23

Part Two:

"The Right People Around You"

Precisely one year later and a bit closer to Lukas' 14th birthday, we were not prepared for a new major crisis involving his mental health. I received another incredibly difficult phone call from his school. Lukas' counselor, Candy Moore, is once again explaining that Lukas is sobbing uncontrollably and has a plan to take his life. It has been almost two years since Reat's death, and our only living son is still writhing in pain.

Lukas recalls this time in his life with this simple statement, "And again, I had a relapse about a year later. Both of these times were around my birthday, about a month before the anniversary of the shooting."

This time, his need for outpatient care lasted twice as long as the first, but thankfully, it proved to be a launching point for Lukas to find his way out of his dark, deep depression. After his second release from the Research Psychiatric Center, Lukas asked if he could go to the golf course. While he didn't play golf yet, his interest in anything outside of our home could be an integral component in his grieving process. Our boy was on the closest golf course within one day!

Managing the pain inflicted upon me with the sudden and violent loss of my oldest child seems to constantly be part of my shifting emotional status. My body yearns to parent someone who wants my parenting, my love. Our journeys toward healing have been a winding road, a rushing river and an angry ocean, at best. I have concerns after Lukas' second release from the medical center because I'm noticing he has become even more withdrawn from me, in particular. His outbursts toward me continue, but only when Len is out of the home. Although the medicine prescribed seems to stabilize him for school and other activities, our relationship is jagged.

Fighting for myself and praying that if I am healthier, Len and Lukas will rise with me ... I kindle a conversation from the past. In 2013, with a healthy family of four, we considered the idea of having a foreign exchange student join our family during Reat's junior year of high school. With Reat ripped from our lives and Lukas spinning out of control in front of us, we agree to host an older male teen to fill a gap, but not replace our son. On August 3, 2016, Saúl Cordero Egido arrived from Spain. We had been extremely transparent about the changing dynamics of our family in 2014, and Saúl still chose us as his American family.

We embraced Saúl as our own, again, not a replacement, but a new teen allowing our care, thoughts and attention to flow his way; and this offered Lukas a much needed break from his new role as our only child. Our dinner conversations and daily routines added new and much-needed layers of responsibilities. As a senior, in Reat's senior class at Blue Valley High School, Saúl made it possible for me to be a parent of a senior. I missed Reat and all that I was expected to provide for him. Now, with Saúl in the same high school, I was able to re-engage with Reat's friends from a different perspective. Without being the strange woman attending high school events with no child present, Saúl provided me a lifeline into being a senior parent. His presence in the senior class and the young adults, whom I had watched grow from first grade, provided me an entrance that I had felt closed with Reat's murder. Saúl's interests were different from Reat's and Lukas', which added much flavor to our lives during the two semesters his presence graced our family. Cross-country running in the fall and then track in the spring became part of our daily vernacular, of which we had never spoken about previously. As a freshman, Lukas wanted nothing to do with us. We caused him such embarrassment just by breathing, which is typical of many teens his age. However, Saúl welcomed our participation in his life, paving a way for my heart to find another path to heal.

Our first semester was difficult, mostly for Lukas. His brain had not heard or retained much information during seventh and eighth grade. Therefore, as he entered his freshman year of high school, I like to say, "The plane took off and Lukas was standing on the tarmac." Saúl helped us to buffer Lukas' emotional outbursts with guy time, throwing the football or on a gaming system in the evenings, and encouraged Lukas to join the cross-country team as a manager. Lukas' social life was holding steady while his academic prowess was nose diving. By Thanksgiving weekend of his freshman year, Lukas independently raised his white flag. He was overwhelmed, underwater and exhausted in his current academic arena, which led us to arrange the majority of Lukas' learning time to be with Accelerated Schools of Overland Park (ASOP). Blue Valley High School principal, Scott Bacon, and director, Jane Curran, of ASOP, worked with us to arrange the best possible scenario for Lukas to finish his fall semester and begin his spring semester as a dually-enrolled student.

The transition these two educators and their staff provided Lukas were monumental in saving him from what he would have felt was personal failure. Meeting him where he was, truly where his brain had stopped learning much, they embraced his loving nature, encouraging him to see daily success.

In the midst of following typical mental health protocol, I was introduced to the concepts of Shaman Healing and Eye Movement Desensitization Reprocessing (EMDR) as possible tools for our long, excruciating journey. Dr. Michelle Robin, a dear friend, chiropractor, wellness provider and author, had been part of our family's healing strategy since the tragedy. She was the first person to actually get me out of my home for a walk in nature and to help me prove to myself that I could once again walk a full mile. She also encouraged me to enter, for the second time, a women's only sprint triathlon. Barely training, I managed to complete the Win for KC 2014 triathlon in late July. There were no records set, but I finished. Physically falling into the arms of caring women at the finish line, they held me tightly, whispering words of support and encouragement. Their words and touch hydrated me as much as the drink placed in my hand. Recovering from the race was less important than recovering my life and that of Lukas' and Len's, and I had a new determination to do so.

I appreciate Michelle for her abilities to hear, believe and encourage her friends and patients to find the healing that works for them. Michelle introduced me to Crystal Jenkins and Cuky Harvey (pronounced like 'cookie'). Crystal's official title includes Director of Teacher Training at the Hoffman Institute, and she is a licensed clinical professional counselor (LCPC). Cuky is a traditional lomilomi practitioner.

Together, these two professional women healed Lukas from the inside out.

Because Lukas' time with his counselor, Crystal, is private, I only have the ability to share that her skill in providing EMDR therapy, her knowledge of teenagers in general and her love for my broken boy helped him find the value in himself. Every parent should have a "Crystal" in their lives.

Before the shooting, I had never heard of lomilomi and likely would have dismissed and invalidated this idea with a judgmental spirit. But when you're drowning, you're willing to grasp at anything that might hold you above water, even for one desperate breath at a time. Willing to try something new to find the internal peace I was seeking and to begin to put little pieces of Lukas back together, I made an appointment with Cuky for Lukas.

Knowing that Lukas will disregard the idea of going to a woman's home for a massage called lomilomi, I told him she was a masseuse recommended for teenagers. He and Reat were treated to a massage on a dock, under a canopy, overlooking the Caribbean when Len and I had taken the boys to Mexico for a spring break trip. I can still visualize the beauty of the day … the breeze blowing the cloths laying over their child-sized bodies, their arms dangling at the sides of the table. I wanted them to bask in the care being provided to them and to understand that our bodies are our temples. After that massage, they were both hooked.

What I wouldn't do to transport us back to that moment—with BOTH boys—in the Caribbean. This massage would look vastly different and serve a very disparate purpose. My trust in Michelle gave me confidence to step into a different world of healing.

I begin to experience Cuky's greatest gift within minutes of her time with Lukas. She can literally feel, hear and see what is going on inside her clients through her touch. Cuky explains to us that as she places her hands on her clients, she feels a streaming from the top of her head. She can accurately visualize or feel the emptiness or brokenness in her clients' bodies. Then she hears the spirit of the body, or possibly the Holy Spirit, while she is working on them.

She asks, "Spirit that you are, move into my hands. Use my hands and use my voice to heal." Cuky, through lomilomi, reconnects the spirit of the soul through deep nurturing. The nurturing softens the body, allowing the spirit to reenter and take its place for the whole self to be one again. Lomilomi has the power to move you from trauma to peace.

Cuky sees her responsibility to reach those in pain. Trauma catapults us into survival mode. Once we are able to begin to slowly make our way out of mere survival, Cuky becomes involved. She enters the healing process when we are ready to be held and touched … to heal our shattered selves.

Using the metaphor "coming upon a train wreck" to describe her work, she assesses the damage, pulls off the pieces that are shattered and laying on the ground and then determines how they need to be placed back together.

Cuky's impact on Lukas is monumental.

She positively helps him retrieve his soul, which had also been shattered. The first four sessions, Cuky doesn't touch Lukas, other than to hug him when he arrives. Explaining that he is too broken to receive the lomilomi, she has substantial work to do before he can be nurtured through touch. I know this to be true from our experiences at home. During his first several sessions, she provides nurturing, care and guidance to Lukas with chanting, singing, vibrations, prayers and speaking to his spirit. His soul begins to listen and find a path to heal.

I only attended the first two sessions with Lukas and Cuky. Weeping silently through both of them, I experienced a spiritual transcendence as his soul was being sought. She transformed the room and our time into a spiritual session that allowed each of us to realize the depth of our brokenness. She offered Lukas a path to the light—to his whole self.

After each session of primarily "energy work," I witnessed my little boy coming back. Cuky is helping Lukas find himself again. She can sense things about him and then utilizes those discoveries to help him walk through the intense fear, regret and anger that plagues his soul. Speaking life-altering, encouraging words into Lukas' soul, she tells him he is a warrior, a fierce warrior who should no longer stand in the shadowy death of his brother. She guides him to visualize a path he can take towards an individualized, healthy future.

When Cuky discerns the time is right, she lomilomis Lukas with oils, hot stones and body work. She calls her work the "nectar needed to feed the spirit and welcome it back into our bodies." She explains, "When we are traumatized emotionally or physically, the trauma ejects our spirit out of our core. Our spirit grabs onto the outside of our body and is hanging on, wrapped around to protect us. We can survive like this and many people do for the rest of their lives. If they don't allow complete healing, their spirit/soul cannot come back inside to give them peace."

Cuky describes how she restores the innate healer within each of her clients. She explains how God created us as survivors with many survival instincts. Cuky says our most effective, God-given survival mechanism is the "healer" within each of us. It guides us into the difficult work of transitioning from surviving to thriving.

With the consistent help from Crystal and Cuky, Lukas seems to be finding his way out of the dense fog. As the year progresses, although Lukas' mental health stabilizes, it is clear he struggles with learning in school, homework and attending class. I begin to consider and openly tell Len that we might examine alternative educational plans for Lukas. Not being a medical or mental health professional but his mom, I can tell there is a disconnect in his brain when it comes to learning, but I have no idea how to mend it.

Encouraged by Cuky and Crystal to feel the flow of anger and sadness leave his soul through action, Lukas started painting. He had asked for some paints, canvas and an easel for Christmas in 2015. Desperate to provide assistance and tangibly share my love for him, it was easy to oblige. Within weeks of Lukas' new interest in painting, I received a phone call from a mother of a young local artist, Jeffrey Owen Hanson. A coincidence, I think not. Julie Hanson, introducing herself to me over the phone, explained that Jeff, whom I had heard of but never met or seen in action, had taken himself to his basement art studio on April 14, 2014, one day after Dad and Reat were murdered, to paint the anger and sadness from his heart. Tormented by the murders of my father, Reat and Terri LaManno, Jeff had immediately stepped into a new creation on behalf of Reat.

Julie and Jeff's father, Hal, were watching Jeff's own sorrow and despair transform white canvas into vibrant pieces of art. His signature style, colorful layered acrylics, making deep crevices and pointed peaks, were blooming with my son's tragically ended life on his mind. Not knowing Reat personally, Jeff was trusting his own spirit and creativity until he felt it was time to learn more about the person channeling through him. Julie was calling me for several reasons. Jeff needed to know more about who Reat was than what they had learned from the news. What was his favorite color? Did he have a preferred number? Was there anything quirky or interesting Reat did? The answers spilled out of my mouth without much thought ... pink, the number 21 and he used to hold his hand in a peace sign in front of his body during photos. She went on to explain that each year Jeff created a piece of art with the intention of giving it to a nonprofit organization to hang in their location. With my details, Jeff would be able to complete this piece of art and because it was dedicated to Reat, we were being asked to choose the nonprofit organization. Two locations came to mind immediately. Operation Breakthrough and the Church of the Resurrection, both of which were ingrained in our lives from the time Reat was about 5 years old. Based on proximity of the church to our own daily living and the fact that Jeff had previously provided a piece of art to Operation Breakthrough, we easily selected the Church of the Resurrection to receive Jeff's annual gift. Because this gift was created with Reat in mind, we asked that the art be hung in the children's wing, where Reat and then Lukas had volunteered their time during church services.

During a time in Lukas' life, when he felt debilitated and blind to joy, a young man declared legally blind showed Lukas the bright colors of life. Friends, Jeff had developed a tumor on his optic nerves at the age of 6 that caused him to lose much of his sight. While Jeff couldn't see the stars in the sky, ride a bicycle or drive a car, he taught himself to paint the most brilliant, beautiful pieces of art. Jeff said, "We all face challenges. It's not the challenge, but rather your response to the challenge that defines you."

One day, in the midst of life with a hurting Lukas, the Hanson family welcomed us into their basement art studio. A tour was given, treats eaten and laughter ensued. My heart melted when Jeff asked Lukas to sit beside him as he worked on a recent creation.

Jeff's core belief is that "every act of kindness helps create kinder communities, more compassionate nations, and a better world for all, even one painting at a time."

With deep sorrow, I must share that recently, we lost our friend and shining light Jeff to a new brain tumor. On December 20, 2020, Jeff met God and I know he found Reat for one of Reat's deeply intentional hugs. Part of Jeff's story is depicted in the book, *Lessons from CLOD: An Inspiring Story of Art, Philanthropy and Entrepreneurship* written by his father, Hal Hanson, M.D.

Throughout my lifetime, I can name several people who changed the trajectory of my life and now Lukas'. The Hanson family unknowingly altered an anger and hate simmering in Lukas with their kindness on a beautiful sunny day in Overland Park, Kansas.

Released from Research Psychiatric Center in 2016, after receiving outpatient care for over 14 days, Lukas shifted his healing modality from painting to golf. Lukas told Len on more than one occasion that when he is on a golf course, in nature, considering his next shot, he feels the peace he is seeking. His finding solace on the golf course soon proved to be a catalyst of change for all of us.

"If you have the right people around you, you can get over it/heal/ move on." Profound words spoken from an 18-year-old who knows now how to advocate for himself.

The irony in this next phase of our lives is that I was not the right person to be around Lukas.

My path to healing and his were clashing and often. Lukas was seeking to be out of the "Reat-and-Popeye-were-murdered" conversation, while I was building a foundation around this very hateful action. Spearheading the Faith Always Wins Foundation to promote dialogue for the betterment of our world through kindness, faith and healing was part of my journey, not Lukas'. In fact, he needed to be far away from the flurry of activity that I was creating.

In late October 2017, Lukas asked us to move him to Florida under the pretense of joining a golf academy and attending private high school in Florida. Overland Park, Kansas, the location of the murders and frankly his life in the home, where his brother should be and isn't, was too painful for him.

Lukas shares his perspective of this period in his life during our interview, "When I was 15 years old during the first semester of my sophomore year in high school, we went to visit the Gary Gilchrist Golf Academy near Orlando, Florida. I just fell in love with it. It was beautiful, awesome. It was hot and not cold and a golfer's heaven."

Len and I were not golfers and still aren't. We had no knowledge of 'who was who' in golfing but had explored with golf professionals in our area of Kansas to ensure this academy was reputable. We didn't realize that Lukas would be taught by "some of the best coaches in the world."

"I mean, Gary Gilchrist, one of my coaches, is literally one of the top 10 junior coaches in the world," Lukas shared with excitement, recalling his time under the tutelage of whom we now call a dear friend.

Touring the private high school, Montverde Academy, I fondly remember our tour guide explaining the many Advanced Placement (AP) classes offered for students at all levels. Knowing how much Lukas was struggling in school, Len and I had concerns about him qualifying for entry. We were all pleased when Lukas passed their academic entrance process, and they had no problems with him choosing to stay in regular classes rather than stretch himself with an AP course.

Lukas flourished under the guidance of adults, other than myself and Len, who offered him a structure that we couldn't and didn't understand was needed. Explaining his daily schedule, Lukas provides this detail, "My daily life consisted of a 6 a.m. wake-up. I would make myself breakfast and had to be on the bus at 7 a.m. If you're not on the bus at 7 a.m., they leave you and then you miss the entire school day. Everything is very time oriented and you have to be there on time. I managed to mostly be at the bus by 7 a.m. and school started at 7:45 a.m. I had five classes until 12:05 p.m. and then I'd have lunch until 12:30 pm." The golfers were bussed from Montverde Academy to the Gary Gilchrist Golf Academy that made its home in the Mission Inn Golf Resort in Howey-in-the-Hills, Florida.

"Golf practice was from 1:30 p.m. to around 6 p.m. or dark, typically." During the evening free time, Lukas developed a keen interest in working out in the gym. The gym became a passion for Lukas, who weighed 270 pounds at 5' 9" when he moved to Florida. "Going to the gym until probably about 8 p.m., eat a little dinner and go home. Then do homework and go to sleep. This would be repeated Monday through Friday. It was tough. I enjoyed it, though."

In the same week Lukas asked to move to Florida, Len hinted at his desire to spend much of his time in Florida near Lukas. For a few days, I allowed myself to indulge in a pity party, feeling abandoned once again by the loved ones in my own home. My parents had raised an independent woman ... now I just needed to find her.

An excerpt from my journal notes on November 29, 2017, illuminates our lives, "Lukas is doing very well in life and school. He is driving himself! Lukas obtained his license today!! Len is tired and stressed. Luckily the weather is only cool and not freezing. Lukas was accepted to Montverde Academy. Camille is moving in with us on January 3, 2018."

It seems my mind rarely takes a pause. Reading *Jesus Calling: Enjoying Peace in His Presence* by Sarah Young daily, listening only to Christian music and journaling daily provided me the opportunity for contemplation. Knowing that Lukas is on his way to Florida for school, golf and most importantly a path to healing, and with Len showing signs of fear of being left alone with me, I asked God for more assistance. Feeling a new and unusual nudge, I reached out to Camille (Coffman) Holland.

Formerly an employee with Boyer Corporon Wealth Management (BCWM), Camille was in her final months of dental hygiene training at Johnson County Community College. Single at the time, she was living with her oldest brother, his wife and two children in a town farther from her classes than my home was. We had met when I hired Camille at BCWM, her first employment out of college. Her first days with BCWM were in January 2014, only months prior to the murders of Dad and Reat. Camille recalls driving Reat to school on more than one occasion and meeting my father during a few of his visits to our office. Of course, she was fond of them. After the murders, Camille found herself in a role closely related to a personal assistant for a grieving, daughter and mother while carrying the typical responsibilities of her corporate positions of Director of First Impressions and then client service representative. While we were friendly, I also kept much of my personal anguish to myself.

With Len's increasing expectations to be near Lukas, I took a leap of faith, leaning into my increasing desperation for companionship from a loving soul by asking Camille to move in with me—us. Having no plans to leave our home or Kansas other than trips to visit Lukas or take vacations, I sought togetherness in a home that was quickly becoming more ghostlike every day.

In preparation of this narrative, I engaged in a text and email exchange with Camille. She provided her perspective in this way, "After two years with BCWM, I left the company to pursue dental hygiene and my communication with Mindy and her family slowly faded. Surprised and excited for the opportunity to reconnect with her and her family and to be closer to my classes, I agreed to move in with them."

"Living with Mindy and her family was a sweet season. I felt like I had gained a new little brother in Lukas, and new mentors in Mindy and Len. I cared deeply about their family." Moving in only one day prior to Lukas moving out, Camille brought a ray of sunshine to my gray heart.

The early months of 2018 found Len traveling between our home in Kansas and Lukas' new home in Florida, as he had planned. These same months found me making final arrangements as the CEO of Boyer Corporon Wealth Management and contemplating my marriage, faith and life itself. Camille remembers, "Mindy and I found opportunities for conversations about life, faith and the healing process. Living in their home allowed me a glimpse into her family's grief and the strength they had, allowing them to walk through that grief." Never close to suicide but thoughtful about every move I was making, I carefully placed people around me, as I had for Lukas, to piece my soul together. "Welcoming and inclusive, I feel blessed to have been able to learn from Mindy and the example she sets of how to lean on faith and community seeking healing and restoration," Camille added. God knew Camille would be beneficial to me, more than I realized. She closed her communication about our time together with this comment, "This season came to an end when I decided to make the move to Virginia, and Len and Mindy decided to make the move to Florida. God knew exactly what we needed and when we needed it, allowing our paths to cross during that particular season. I will cherish our time together and know I always have a second family in the Losens."

During sessions with Cuky Harvey and in couple's counseling with Len, under the care of W. David Disney, LMFT, a path I didn't want to take began to appear before me. Fall of 2018 found Len and me moving to Howey-in-the-Hills, Florida. This was Len's plan. He dragged me, angry, kicking and screaming from our home of 13 years to be closer to Lukas. To stay married and willing to work on my relationship with Lukas, I agreed to sell our home and move from where my mother and one brother and his family lived, as well as the location of the murders, which were so integral in my life.

Cuky, who had enriched Lukas' life enough to assist him with healing, had now started her work on me. She explained during one of our sessions that Len was rowing our 'family canoe' to the light. He may not even realize this, but he was following a path for the benefit of our family. Frankly, she told me, "Get in the canoe and allow him to take you where you are supposed to be." Funny thing, in this same session, Cuky told me I should not be holding on to dead flowers, which I was. Going home after this session with Cuky, I knew my responsibility as a mom needed to transfer more clearly to my living child and away from my deceased child. Every dead flower I had been keeping from their funeral was thrown away, freeing my soul ever so slightly.

Camille moved from our home to her new life in Virginia only weeks before we left our home in Stilwell, Kansas for the final time. Awaiting her was a new career as a dental hygienist and a boyfriend who soon became her spouse. Each of us contemplated the Scripture, "For I know the plans I have for you, declares the Lord. Plans to prosper you, not to harm you, plans to give you hope and a future." Jeremiah 29:11.

Lukas was flourishing under the tutelage of the coaches at Gary Gilchrist Golf Academy and the teachers and counselors at Montverde Academy. He also had decided to lose the weight that had placed him in an obese category for his age and height. Seeing the positive changes in his emotions, demeanor and physical presence, I didn't want to interfere. I did, however, want to be supportive of his regimen, new work ethic and planned diet. One of the first tangible ways I could support him after my own arrival in Florida was to introduce him to friends of mine and owners of Hitch Fit Online Personal Training from my connections in Kansas. Diana Chaloux-LaCerte and her husband, Micah LaCerte, were instrumental in helping Lukas with his health, weight and confidence.

Over a period of five months, Lukas lost 50 pounds. "I started playing really good golf and getting college attention. I was locked in and zoned out from the rest of the world. I was not social whatsoever or going out at night and I was not really doing anything fun. I was focused on losing weight and playing golf and was doing really good at both," he shared on my podcast in December 2020.

School continued to be challenging; but with the help of key individuals at Montverde Academy, Lukas was able to catch up in many areas. His recollection of this difficult time is uplifting to hear, "I mean, they walked me through my junior and senior year with so much guidance. They taught me how to study. They taught me how to take tests and basically how to live an academic life. This is what got me into college. Honestly, I would have had to go to community college if it wasn't for those two women. I mean, they really did reteach me the whole academic system in a span of a year and a half. And, they focused on me as a main priority because they knew that I cared, and I worked my butt off. I give all the credit in the world to Victoria Hall and Maureen Kesselring. You know, my two ladies at Montverde Academy."

While academics were an uphill climb, Lukas departed Montverde Academy with two awards, proving himself a leader, passionate for knowledge and a young man with high character. No less than their mission for each graduating senior. Lukas won third place for his senior speech titled, "Overcoming Adversity" and the Dalton P. Monroe Award, honoring the fact that adversity would not conquer Mr. Monroe's spirit and humor. Lukas was seen as the student who sees the positive side, keeping his sense of humor in the face of adversity; conquering adversity and maintaining success at MVA.

Our family and friends have walked alongside us, helping to care for Lukas, encouraging him every step in his journey. Several times, it was beneficial for me to step away from Lukas, allowing each of us time to just be. Never was he alone in his journey. When we sent out Lukas' 2020 high school graduation announcements, they were sent to Team Lukas. Len and I know we spearheaded, pushed, cajoled, cried with, lifted up, physically moved and walked through the fire with Lukas. We also know, "If you have the right people around you, then you can get over it quicker. If you have the wrong people around you, you may never even move forward. And you always have to have support," which was a quote from Lukas Losen, himself, achiever extraordinaire!

Today, Lukas is attending the University of Arkansas as a business major. He says that he has plans to "live life to the fullest!" His dad and I, along with Team Lukas, are so very proud of him and will be encouraging our charismatic, nurturing, thoughtful young man every step, class and putt along the way.

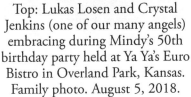

Top: Lukas Losen and Crystal Jenkins (one of our many angels) embracing during Mindy's 50th birthday party held at Ya Ya's Euro Bistro in Overland Park, Kansas. Family photo. August 5, 2018.

Top Right: Mindy, Len and Lukas with Zach, Josh, Olivia, Mike and Shelly Miller—Super Bowl LIV. Every new memory is to be lived to the fullest. "Live life to the fullest and never give up." –Reat Underwood. Family photo. February 2, 2020.

Middle: Cuky Harvey poses with Dr. Michelle Robin, two key individuals involved in healing Lukas and Mindy from the inside out. In Overland Park, Kansas. Photo courtesy of Cuky Harvey. 2018

Lukas Losen, Mindy Corporon and helpful friend, Denise Kruse, attending the Kansas City Chiefs football game in which Mindy was honored to sit in the Lamar Hunt Legacy seats. Photo courtesy Denise Kruse. December 2020

ADL In Concert Against Hate honorees and guests included (front row, from left) Lukas Losen, Mindy Corporon, Melinda Corporon, Alissa LaManno, and Jim LaManno. Second Row: Patricia Mills, Billy Mills, Barbara Fox, Jean Baptiste Rudatsikira, Jacqueline Murekatete, Len Losen, Gian LaManno and Brian Fowler. Hosted by David Friedman, ADL Washington, D.C., Regional Director (not pictured). Photo courtesy ADL of Washington, DC. October 27, 2014.

Athena Sullivan, Roxana Rogers Lemon and Mindy Corporon volunteering at the Blue Valley Middle School Outdoor Learning Center created in memory of Reat and Bill. Not pictured are the numerous family members and volunteers who helped create this beautiful space. Photo courtesy Athena Sullivan. October 2015.

Melinda Corporon, Katy and Andrew Corporon, Mindy Corporon and Jim LaManno gather during the dedication of "Three Ripples" created by artist Jesse Small in memory of William, Reat and Terri. Commissioned by and located at the Jewish Community Center in Overland Park, Kansas. Photo courtesy *The Kansas City Star*. April 21, 2016.

Friends since the 1991 Kansas City Chiefs Cheer squad. Back row: Susie Bond, Tandi Ball. Front row: Mindy Corporon, Tarra Freberg and Liz Barnard enjoy one another on one of Mindy's favorite places to be, Ambergris Caye, Belize. Photo courtesy Liz Barnard. February 2018.

24

God's Healing Through Others

While God placed these words, "I am with you," specifically in my darkest moments, in my head and in my heart, He actually showed up through people, most often.

I have some concerns that someone will be forgotten. A gift so meaningful and heartfelt, now wrapped carefully to protect it from time and every move we have made since 2014, it might not be on the top of my mind. An action, a smile, the hug I needed just when it was provided … there is no way to remember them all individually. Collectively, those around our community, nation and around the globe lifted us back into the world of the living with good thoughts and prayers. Having been prayed for by what could have been thousands of people, maybe even reaching close to one million prayers, I know the tangible feeling of being lifted. I lived through the much-needed "prayer lifting" days, knowing that I was not willing myself, to walk and talk. Others were alongside me—some of whom I knew and knew well, others whom I most likely will never know or meet. What they offered was kindness, faith and hope to us when our own well was bone dry.

The following actions and people who made them happen are in chronological order, to the best of my knowledge. Without them, undoubtedly, I would not have written my memoir.

Much later on April 13, 2014, after finding my father dead in the parking lot of the Jewish Community Center, hearing from a Jewish emergency room doctor that "the young man in the ambulance did not survive," sharing sorrow in my mother's home and speaking at the student vigil holding just as many adults, I found myself back at my mother's home. One clear recollection is of my mother's second youngest sister, Barbara Fox, whom we call Barbie, walking through the door with a small suitcase in one hand and a jacket in the other, looking breathless and relieved to be with us. Living near Dallas, Texas, Barbie had received the same frightening phone call from Len that he had made to my mother and brothers. As Barbie and I talked through her recollections, she shared with me that Len was the first to call her. Len only made phone calls from the time I initially phoned him until he and Lukas found me at the Jewish Community Center. Because Lukas was in the car with Len, this confirms that Lukas' trauma started earlier than his viewing of Terri LaManno's deceased body in the parking lot of Village Shalom. My 12-year-old Lukas, recently disappointed about a canceled lacrosse game overhears up to five phone calls on the topic of his grandfather and brother being shot.

Quickly departing her current location, Barbie was on her way to the airport for a quickly scheduled flight from Dallas to Kansas City, before she reached my sister-in-law, Dana, to hear that my father had been murdered and Reat was in an ambulance. And now, she was here in my parents' home. Of course she was. Much of her young adult years had been spent with my parents, Will and me. Her face was taut with a fearful and sad expression as we locked eyes. Embracing her, I said, "I can't believe this has happened. Thank you for being here."

Peculiar thing about trauma … Len has no memory of calling Barbie.

Arriving at my own home, now, my heart as dark as the sky, I am surprised to find a gathering of friends sitting around our round dining table and in our kitchen. Dominic DeCicco and his older son, Dante, who is Reat's age, are at the round table. Mike Miller is in the room and soon makes an offer to spend the night. Dewey and Niki

Neal are present. This is the first night of many to come with a similar group of friends and tone of conversation. We have lost a child. We lost my father. The conversations are jilted and unsteady. None of us know exactly what to say, how to say it or when to say it. It is okay to not know what to say. Words are not mandatory. Purchased gifts are not mandatory. Frequently, simply being with a friend, colleague or even a stranger in need of compassion and empathy is best.

Another clear memory is of me needing to lie down. Feeling as if a Mack truck had run over me from the time I found my father in the parking lot and as if a building had fallen on me as we listened to the unbelievable message that Reat had not survived, I wanted to take back this entire day.

Actually afraid for the day to end because then there is no way to get it back or to make a change ... I am fearful of sleep. My shaky, unstable legs begin to quake under me as Niki takes me by an arm and most likely by my torso, too, and leads me to my closet. I have become a child. She gently and carefully helps me undress and redress into my pajamas. All the while, I am muttering to myself, yet aloud, that this just cannot be. How could this be true, any of it? Her calm, sweet voice and her caring hands hold me steady while I lift one leg slowly into a pajama pant leg and then the other. Concentrating on staying upright, I feel turned upside down and inside out.

Niki prepares my bed and a comfy pallet on the floor for Lukas to sleep next to me. This will be the first night of a four-month (and then some) sleeping arrangement. Lukas is wrapped, as if in a cocoon or burrito, reminding me of him as a baby—always wanting to be wrapped tightly for sleeping. We are babies again, infants in need of much care.

Many friends had shown up at my mother's home during the evening of April 13, 2014. Past neighbors Jim and Shelly Maxwell were shoulder to shoulder with a number of influential women who were members with me in Women Who Mean Business (WWMB). One such woman, Margaret Reynolds, slipped a piece of paper in my hand with her number on it and said, "Please call any time." I had attended Margaret's daughter Alison's funeral only one year ago. While Alison had passed from natural causes, she was a beloved daughter and sister in the Reynolds family. Sorrow had been with Margaret for a full year.

Sleeping fitfully, I consider, how on earth will I survive? How will we all survive? Finding the slip of paper with her phone number on it, I called my friend. Her phone rang at 5 a.m. "I need you. I need your help," was all I could manage to say. She arrived at my home before 6:30 a.m. Our home was still quiet as Len and Lukas slept. We had taken Mike up on his offer to stay the night and now he was on the couch with his laptop. Once Margaret arrived, I encouraged Mike to go home and start his day. He had been in conversation with me in the wee hours before dawn, remembering Reat and my father and the love we would always hold for them.

Margaret offered guidance and thoughts on logistics, which was what I was seeking. Her steady, knowing voice prepared me for navigating the next few days of our lives.

Later that morning our doorbell rang, disrupting the fog in my brain like the sand falling from a shaken beach towel. Concerned about who I might find at our door out of a new fear I now have for my family's safety, I peek out the window. My fear is set aside as I welcome Kathy Schikevitz, another WWMB friend, into our home. Kathy was at my mother's home with her husband, Ron, and another WWMB friend, Lori Mallory, the previous evening. Also attending the vigil, Kathy shared with me, "We sat in the back with many other members of the Jewish community and cried as our hearts broke for you, our friend. Lori and I talked after the vigil and decided to meet at your home the next morning. We didn't know what would be needed, but we knew we needed to help. It became immediately evident that I should 'man' the command center for the activity that was now starting to take place around the family and your home. Local and national media were contacting the home, which needed to be assessed and forwarded to Will. Funeral plans needed to be coordinated."

I heard her explain that she is part of a team of people who will be coming in to help run our household. My foggy brain continues to linger and I shake my head on my own, seeking more clarity, not to say no, but to confirm I heard her correctly. There may have been an opportunity for me to say yes or no, but I don't recall. I simply watched as she unfolded her laptop and set up "office" at our kitchen table. For the next 10 days, including the weekend, I watched Kathy and our other WWMB friends orchestrate life for our family. Kathy explained further, "Being Jewish myself, I was able to help the family understand the position of the Jewish community and coordinate communication with the Jewish community director throughout the week."

These amazingly savvy business-owning, company-running, distinguished women halted their lives to breathe life back into our family.

On about day three or four, when our friend Kathy Koehler (K.K.) was headed to our house for her shift, she inquired as to whether I had moved beyond eating Snickers and drinking Coca-Colas. I told her I would love some shrimp cocktail. She obliged and I finally ate "real food" as she poked it into my mouth between conversations pertaining to the care of Lukas, our home, our dog and funeral planning.

During the first few days after the murders, we manage to juggle funeral logistics, daily life and insurmountable grief. As we begin to sort through logistics of the funeral, several businesses stepped forward with assistance. Kat McDaniel and MEDiAHEAD took on the creation and printing of our funeral programs while Gina Danner and NextPage enlarged selected photos of Dad and Reat for the funeral, itself. We also realize Lukas needs an outfit to wear to his grandfather's and brother's funeral. Again, Mike Miller and his wife, Shelly, volunteer to take him shopping. Our household team from WWMB are staying on top of our laundry, feeding our dog, Lucy, and taking messages from Len's phone. They accept every delivery to our home, document the giver and the best way to provide a thank-you in the coming weeks.

For 10 consecutive days, we had two women in our home on a two-hour rotation during the hours of 8 a.m. to 8 p.m. They gave our home "life" in the days we felt lifeless. Their aching hearts worked to take some of our own pain and carry it for us. Pastor Adam Hamilton has called this type of help—these "angels on Earth"—stretcher bearers. Len, Lukas and I were on our own stretchers and these highly skilled, capable businesswomen shared time out of their lives to carry us. Lukas was cared for as if he were their own. Even now, each woman who spent time with Lukas shares their memory of my 12-year-old—his sadness, his love of his older brother and grandfather, the concern he had for me and all the crying in his home and thankfully, his resilience to live.

Another evening after the murders and prior to the funeral, a large prepared meal arrived at our home along with warm, caring faces and hugs. Clients and friends of mine, the Weinberg, Stolzer, Robinson and Ellis families—all Jewish, mind you—collectively brought nourishment in the form of food, love and empathy into our home. Kay Stolzer reflected about her engagement with the restaurant from where the food was purchased. They understood the meal was to be for our family and would not allow Kay to pay for the meal. The full cost was covered by Bravo! Italian Kitchen. "Of course, this will be on us. We're all in this together," is what she heard from the manager as they provided her a hug and many sacks of delicious food.

This occasion, meant for our entire family, brought my mom to our home with her three sisters. Joining Barbie, Dena Berquist and Jilda Elk had arrived to grieve alongside my mom, offering support to all of us. My mom, the oldest sibling in her family, was the first to be married, so her sisters had grown up knowing and loving my father since they started dating in high school.

In the midst of this same week, my sister-in-law Dana's employer, People's Bank, planned a dinner at a local restaurant for all family members coming to pay their respects to help them share stories and try to find some sliver of good from these heinous murders. Once again, from the perimeters of our lives, people offered care as well as they could. A community aching from the blast that seemed to have an epi-center everywhere I turned, reached inward to help us heal. The room was crowded with Corporons, Gordys (my mother's maiden name), Losens, in-laws and out-laws, as my father and his siblings used to tease one another … all were present. Relatives traveled from Arizona, Colorado, Florida, New York, North Carolina, Oklahoma, Tennessee, Texas, Virginia and Washington State … there might have been more, but my new friend, brain fog, was with me everywhere I went. I know for sure that "mom 2" was there for me. Janet Loveless, Kyle's mother, had made the trip with my longtime sister/friend Lynn-a-bee.

It was during this dinner when two other WWMB, Denise Kruse and Merrie Jo Pitera, put their child sitting skills to work for the ben-efit of Olivia Corporon, my brother Will's youngest child, who was only a toddler at the time. These ladies kept Olivia at my home busy and happy, as any almost-2-year-old should be. Denise also hosted the first gathering of volunteers to assist in writing thank-you notes to hundreds of well wishers who had sent gifts. This particular afternoon, the attendees witnessed us receiving a "message" from Reat. Denise was offering instructions to everyone in attendance while Pandora was softly playing random songs in the background. "Hey, Soul Sister," a song by the musical group Train, started playing. The familiar tune and lyrics found my mother and I looking at one another with gaping mouths. This was the first song Reat had performed live. Distinctly, we knew this to be a "message," that Reat knew exactly where we were and what we were doing. We choose to believe, having faith, that he and my father walk with us, daily.

The amount of decisions that need to be made prior to a funeral are immense. One such decision was to select what clothes Reat would wear in the casket. Susie Walker Bond, another longtime friend from cheerleading camps and the Kansas City Chiefs cheerleaders, provided strength and comfort while I looked through his clothes. She had taken a shift to be in our home on this particular day when the funeral home called, asking for clothing. Not thinking through the gravity of what I had to do, I only knew how appropriate it was for Susie to be with me when this task had to be completed. We had experienced so much life together, as we met when we were both teenagers. I am appreciative she was with me during this unbearable task of choosing Reat's clothes.

After making the selection, I hold up Reat's clothes for Susie. Looking at her face, I can see sorrow seeping into the crevices of her eyes. Joining her in this feeling, we both break down in a watershed of tears. She holds me in the middle of Reat's room as I sob and sob, again. It feels surreal that I am picking clothes for my son's funeral. This is a job no mother or parent should ever have to complete.

Facing the daunting task of crafting Reat's obituary, I know my mom is doing the same for my dad. Grateful that she, my brothers and aunts are combining efforts in creating my dad's obituary, I am having trouble sitting down to complete this task on Reat's behalf, so I keep delaying. An obituary illustrates finality and I would simply rather not be part of this illustration.

I am blessed with many dear friends from my college sorority, Delta Delta Delta, at the University of Oklahoma to my Kansas City Chiefs cheerleaders, female and male, and my Women Who Mean Business powerful friends. They all kick ass in one way or another. Liz Crawford Barnard, from my KC Chiefs cheer squad, is my selection to assist me in memorializing Reat's short but full life through his obituary. A talented writer herself, Liz and I have toyed with the idea of writing a book together about the "unbalance" of working women and families.

Liz sat by my side, typing, while I worked to formulate the love story I felt needed to be shared. She recalls it this way, "It was hard to grasp what had happened. I was at your home the day after the shooting; it was late. All of the visitors had left and your family had gone to bed. You were wearing a fluffy white bathrobe and sitting with me at your kitchen table. It felt as though you were relaxing. Our friendship spanned 20 years, which included many experiences together. When you asked me if I would help you write Reat's obituary, I said, of course, and we hugged one another." It had to have been so painful for Liz sitting with me as I tearfully documented as much as I could recall about my loving, cheerful, talented and humorous son. Liz helped me by suggesting, "We start by saying that a young man with much promise was lost too soon." Reat lived life to the fullest and never gave up.

Undoubtedly, as I walked through each of these difficult steps, I was not thanking God for any of the hardships. I am fairly certain that I wasn't thanking God for my blessings, either in the form of families who were providing food—Denise, Susie or Liz at the time. A horribly dense brain fog, a broken heart and a shattered soul don't lend themselves to showing much appreciation. Hugs and simple thank-yous were what I could offer. Drained and depleted, I couldn't give back to them or anyone during this week or the next. Yet, they were there. One person for one item needed, sharing each of my burdens to lighten my load, even if only a smidge. They were there because their spirit, whether it be God, Allah, Yahweh or any other energy source in which they believed, helped build a bridge for me to escape the raging, frightening, crushing river swirling around me.

For the better part of these same 10 days, I was driven anywhere I wanted to go or needed to be. Tarra Freberg held my hand during the vigil as I spoke publicly for the first time after the murders. Our friendship kindled in a similar fashion to others in my life. We found one another on the 1991 Kansas City Chiefs cheer squad and have never let go. Often, I refer to Tarra as my own personal "Martha Stewart." Not only can she cook a "mean" anything-you-want, she can teach you how to do it on your own, all the while with joy in her heart. In 2001, as a mother of two, Tarra watched Reat for me on a regular basis during my single working mother days. She and her husband Eric grew their family, adding two more Frebergs—all of them amazing young people.

Shelly Miller (Mike's wife and Josh's mom) assigned themselves to this position on rotating days. Donna Osterlund, whom I befriended while pregnant with Lukas, greeted our guests and organized gift and meal deliveries, which meant she spent significant hours close to our chaos and overseeing our daily progress. Donna, Tarra and Shelly were highly involved in running our home alongside my cohort of WWMB, and new friendships were formed between many of them. These women spent days after the murders and time beyond the funeral with Len, Lukas and me. I had significant friend withdrawals when they left our home for their own.

Two days prior to the funeral, via my personally assigned driver, I arrived at Wesley Chapel, adjacent to the Church of the Resurrection, for what you would call a "laying on of the hands." So much pain in our community from this senseless murder spree sent ripples of love flowing from all areas of our lives, via friends, relatives, connections and acquaintances currently in our lives and from years past. A current friend from WWMB and a Scouting mom of a teen in Reat's troop, Lori Mallory arranged for me to physically receive prayer through word and touch from other women within our circle of friends at Wesley Chapel, which later played a significant role in my personal grieving. God was with Lori when this idea came to her. Her spiritual maturity continues to teach me how to listen and walk with faith. In 2016, Lori was my travel mate on a meaningful trip to Israel where we each received profound messages from the Holy Spirit and ate a massive amount of hummus!

Another enormous meal was prepared for each and every family member and friend who had traveled from anywhere to Overland Park, Kansas, for the funeral of William L. Corporon, M.D. and his grandson, Reat Griffin Lloyd Underwood. Similar names from the previous meal at our home and now new ones joined in to assist in lifting not only my now small family of three but also our extended family of hundreds, who were reeling in similar fashion to me. The Alpert, Cloud, Ellis, Isenberg, Robinson, Stolzer, Thalblum and Weinberg families were responsible for this huge undertaking in so little time and for so many people. You see, God appeared often and through humans who offered their mitzvah—a Jewish term meaning a good deed done from religious duty—over and over and over to us.

The murders of my father and son took place on Palm Sunday. Their funeral was held on Good Friday. As Easter Sunday approached, the enormity of this drastic change in our lives was taking a toll on me. Kathy, Dr. Michelle Robin, Lori, Denise and other friends reconvened once again coming to our aid. With yet another act of courageous kindness, they provided an Easter Sunday family meal. Kathy explains, "The following Sunday was Easter. I coordinated and catered a lovely Easter dinner at my clubhouse for all of your family who were still in town. We wanted to provide you another environment in which you could be with family during your Christian holiday."

Our family met President Barack Obama during the summer of 2014, as he made a stop in the Kansas City area. He had graciously requested to meet us. We passed the security clearance and now have photos and his presidential coin to prove we met. He was compassionate, kind and genuinely offered his condolences. He hugged Mom and me and shook hands with Len, Lukas and my brother, Tony.

Art was made, paper links were created and poems were written for Reat and Popeye by students and adults ... Mitchell McCroskey, Kara Choate and Madilyn Veatch shared their sorrow through poetry.

"POPEYE'S PASSAGE"

Husband, dad, Dr. Corporon, friend,
Son, brother, uncle, and Popeye all roles occupied by him.
The love for his family no one could explain,
Not enough words to describe it, for always it will remain.
The reason he was taken we will always ask why,
Every one of us has our time and with God only does that lie.
His life full of purpose, reason, and love,
Now with his Lord and Grandson in Heaven above.
The tears will fall and that is okay,
Just remember you will be with him again one day.
In a place where sickness, sadness, and evil cannot reside,
Where the Lion lays with a Lamb by his side.
There will be hard days and God will be there,
To carry you through the heartache and pain that you bare.
So remember your special times, his laugh, and his smile,
How it went on for miles and miles.
Know that he is with you each and every day,
No 'Goodbyes' just a "See You Later" you can say.
For he will be at the Gates with arms opened wide,
Him and Reat waiting to embrace you inside.
What a Glorious day that will be,
God gives us that promise, for it is in Him we Believe.

-Kara Choate

"REAT'S ROAD"

A Precious life called to his "FOREVER" home above,
Talented beyond his years and full of love.
He had a smile that lit up any room,
For us left behind, his life ended far too soon.
His life will live on far beyond what we can see,
His memories in our hearts forever will be.
God wasn't surprised by what happened on that day,
He will bring blessings from this tragedy in all kinds of ways.
It will not be easy without him here,
Hold on tight to your strong faith even through the tears.
He promises to never give us more than He can bare,
Even though right now our hearts continue to tear.
Reat's wrongful passing was not in vain right now God only knows,
What this handsome young man's legacy has to show.
For Mindy, what a precious mother you are and no greater trial will you face,
It is beyond a mother to bury her child no matter the case.
I know your faith in the Lord, it is strong, evident, and shows,
Grip it tight as ever and don't let go.
He will carry you when one step or breath you think you cannot take,
This is part of the journey He has for you to make.
I am not going to lie and tell you it gets better,
For that isn't true, not one single letter.
What I will tell you is every day God will give you strength to live,
To show this world all your love and the love your son had to give.
Remember Goodbye you will not say,
Just a "see you later, be good with Popeye, I'll meet you one day".
He is watching over all of you with our Lord and your dad,
Perfect in peace not wanting you sad.
For one day it will come and united you all will be,
Your Precious Son, your Dad, you SAVIOR, WOW what a sight to see.

~KARA CHOATE~

In Memory of Reat Underwood

Remember the grin
Remember the joy
Remember the life of that little boy
Stay in our hearts
Keep things simple
Never forget those cute little dimples
Fly with me now, to the morning sun
Soar through the sky, hit the ground and run
Nothing can stop us
Not even one man
Try to knock us down. Together we stand
Try to hold it in
Although it stings
Reat will always be there; the wind beneath our wings.

He flew, he ran
He slid, he soared
He reminded us all; love is an open door
The shells on the sand
His hand in our hands
The man never let one person just stand
Home of the Tigers
Stay with us all

He smiled and passed as we walked through the halls
He sang with you
He sang with me
We knew he would never miss a beat
He stays with us now
He lives close not far
He lives in the wonderful place in our heart.
Work like he did
You know you should
Try to live like Reat Underwood

Poem by Mitchell McCroskey

For the first time, I've seen the light.
For the first time, I've seen true evil.
For the first time, I want to be more like you.
For the first time, I can make good from bad.
For the first time, I want to know you more.
For the first time, I can see your true beauty.
For the first time, I can feel your love.
  Now you are the sun, stars you are the light
and with the clouds, with the stars and sun.
Now I see that you are gone, my light is lost.
But then you gave me a new one. Now I can
see again, see myself, and now you.
  For the first time,
I can see your beauty.
For the first time,
I can feel your love.

By Madilyn Veatch
MEV

Reat had a star named after him by a friend from high school, Megan Duggan. His kindness on her first day in school impacted Megan so greatly; she took actionable steps to share with us who Reat was to her.

Jake Goldman, at the age of 16, sought me out for a discussion on how we might join forces for good and kindness. Jake had been taunted for his Jewish faith prior to and now after the murders during several racist bullying incidents at his school. He was seeking to take action and had a keen interest in exploring ideas with me. Jake was the perfect young person to lead our Faith Always Wins Foundation Youth Advisory Board, and he did so during his junior and senior years in high school. Reminding me of Reat during our initial meeting and today, I admire Jake's strong leadership skills and courage to take on a difficult topic of conversation and task with nothing but good intentions for all involved. Caring about justice, equality and human-kind above himself, I could be speaking of Jake or Reat in all of these sentences.

Len has had encounters with God through people during the years following the murders of Dad and Reat. One such "encounter" lasted for a few years, which began with an Alpha Course. The Alpha Course is a 10 session practical introduction to the Christian faith that began at Holy Trinity Brompton Church in Central London. What began in one church over 40 years ago has now been experienced by over 35 million people in over 100 languages all around the world. All questions are welcomed. I dubbed it "Christianity 101." The gaping chasm between Len's knowledge of the Bible, Christianity and walking in faith was vastly different from mine. Unlike me, Len had not "grown up" in the church. Pastor Jeff Kirby, a teaching pastor at the Church of the Resurrection, who was soft spoken and always offered a warm smile and a large hug, taught the session Len joined. Within a few weeks and certainly by the time the course had ended, Len could say he had a friend who also happened to be a man of the cloth. Pastor Kirby encouraged Len to attend a men's Bible fellowship that met every Wednesday morning. The men involved in this Bible fellowship embraced Len where he was in his knowledge of the Bible, God and faith. Moving even one step further into an unknown space, Len attended their annual weekend retreat. I was overjoyed to hear Len describe his positive, spirit-filled, "life-changing" experience during a weekend retreat he had initially not wanted to attend. Upon returning home, Len divulged that it was an "unexpected emotional two days." Explaining that he had not realized how broken he was before entering the weekend, he had deep conversations, bouts of crying and received significant emotional support. Len said these men, along with Pastor Kirby, helped him shift his outlook on life.

One huge shift was his learning to appreciate what we had in our marriage. He considered how difficult life would be without me.

Open to the possibility of documenting, even if only through simple blogs, the monumental steps we had to take to keep our marriage intact, I've chosen not to discuss the normal difficulties of our marriage before or the enormous difficulty of holding a marriage together after our child's death and that of my father, in this memoir. Some might say then that this memoir is not complete. I would respond with, I am not complete.

Athena Sullivan, a gifted education teacher at Blue Valley Middle School and one of Reat's former teachers, explained to us that while Reat was in her class, he and his classmates had discussed the topic of "fixing up" the outdoor area to make it more conducive for learning. Athena wondered if we would be interested in tackling this creative outdoor project as a memorial for Reat and Bill. At the same time, Len realized that he felt much closer to Reat and Dad when he was outdoors. Our beautiful home landscaping was a testament to his meticulous nature and his desire to be outside. Athena, Principal Roxana Rogers Lemon, Len and my brother Tony's family, along with school district officials, concrete and landscaping companies, Joe Donnelly of Complete Pools, a grant, numerous meetings and effort were all needed to create the full-sized, outdoor classroom in memory of Dad and Reat! Blue Valley Middle School students enjoy classes throughout the year in a beautiful natural setting thanks to Athena listening to her spirit and God. Her willingness to act on this nudge provided healing for all of us and, in particular Len and my brother Tony.

Next to strawberry rhubarb pie, fudge was Reat's favorite sweet! My father's youngest sibling, Gael Martin, celebrated Reat's 15th birthday, (arriving five weeks after his murder) by making homemade chocolate fudge. He would not turn 15 and we would not be able to celebrate with him at his high school or our home. Therefore, along with Blue Valley High School principal, Scott Bacon, and a lovely man named Charlie, head of their food services and the school Family and Consumer Science Classes, fudge was prepared for all 1,400 students. All the fudge made, Gael's and the school's, was a message flowing from their hearts to ours that Reat was remembered and loved.

When you hear of a sorrowful tragedy, a loss that seems unimaginable and you feel a nudge to take an action … do it. Though I was aware of Fred and Candy Merrill through the lease agreement Boyer Corporon Wealth Management held with Merrill Companies, I was unaware of the magnitude to which the murders affected them. Creating the entertainment, eating, dining and living space of Prairiefire at precisely the same time that Dad and Reat lost their lives, the Merrills felt a nudge to take action. On the winding path through the Kansas tall grass and butterfly oasis, just north of the Museum at Prairiefire are two oak trees planted in memory of Dad and Reat. The inscription on an uncomplicated plaque states "Bill and Reat, Strong as Oak."

Yes, Reat and Dad were murdered by gunfire, so it may seem crass that we allowed a BB gun range to be dedicated in Reat's memory. Stay with me, please. As I have previously stated, our son loved Scouting.

He learned to shoot a BB gun at the Theodore Naish Scout Reservation during his Cub Scout years with either me or my dad by his side. We selected the Heart of America Council as one option to receive financial donations after their murders. When the funds trickled to a stop, there were enough funds available to almost cover the full cost of a newly designed and almost complete BB gun range at the very campsite where Reat loved to camp, enjoy his buddies and learned to shoot a gun, a bow and arrow, whittle a stick, make yarn bracelets, save a drowning human and much, much more! This was 'something good', made possible for future scouts, now boys and girls, as they engage in outdoor learning activities with supervised training—activities my son relished.

In the event you find yourself on the campus of the University of Oklahoma, there is a specific picnic table, hosting a plaque beginning with the words "In Loving Memory of … " dedicated in memory of Dad and Reat. Standing only feet away is a peaceful, tall and strong tree planted in efforts of beautification and I think to keep the table company. One day, this tree may provide a much needed shade to whomever takes a seat. Both of these gifts were made possible on February 28, 2015 with the efforts of my older brother, Will. Will made a request to a longtime friend and fraternity brother, JP Audas, who in turn found the team to take a thoughtful idea and turn it into a tangible healing step for our family. Karen Renfroe, associate vice president of advancement at the University of Oklahoma, along with Allen King, director of landscaping, and the ever gracious, Mrs. Molly Boren—all with the University of Oklahoma during this time, heard and acted on the story of Bill and Reat. Our family ties to Oklahoma and the Sooner campus were also shared with Oklahoma Basketball Coach, Lon Kruger. A friend of JP's, Coach Kruger and his staff arranged for our family and everyone in attendance at that weekend's basketball game to hear Reat's recording of the National Anthem. A large group of family and friends gathered with us for these remembrances. Namely, one of my Tri Delta sorority sisters, Dawn and her husband, Kenny Sullivan, who hosted Reat at what would be his final OU football game in the fall of 2013. Sharing in the lives of Reat and my father and now in memories, we have been blessed with deep friendships.

I have found that covering myself with love and memories of my father and Reat help me to feel their spirit and love for me. Ever thankful for the friends who provided me memorable ways to cherish them, there are several pieces of jewelry that adorn me on most days: A necklace bearing the inscription "Popeye" on a larger metal circle and "Reat" on a layered, smaller metal circle. Nestled inside these is a heart. Given to me by Merri Jo Pitera, a WWMB who offered her childsitting talents for Oliva Corporon alongside Denise Kruse and has continued to be a valued friend. A silver bracelet with an outside inscription reminding us to "Live life to the fullest and never give up!", which was a statement Reat made to everyone from his newly created social media accounts at the age of 14. Liz Barnard thoughtfully added an inscription to the inside, as well … "Romans 8:28" and "v xxi mcm xcix," Reat's date of birth, May 21, 1999.

When you feel a nudge to give … give.

In a conversation on my podcast, "Post-Traumatic Stress Disorder" with my younger brother, Tony, he shared how his children's school staff walked alongside his family during the dark months following the murders of his father and nephew. "The kids were so young when this happened that we were concerned." Andrew and Katy were 7 and 5, respectively, and had been in the car with their parents as they arrived at the Jewish Community Center, searching for answers about the whereabouts of Dad and Reat. "We were so very blessed to have strong personalities, strong willed, caring, empathetic teachers in their lives," Tony continues. "These teachers and counselors, in their lives, made sure that they were loved when we couldn't be there to love them." Breaking my heart, this speaks directly to the difficulty I had in parenting Lukas in my own broken and shattered state. "Their school

rallied around them and still does to this day as we celebrate SevenDays®
Make a Ripple, Change the World, with kindness in memory of Dad
and Reat. Sunrise Point Elementary and the professional staff that
are there now and that were there then, were just phenomenal," Tony
reflected.

It may have been their job or their training from years of education that made the teachers, counselors and staff readily available
to Andrew and Katy and therefore to Tony and Dana, their parents.
However, I can hear in Tony's voice that what the staff at Sunrise Point
Elementary offered them was not simply from training. It was from
their heart source, energy or faith—whatever you want to call it. These
staff members and I know countless others who make themselves
available, leave themselves vulnerable to a new pain each and every
day as they feel called to do so when one of their flock is injured.

My older brother, Will, reflected warmly on two aspects that I
believe God placed on his heart during my podcast interview with
him titled, "The Eye of a Hurricane." Specifically speaking about the
funeral, "We were just trying to hang on and do the best, the best
we can do. But, you know, that week one of the things that I always
remember fondly is the funeral … leaving the house and going to
the funeral and the church, being surrounded by I don't know how
many thousands of people. The church being completely full and then
finding out later that the online service had been watched and viewed
live in something like 40 countries."

Who were all of these people and what took them to the funeral?
Perhaps this is the reason: Isaiah 43:2, "When you pass through the
waters, I will be with you; and when you pass through the rivers, they
will not sweep over you. When you walk through the fire, you will not
be burned; the flames will not set you ablaze."

As Will stated, thousands of people showed up to walk through our
fire with us. This is what humans with hearts do. In this same interview, Will shared how he found solace, "Fortunately, through prayer,
Heather and family," they made it one day at a time.

If Peyton Palmer had not spoken to her mother about Lukas' intention of taking his own life, we might have lost our second son, his precious life, to the same hate that took his grandfather and brother. Lukas spoke to the importance of the help he received from his friend Peyton and many others during our final minutes of my podcast titled, "In Conversation With Lukas," released December 19, 2020. "Yeah, don't just talk the talk, you should walk the walk. And do not be afraid to tell someone's parents if they're suicidal or even if they say 'don't,' I mean you should, you 100% should tell someone. They will forgive you in the long run. It'll be better in the long run." If your intention is to help someone, Lukas explains, "Let them know you're there for them is number one, but only do it once or twice. Don't overbear it. Don't keep saying I'm here for you. I'm here for you. If you're really there for them, show it. Do something for them."

Beyond his age in maturity and wisdom from a heinous atrocity committed over six and half years ago, Lukas has learned, "There is really no reason to be mean to people in life. Seek the inherent worth in each person you meet. When you figure out that person's worth, sometimes it's pretty cool to get to know them more."

I am told I provide inspiration to people because of the words I used after the murders. I used words like, "We were living life. We will live life again."

"We want something good to come from this."

"God did not kill them, a person with a gun killed them."

I am frequently questioned as to how I said such things. From where did I find this strength to speak of good and God in a time of such sorrow and despair? Perhaps the pragmatism from my father's rearing, from the Bible verses I heard but could never memorize and from my DNA are where I found these words. Maybe life experiences, such as Kyle Loveless' death when I was 15, my years being in front of crowds urging them to cheer loudly for my teams and, yes, from finding my beloved father, himself deceased, and Reat near death, were all key components.

For me to have hope and inspiration to speak of these tragedies and explain how inherently wrong they were, I found strength from others who walked with me. For an entire year, I stepped inside Wesley Chapel on the campus of the Church of the Resurrection, alone and seeking guidance from God. Why? Why would this happen to me, to us? The messages I continued to receive were a redirection in nature. What I discovered is that for me to find peace and to find myself whole again, I was to "Bring God's People Together." This didn't answer my question of "why." I know the "'why." "An idiot with a gun" was allowed to continue spewing his hate on our sacred planet.

Carrying hate in my heart would only hurt my heart. Allowing anger to fester in me will not bring my son or my dad back to me. I know where they are and will see them when the time comes. I felt this way from the time I knew they had both died—yet, that doesn't make the journey less difficult.

Every day we have a choice to make. For me and my tribe, we choose courageous kindness.

Kansas City KSHB News Anchor Christa Dubill, Mindy Corporon
and Kansas City Mayor Sly James opening our SevenDays® Kindness
Walk with hundreds of 'walkers' ready to show their kindness.
Photo taken in the historic Union Station in Kansas City, Missouri.
Courtesy of Faith Always Wins Foundation. April 24, 2017.

Top: A weekend of reuniting with Delta Delta Delta pledge sisters. From the left: Mindy Corporon, Mary Ann Kellam, Denise Martin, Lori Wilson, Dawn Sullivan and Laura Waits. Sisters in life have buoyed Mindy when the waters are too deep to swim alone. Photo courtesy Mary Ann Kellam. Frisco, Texas. October 2018.

Bottom: Volunteers and Button Art Competition winners promoting SevenDays® Make a Ripple, Change the World at the press conference hosted by AdventHealth Shawnee Mission in Merriam, Kansas. Photo courtesy of Faith Always Wins Foundation. January 2020.

Top: Faith Always Wins Foundation Interfaith Planning Group on a Zoom call. Photo courtesy of Faith Always Wins Foundation. November 2020.

Bottom: Gathering for cross-racial conversations in a group Mindy named, R.E.A.T. Black and White Women Friendships. Top row from left: Dr. Nicole Price, Lisa Pleasure, Mindy Corporon, Dawn Collins, Lori Wilson. Second row from top, from left: Mary Ann Kellam, Dawn Sullivan, Laura Waits, Chris Oneschuk. Third row from top, from left: Denise Martin, Michelle Wimes, Cleo Brager, Susan Bro. Bottom row, from left: Stephenie Smith, Melanie Miller, Kiona Sinks and Doris Rogers. Members now named R.E.A.T. Sisters. Respect, Engage, Appreciate, Trust—We are changing the world in which we live. Photo courtesy Mindy Corporon. 2020/2021

25

Gathering to Shine
a Light on Peace

December 4, 2020.

Watching a stunning sunset from the end of the Belizean Shores Resort pier on the island of Ambergris Caye, Belize, took my heart back to 2013. Only seven years ago, I was in this same space on a pier off the same resort photographing my two boys—Reat and Lukas—before we boarded our water taxi for the San Pedro Town, Belize, airport. Len and I found Ambergris Caye on our honeymoon in 2001. We have returned numerous times, finding comfort and extended family through deep friendships and a simple way of life. 2013 was to be the first of many family trips.

Without warning, our lives were altered, forced into a turbulent transition from the enormous adversity thrust upon us—our lives broken, my soul shattered. How did I pick up the shards of my life without also inflicting more wounds? I didn't. Picking up every piece I could find also wreaked havoc on my shaken spirit and the lives of those I love. During my search for a pain-free heart, hope found me. Hope found me in the Scripture that Josh Miller placed on the white bracelets he created only days after the murders shook the stability in life we thought we had; Josh believed in Romans 8:28, "And we know that in all things God works for the good of those who love him, who have been called according to his purpose." Hope found me through yoga, lomilomi massage and energy sessions.

While suffering was draining, forgiveness was filling me.

Inspiration found me in the Scripture I tattooed on my left wrist underneath a beautiful yellow butterfly, representing Reat, "Abraham found righteousness in God" (Genesis 15:6). Inspiration found me with every smile, hug, poem, song and note of shared anguish and encouragement to continue living.

Peace found me when I followed the path laid before me.

Just as family and friends were instruments of God, available to breathe life into me, I have picked up my own cross to pay it forward to help others find healing, hope and inspiration.

Today, my days are spent on Workplace Healing, LLC; the Faith Always Wins Foundation; SevenDays® Make a Ripple, Change the World and the *Real Grief—Real Healing with Mindy Corporon* podcast … none of which existed in 2013. All were created from the shattered pieces of my soul, blown up by hate on April 13, 2014.

Workplace Healing, LLC, a for-profit company and my most recent creation, was co-founded with Lisa Kolias Cooper in 2018 to change the way corporations respond to employees whose lives have been disrupted. My personal experience, returning as the chief executive officer of Boyer Corporon Wealth Management after Dad and Reat were murdered, serves as my guide and passion to helping other business owners measurably reduce presenteeism in their workplace.

The Faith Always Wins Foundation promotes dialogue for the betterment of our world through kindness, faith and healing. We received our 501(c)3 status in May 2015, 13 months after the murders, which catapulted me and my family into actionable steps to bring people of all faiths together for civil dialogue and understanding. Through our kindness pillar, Faith Always Wins produces an annual experience: SevenDays® Make a Ripple, Change the World.

Commonly referred to as SevenDays®, our experience provides opportunities encouraging all people to increase kindness through knowledge, mindset and behaviors. Our seven themes, LOVE—DISCOVER—OTHERS—CONNECT—YOU—GO—ONWARD, each provide meaningful activities for students, adults, businesses and schools to engage in fun, safe spaces for learning with and about one another. The formation of our Kindness Youth Leadership Team (KYLT) gathers interested high school students from across the Kansas City metropolitan area interested in making our world a better place. Paired with an adult mentor, our KYLT members personally assist with the creation and implementation of SevenDays® and participate in community service projects during their seven-month commitment. My friend and director of SevenDays®, Jill Andersen, works full time for part-time pay; and she is dedicated to preparing our KYLT members with skills to enrich their own lives and that of any community in which they choose to live.

Each of these entities has been created with God's message to me emblazoned in my mind, "Bring My People Together." Focusing significantly in the genre of faith and deliberately staying away from a racial discussion was possible until May 2020.

A white man, a white supremacist, murdered three white people who he thought were Jewish on April 13, 2014. Since it was a white-on-white crime, there was no need for commentary or attention on the racial aspect of this hateful act. There was no racial aspect. This crime was a hate crime based on the intention of the shooter to murder Jews. In much of my early commentary, I felt uncomfortable explaining to an audience of any kind that my family members were Christian. It is true they were Christian. But saying, "He wanted to murder Jews and he murdered three Christians instead," or "He was there to murder Jews but made a mistake in murdering Christians," is as abhorrent as saying, "He murdered the wrong people." No one should have been murdered. My family and I hold true to this statement. There was no reason for anyone to lose their lives because of "an idiot with a gun."

Appropriate uproar about this atrocity stretched from our local community to the White House and gained international attention. Everyone who heard the stories of "the grandpa taking his grandson to a singing audition, ambushed by gunfire in the parking lot of the Jewish Community Center by a deranged neo-Nazi," and the "woman visiting her mother at a retirement community gunned down," felt an ache for our families who were shattered by violence.

The shooter was captured, a trial was held and he was sentenced to death row by a jury of his peers in Johnson County, Kansas. The death penalty had been reinstated in the state of Kansas on April 23, 1994. District Attorney Steve Howe told our family and the LaMannos, "If I didn't request the death penalty on this case, then when would I?" Each family member present was asked our desired outcome for the shooter's potential sentencing. Without discussing among ourselves any specific answer, we each voiced our intent for his vile rhetoric to be silenced. District Attorney Howe provided this commentary to us as a group after hearing our requested opinions, "Obtaining the death penalty would eliminate his ability to spread his hateful message to others or have access to the media. While on death row, he will be in a cell by himself 23 hours a day. He will have very little time out of his cell and will not interact with the general prison population. This means he would not be able to preach his twisted view of the world to them and potentially cause problems within the prison population. He will not have the audience he desperately wants and he will disappear within the prison system and never be heard from again." So far, so good. This statement has rung true, allowing our families a glimmer of freedom to continue chasing kindness.

There will always be a part of me missing … only to be filled when I reach Heaven, to be with Jesus, my father and Reat. Therefore, when I talk about healing, my intention is not to portray that I have no pain, tears or continued sorrow for their lives lost. On the contrary, I have sorrow for their lives lost, as well as ours. We lost segments of our lives and continue to with each new memory that we make without Dad and Reat. Many lives suffered greatly from the ripples of evil created from one man's hatred of another.

This should not have been. This should not continue.

I have become well aware of when God is talking to me. Yes, to me. I may hear it in song, through the message of another or directly into my heart. Initially, the clarity of what He wanted from me was painfully frightening. I left a career I built and loved. The creation of a foundation built on promoting dialogue through kind actions bringing people of all faiths together has been challenging. Not many people find interest in funding such an endeavor, all the while saying how important our work is. Supporting my second and only son's decision to move 18 hours away for purposes of creating a safer environment for his healing and placing myself in the "canoe of life" with my husband, Len, to find myself and the peace I sought were stressful and complicated times in my life. With each change, I had previously heard a call to action from the Holy Spirit. With trepidation and courage, I took each step.

It was this bravery and nerve that prompted me to understand more about how a person might choose to become a white supremacist. Irv Robinson, friend and recent board member of Faith Always Wins, sent me a link to Christian Picciolini speaking at the November 2017 TEDxMileHigh. His talk was titled "My descent into America's neo-Nazi movement—and how I got out."

Christian and I have since met in person twice and carried on countless email conversations about his work in helping those "in the hate movement," to not only get out, but also get out safely. Through his two books *White American Youth* (2017) and *Breaking Hate* (2020) both published by Hachette Books, a featured documentary series on MSNBC, titled *Breaking Hate* in 2018, countless podcasts and speaking engagements, Christian works to undo the wrongs he himself fueled as a teenager and young 20-something. He has been a leader in the white power movement in Chicago, Illinois.

I view Christian's work as "in the trenches with the dark and dirty haters," while my focus is on bringing people together using kindness as a bridge, linking faiths to one another. We want the same thing, peace for humanity; and we reach for it differently, based on our personal experiences.

I believe God had another intention for me meeting Christian. An introduction to Chris Oneschuk and Susan Bro, both mothers who also lost a child to violent murders from inside a world of white supremacy, neo-Nazism and hate, came by way of Christian due to his documentary productions, which opened a path I had not considered for my healing journey.

Gathering these two grieving mothers, who had experienced sorrow more recently than me; Andrew Oneschuk was murdered May 19 and Heather Heyer was murdered August 12, both in 2017; on a

Zoom call in April 2020, we chatted openly about our children when they were living and in the bosom of our family and now as victims of a hate none of us can comprehend.

Loss is universal, while grieving is individual.

Each of these women are paving their own paths to shine a light on peace. Chris has been surprised and excited to find that she has healing abilities of her own. Placing her hands on clients, surrounding herself in energy work, she reminds me of my own healer Cuky Harvey. Chris has explained that she feels a deep connection with her son, Andrew, during her clients' healing sessions. Realizing her newfound skills, Chris is finding she is healing herself while helping others do the same.

Susan Bro was rocketed into international attention, the media and government hearings, when her daughter, Heather Heyer, was killed by a vehicle purposefully driven into a crowd of people during a so-called "alt-right" rally in Charlottesville, Virginia. The Heather Heyer Foundation was subsequently formed, creating a scholarship program to provide financial assistance to individuals passionate about positive social change.

This takes me full circle to Reat's 21st birthday on May 21, 2020. While my baby boy, his dimpled smile and starlit eyes shining with every smile, turned 21 in Heaven, I bravely opened a Zoom meeting with eight Black women, some whom I knew well and others by acquaintance, along with seven other white women. R.E.A.T. Black and White Women Friendships was formed: Respect, Engage, Appreciate and Trust. Prompted by the specific murder of Ahmaud Arbery on February 23, 2020, the Holy Spirit was stirring in my heart. Our initial conversation was followed only four days later with the heinous public murder of George Floyd in Minneapolis, Minnesota.

"Bring My People Together" has a new meaning for me. Initially, I chose what I call the "faith" lane due to the nature of the murders that took the lives of Dad, Reat, and Terri. My efforts were involved in bringing people of differing faiths together for the purpose of dialogue and hopefully a clearer understanding of one another. Lack of knowledge can breed fear. Fear could easily be moved to hate. I live with what happens after hate arrives.

There will always be good work to be accomplished in what I call the "faith" lane and interfaith dialogue. While not abandoning interfaith work, I feel and hear God asking me to add a lane to my conversational repertoire and to use what platform I might have allowing for conversations about biases, racial profiling and systemic racism. Could it be that shining a light into this cave of oppression might also highlight from where the white anger comes? Will I also find the cure for white supremacy and neo-Nazism? One day will I understand the "why" that shattered my own world into millions of shards? No, I will not. But this won't stop me from trying to move people who are filled with hate for another because of their faith or color to an understanding and a respect for each other.

Six months walking in this new lane, I am embarrassed by my own biases and racial tendencies. I suppose 52 years of learning, seeing, talking and engaging with mostly white people will take more than six months to untangle my perspective and open my eyes to the Black lives who have been in front of me, but not truly seen.

Friends, thank you for joining me on this journey of courageous kindness. Together, I expect to cry more than I think I should, feel my heartbeat with sorrow and joy simultaneously, forgive rather than hold anger and believe, oh yes, believe I will share a deep and long-lasting hug with Reat and my father, when the time comes.

Acknowledgments

With the assistance of numerous family members, most of whom did not need to write a memoir as part of their healing process, details were provided, blank spaces were filled with color and raw feelings were shared. Whether via conversations at our dinner table, during family holidays or being interviewed on my podcast, they allowed me to squeeze as many feelings and remembrances from them as I could. Many times, a memory from one would lead to uncovering a memory of another. Their insight regarding the day of the murders and their personal journeys in healing were of utmost importance to share. While we each experienced the trauma of losing two family members, we also experienced the tragedy on April 13, 2014, differently. Grieving is universal. Finding our path to move onward is individual.

Thank you to my spouse, Len Losen. In good times and bad, for better or worse. The death of a child causes a storm unlike any other in the life of a marriage. Your strong and quiet hugs, hand holding, empathy, and compassion, your willingness to walk in your own pain and share mine … all of these and so much more, provided the necessary support I requested for this healing journey. Thank you for the fun, vacations, memories and rowing our canoe to a healthy destination for the three of us. I love you.

Lukas Losen—My baby boy ... your momma bear loves you to the moon and back and again and again. Thank you for trusting me during the most difficult time in our lives to assist you in finding opportunities for healing. I will always offer you unconditional love.

Melinda Corporon—I love you, Mom. My tenacity took hold. Thank you for your persistent love of family and me. You are important to so many of us and I pray you continue to walk your healing journey knowing more joy can be found.

Will Corporon—I love you and appreciate your care of me as your little sister. Thank you for your willingness to interview, send photos, discuss copy and be a steady voice in the chaos during the days following April 13, 2014. Together, we will continue going east.

Tony Corporon—I love you little brother. Thank you for sharing a vulnerable time in your life on my podcast and allowing me to print the same in this memoir. I commend your brave decision to identify Reat's body, skills to navigate the immediate conversations with law enforcement and be the loving husband and father you are for your family.

Dana Corporon—Your calm understanding of me and our family is an adhesive for which I am grateful. Thank you for your continued love and care of Lukas, as your own and allowing me to parent Andrew and Katy as mine, too.

Heather Corporon—I am grateful you found Will and he found you. Adding you, Alli, Sam, Hanna, Maggie and Olivia into our lives has been a continuous blessing.

Gael (and Dave) Martin—With love and encouragement you lift me, always. I appreciate you both, immensely. From a room in your home to an interview on my podcast, keep the humor flowing so we can laugh through our tears. I hope to join you the next time you make Reat's fudge.

Dena (and Dr. Kent) Berquist—With love and gratitude, thank you for your interest in and mentoring of my spiritual care, and knowing when to call me MindyDoll. Your willingness to read and review two manuscripts providing meaningful edits was a sweet surprise, too!

Barbara (and Jeff) Fox—From card playing to horseback riding, from dog training to nutritional conversations, we have an ease about us. I love and appreciate our relationship and more importantly the relationship you offer our whole family.

Jilda Elk—My sweet Jilda ... we share the same heartache and wish we didn't. Your love notes, spiritual guidance and prayers always arrive just when I need them. I pray to be as helpful to you as you have been for me.

Yvette Manessis Corporon—My dear cousin, friend, and soul sister—thank you for your personal accomplishment in explaining the atrocities of April 13, 2014, in *Something Beautiful Happened*, a story of survival and courage in the face of evil. Your work to uncover the mystery of your grandmother saving the lives of others is a meaningful tribute and guide to the rest of humanity. I appreciate your love and care of our family, our story, and my own path to completing this memoir.

The Rev. Kirby Gould—I love that we share our love of philanthropy, foundation development and spiritual conversations. Mostly, I love that we share our DNA. Thank you for your guidance, compassion, and empathy during the most difficult time in my life.

Beyond DNA, my family extends to Ambergris Caye, Belize. Capt. Steve Rubio of the No Rush catamaran—your heart for Reat's time with us on the island and the spreading of his ashes are indelible memories—I am forever grateful that you are part of our lives. Jorge Lopez, Amarillis Peña, Anthony Vasquez, Amariany and Jazlyn Lopez, we are grateful to embrace and be embraced by you as family. To the staff at Belizean Shores Resort, your time, attention and care of my nutrition, internet connections, laundry, massages and time just being ... thank you.

When it came to the painstaking process of proofing this manuscript, I am thankful to have all these eyes helping me by offering the best grammar and spelling and as importantly, assist me in portraying the most accurate of remembrances. While some stories were remembered differently, we all know the catalyst that turned our brains to mush and shattered our hearts. With heartfelt gratitude, I was able to finish my story, my memoir with your assistance. Thank you for your efforts and encouragement!

Brooke Brundige, Christine Oneschuk, Dena Berquist, G.W. Corporon, Mary Ann Kellam, Mahnaz Shabbir, Dan Stringfield, Thomas Bates, Mickey Blount, Melinda A Corporon, Will Corporon, Tony Corporon, Gael Martin, Lukas Losen, Christine Hamele, Irv Robinson, Gail Weinberg, Jeri & Josh Gardner, the Rev. Gar Demo, Rabbi Jonathan Rudnick, Shelly & Mike Miller, Dominic DeCicco, Jacqueline Murekatete, Laura Carley, Alana Muller, Jo Turner, Nancy Corporon, JP Audas, Karen Renfroe, Mat Forasterie, Tandi Ball, Tarra Freberg, Liz Barnard, Susie Bond, Cindy Wysong, Denise Kruse, Kathy Schikevitz, Lori Mallory, Sunayana Dumala, Kati Farney, Jake Svilarich, Dawson Gardner, Jennifer Douglas & Mark Ephraim, Kala Pelate, Anne Blessing, Roxana Rogers Lemon, Athena Sullivan, Candy Moore, Janet & Leroy Loveless, Lynn Loveless Price – the Rev. Steve Langhofer, the Rev. Karen Lampe, Stacey Kelly, Shelly & Jim Maxwell, Jim LaManno, Alissa LaManno, Gian LaManno, the Rev. Jeff Kirby, Dr. Don Fishman, Cuky Harvey, Dr. Michelle Robin, Kim Harrison, Rondi Furgason, Jay Dodds, Josh Miller, Shirley Doyle, Camille Holland, Saúl Cordero Egido, Crystal Jenkins, Dr. Hal & Julie Hanson, Gary Gilchrist, W. David Disney, Diana & Micah LaCerte, Gary Underwood, Victoria Hall, Maureen Kesselring, Margaret Reynolds, Donna Osterlund, Mitchell McCroskey, Kara Choate, Madilyn Veatch, District Attorney Steve Howe and Beth Roller.

With a grateful heart, I thank Richard W. Boyer and my team from Boyer Corporon Wealth Management; Pat Burns, Laura Carley, Eric Clark, Brian Hackleman, Cindy Wysong, Cory Bloodgood, Sean Easterly, Jen Barker, Brittany McCormick, Mark Milosovich and Courtney Rowe.

Coming into my life as I worked to piece together my shattered soul, the humans mentioned below have experienced the aftermath of my storm. Knowingly, and some unknowingly, they entered a vortex of pain and grief. Yet, each always offered me empathy, compassion, and time for processing. Thank you to each of you for so very much: your heart, energy, listening ears and most of all your willingness to walk with me during the hardest days of retelling, reliving, and feeling all the heartache, again. Each of you helped to create the platforms desired to "Bring God's People Together."

Meghan Kempf—Director of Operations for Mindy Corporon, LLC

Jill Andersen—Director of SevenDays® Make a Ripple, Change the World

Ruth Bigus—Public Relations for Faith Always Wins and the Corporon family

Lisa Cooper—Business partner and co-founder of Workplace Healing LLC

Julie Myers—JM Marketing Solutions and website guru

Dina Davis—People People consultant, personal book

The Rev. Cynthia Alice Anderson—Experience of the Soul Podcast channel

Dave Kropf—Experience of the Soul podcast producer

Team at Real Media KC

Team at REACTOR

Vivian Nazzaro—Photographer website and podcast

Eric Campbell—Photographer book cover

Babs Lowenstein—Artist, The Swirling Ocean Painting used for the book cover and jacket

Friends of the Jewish Community Center—Herbert & Bonnie Buchbinder, Felice Azorsky, Jim Sluyter, Tammy Ruder, Sieglinde Othmer & posthumously, Dr. Ekkehard Othmer.

R. Lee Harris—Helzberg Entrepreneurial Mentoring Program, mentor, and friend

With gratitude for your time, energy and compassion for the Faith Always Wins Foundation and our monumental experiences produced as *SevenDays® Make a Ripple, Change the World*. Past and current board members include: Melinda Corporon, Irv Robinson, Gail Weinberg, Kelsey Parker, Dr. Hibba Haider, Alana Muller, Mike Miller, Muhammad Chaudry, Keith Kennedy, John Prutsman and Tony Corporon.

Offering me a higher knowledge of God, faith and religions, special thanks to Pastor Adam Hamilton, Rabbi Arthur Nemitoff, Rabbi Jonathan Rudnick, Pastor Gar Demo, Pastor Karen Lampe, Pastor Steve Langhofer, Pastor Jeff Kirby, Pastor Cheryl Jefferson-Bell, Pastor

Daryl Burton, Rabbi Alon Goshen–Gottstein, Dr. Nicole Price, Bill Tammeus, Mahnaz Shabbir, Sunayana Dumala and Belal Jamil.

Thank you to Jon Willis, founder of KC Interfaith Youth Alliance for your interest in interfaith understanding and allowing me to join you in your vision. With appreciation to Clare Stern-Burbano for walking alongside me during my interfaith infancy.

We are members of a club no one else should have to join. We understand more than we would like about hate crimes, neo-Nazism and white supremacy. Each of these are the common threads among us. We are choosing to band together with love, the everlasting glue for humanity. Thank you, Susan Bro, Dawn Collins and Chris Oneschuk for your strength amid pain, your fortitude in the middle of your own storm and your friendships which will carry us all to a more just and peace filled world.

Thank you to Christian Picciolini for your work to combat hate crimes, help those in the depths of darkness find their light and your introduction of me to Chris Oneschuk and Susan Bro.

Thank you for trusting in me enough to join a group of Black and white women for more than a "book club." You make me a better person. Together, I pray we lift one another up ... as one woman rises, so do others. Members of R.E.A.T. Sisters: Cleo Brager, Susan Bro, Dawn Collins, Mary Ann Kellam, Denise Martin, Melanie Miller, Chris Oneschuk, Lisa Pleasure, Dr. Nicole Price, Doris Rogers, Kiona Sinks, Stephenie Smith, Dawn Sullivan, Laura Waits, Lori Wilson and Michelle Wimes.

David Crumm, Susan Stitt and my project manager, Dmitri Barvinok with the Front Edge Publishing team—Because of your belief in my ability to carry this story to full publication, the tragedy that shattered my soul and tore the fabric of countless lives will be shared ... carrying with it, the hope that we can find an end to hate crimes and journeys to healing. I know there are many more on your team working behind the scenes and I offer my full thanks to each of them as I praise you for your gallant efforts in assisting me with the launch of *Healing a Shattered Soul*.

About the Author

An entrepreneur and thought leader, Mindy Corporon's professional career includes serving as CEO of a successful wealth management firm. Reaching the pinnacle of her professional career, Mindy was in the middle of raising two talented boys when tragedy struck. Mindy's father and oldest son were murdered by a white supremacist intent on killing Jews.

Mindy's life purpose changed from guiding people financially to helping people find space to learn about our differences and discover commonalities. With compassion and forgiveness Mindy shares with audiences around the world, encouraging people to overcome life's challenges, one day at a time.

Along with her family, Mindy started the Faith Always Wins Foundation promoting dialogue for the betterment of our world through kindness, faith and healing. The Foundation engages communities, businesses and schools in SevenDays® Make a Ripple and Change the World experiences. As a co-founder of Workplace Healing, LLC, Mindy is helping to change our corporate culture from primarily a head-based environment to include a path for heart-based conversations. Life disruptions touch every human. Our co-workers have the unique ability to be part of our healing strategy when they know what to say and when to say it.

Most recently, Mindy started a podcast called *Real Grief—Real Healing with Mindy Corporon*. Her programs welcome real people to talk about their life-altering experiences and what steps they take to find healing. She also formed a group named R.E.A.T. Black and White Friendships (Respect. Engage. Appreciate. Trust.), which is dedicated to creating friendships that will change the world for the better.

She believes: Each of us can always do more, to shine a light on peace.

For additional photos of William L. Corporon, MD and Reat Underwood please enjoy a slideshow of cherished family memories at www.MindyCorporon.com.

Are you ready for your own courageous journey of kindness?

Acts of kindness can be grand or small, ordinary or unique. The most important thing is to get started and to make the journey your own.

Are you ready to help promote dialogue for the betterment of our world through kindness, faith and healing? Mindy started the Faith Always Wins Foundation which engages communities, businesses, cities and schools in *SevenDays® Make a Ripple, Change the World*, an experience which provides opportunities for all people to increase kindness through knowledge, mindset and behaviors. At the Faith Always Wins website you can make a donation to support their mission or get more information about joining *SevenDays® Make A Ripple, Change the World* experiences.

Are you, or is someone you know, grieving? Sharing Mindy's podcast, *Real Grief—Real Healing with Mindy Corporon* is an act of kindness for yourself, a friend or a colleague who needs to hear it. New episodes are published twice a month and are available on all of the major podcast services or at www.MindyCorporon.com. In each episode, Mindy explores real grief and real healing, often with a special guest who shares their unique experiences and strategies for living with grief.

Is your event looking for an in-person or virtual keynote speaker? Mindy Corporon is a motivational speaker and thought leader who is available to speak to corporations, conventions and faith communities. She encourages and motivates audiences to overcome life's challenges, one day at a time. To arrange for Mindy to speak to your group, contact her at Mindy@MindyCorporon.com.

Are you an employer interested in the well-being of your organization? As co-founder of Workplace Healing, LLC, Mindy's vision is changing how corporations respond to a grieving employee whose life has been disrupted. Corporate leaders, managers and teams all have the ability to be part of a healing solution when they understand the need for a balance of head-based and heart-based communications and initiatives. Life disruptions touch everyone. Do something kind for your employees and reach out to Workplace Healing. Their innovative training will provide your company with the knowledge and tools needed to restore an employee's productivity following a grief event and ensure that business and life continue to prosper.

Would you like to find inspirational messages from Mindy in your inbox? You can sign up for Mindy's monthly newsletter at www.MindyCorporon.com.

To add kindness to your social media feed and to keep up on the news about *Healing a Shattered Soul*, follow Mindy Corporon on Twitter, Facebook and LinkedIn.

Twitter: Twitter.com/MindyCorporon
Facebook: Facebook.com/Mindy.Corporon
LinkedIn: Linkedin.com/in/MindyCorporon/

If reading *Healing a Shattered Soul* touched or inspired you, you can support Mindy and the book by leaving a review on the platform where you purchased your copy. This is a kind way to let others know about this amazing and healing story.

CPSIA information can be obtained
at www.ICGtesting.com
Printed in the USA
LVHW032341250421
685422LV00006B/389